Serials-ly Speaking

McFarland Classics

1997–1998

Archer. *Willis O'Brien*
Cline. *In the Nick of Time*
Frasier. *Russ Meyer—The Life and Films*
Hayes. *3-D Movies*
Hayes. *Trick Cinematography*
Hogan. *Dark Romance*
Holland. *B Western Actors Encyclopedia*
Jarlett. *Robert Ryan*
McGee. *Roger Corman*
Okuda & Watz. *The Columbia Comedy Shorts*
Pitts. *Western Movies*
Selby. *Dark City*
Warren. *Keep Watching the Skies!*
West. *Television Westerns*

1999–2000

Benson. *Vintage Science Fiction Films, 1896–1949*
Cline. *Serials-ly Speaking*
Darby & Du Bois. *American Film Music*
Hayes. *The Republic Chapterplays*
Hill. *Raymond Burr*
Horner. *Bad at the Bijou*
Kinnard. *Horror in Silent Films*
McGhee. *John Wayne*
Nowlan. *Cinema Sequels and Remakes, 1903–1987*
Okuda. *The Monogram Checklist*
Parish. *Prison Pictures from Hollywood*
Sigoloff. *The Films of the Seventies*
Slide. *Nitrate Won't Wait*
Tropp. *Images of Fear*
Tuska. *The Vanishing Legion*
Watson. *Television Horror Movie Hosts*
Weaver. *Poverty Row HORRORS!*
Weaver. *Return of the B Science Fiction and Horror Heroes*

Serials-ly Speaking

Essays on Cliffhangers

by
William C. Cline

McFarland & Company, Inc., Publishers
Jefferson, North Carolina, and London

> The present work is a reprint of the library bound edition of
> Serials-ly Speaking : Essays on Cliffhangers, first published
> in 1994. McFarland Classics is an imprint of McFarland &
> Company, Inc., Publishers, Jefferson, North Carolina, who also
> published the original edition.

Library of Congress Cataloguing-in-Publication Data

Cline, William C.
    Serials-ly speaking : essays on cliffhangers / by William C. Cline.
        p.   cm.
    Includes index.
    ISBN 0-7864-0918-5 (softcover : 50# alkaline paper)
    1. Motion picture serials.   I. Title.
PN1995.9.S3C58   2000   791.43'75—dc20   93-32499

British Library cataloguing data are available

Cover image: A still from the 1953 Republic serial *Commando Cody* (courtesy Photofest).

Frontispiece: In March 1941, America learned that a man could fly!

©1994 William C. Cline. All rights reserved

*No part of this book may be reproduced or transmitted in any form
or by any means, electronic or mechanical, including photocopying
or recording, or by any information storage and retrieval system,
without permission in writing from the publisher.*

Manufactured in the United States of America

McFarland & Company, Inc., Publishers
  Box 611, Jefferson, North Carolina 28640
    www.mcfarlandpub.com

To Oliver Drake,
an "unsung hero" of serial making,
whose work meant more to me than I knew—
until I knew—and then it meant even more

CONTENTS

FOREWORD (Frank Coghlan, Jr.)		ix
PREFACE		xiii
1	"What's a Serial, Daddy?"	1
	The Question and an Unseen Friend	1
	Of Trash and Treasure	6
	The Magnificent Curse	12
	The Captive-ated Audience	17
	The Echo-ing Sound of Adventure	21
2	"Didn't You Used to Be Don "Red" Barry?"	27
	The Circuit Riders	29
	From the Horse's Mouth	37
	The "What-If" Time Warp	43
	The Cliffhanger Revisited	48
3	"Sure, I Can Do It.... Do What?"	51
	The Way You Do It, Making Movies	51
	Gentle Deception	56
	The King of the Hill	60
	"Directed by Spencer G. Bennet..."	63
4	"Do It As Well As You Can, But Do It Only Once!"	71
	Masters of the Shoestring	73
	An Unsung Hero	77
	Coming Back Like a Song	81
	Tom-Tom: Anonymous But Not Unknown	87

CONTENTS

- **5** *"Imagine, Kid, by Labor Day You'll Be a Star!"* — 95
  - THE COWBOYS AND THE CLIFFHANGERS — 95
  - ONE-SHOT WINNERS — 101
  - THE MAN WHO BECAME WILD BILL... — 107
  - A TRIPLE TREASURE — 112
  - REX BENNETT REVISITED — 119

- **6** *"Look, All You Gotta Do Is Shave the Moustache!"* — 123
  - GOOD AT BEING BAD — 123
  - WHO'S BEHIND THAT MASK? — 129
  - WHEN THE LEOPARD CHANGED ITS SPOTS — 137
  - THE DOUBLE TAKE — 141

- **7** *"Who Knows What All This May Lead To?"* — 148
  - THE FUTILE WISH — 149
  - KEMO SABE AND THE CLIFFHANGERS — 154
  - THE START OF SOMETHING BIG — 160
  - REMAKES AND SIDE EFFECTS... — 164
  - THE BEAT GOES ON — 170

- **8** *"Well, Maybe We Could Just Flip a Coin"* — 175
  - THE DEVIL'S DUE — 176
  - THE COMPARISON URGE: CURSE OF THE INFIDEL — 179
  - THE 228 BEST SERIALS EVER MADE — 183
  - A SECOND LOOK—AND WRONG AGAIN — 189
  - YOUR VIEW OR MINE — 193

- **9** *"But, Dad, That's Not What You Said a Serial Was!"* — 201
  - COUNTERFEIT CLIFFHANGERS — 202
  - JUST SAY IT WASN'T SO.... — 207
  - COUNTDOWN TO DESTRUCTION — 213
  - ILLUSIONS AND DELUSIONS — 216

- **10** *"It's Been a Long Tunnel, Guys, But There Is the Light!"* — 222
  - SAGA OF THE FIRST BAPTIST CHURCH — 223
  - KEEPERS OF THE FLAME — 226
  - THE EXCITEMENT OF WONDERING — 233
  - ALIVE AND WELL—AND GOING STRONG — 238

INDEX — 245

FOREWORD

In his 1984 book *In the Nick of Time,* William C. Cline tells how, at the age of eight, his older brother let him tag along with the bigger boys to the Saturday matinee at their local theater in Concord, North Carolina.

Though they went mainly to see a Buck Jones western, it was the serial preceding the feature film that left him clutching the back of the seat in a row in front of him and, as he says, "hooked" him for life on the action-packed chapter films with their weekly "cliffhangers."

The same thing happened to me, but I was much older. For me, the year was 1925, and I was nine. Up to that time the only motion pictures I had ever attended were at night in the company of my parents. Finally, when I was nine, my mother thought I was mature enough to join three other pals and walk the four blocks to the Apollo Theater on Hollywood Boulevard to see my first unattended Saturday matinee. My circumstances were much different from Bill Cline's. I had just been signed to a five-year contract by Cecil B. De Mille. De Mille was then starting his own studio and had selected me to be the kid actor in his stable of contract players.

At that time I was earning $85 per week on my new contract, which was more than my father was making as a clerk for the Pacific Electric Railroad. In spite of my then-large salary, my mother gave me 15 cents for the afternoon, 10 cents for admission to the theater, and 5 cents for candy. I thought it was a real treat.

Though under contract to De Mille and already playing important supporting roles in his films, on this Saturday I could hardly wait to go to the theater to see my first solo movie. I might add, by this time I had been working in motion pictures for five years and felt I was well versed in what went on in films, both in front of and behind the camera.

Like Bill Cline, I went to the theater to see my favorite cowboy star Tom Mix in one of his western thrillers. Before the feature film I was pleased and surprised to see a serial, *The Riddle Rider,* come on the screen.

I sat there transfixed with what followed. When William Desmond donned his disguise to wreak havoc on "the bad guys," the whistling, yelling, and stamping of feet in the crowded theater was almost deafening.

At that moment, I, too, was "hooked for life" on the serial form of entertainment and the cliffhangers that were to follow each week. The next two serials that became my weekly fare were *The Green Archer,* based on a novel by Edgar Wallace, and *Hawk of the Hills*—both of which starred Walter Miller and Allene Ray.

Of interest here is that the dastardly villain in both was played by Frank Lackteen. Only two years later, when I was playing in *The Last Frontier,* a feature film with my idol William Boyd, Lackteen was the crafty chief of the Sioux Indians. In the big raid on our wagon train that climaxed the film, I distracted Lackteen with a well-aimed rock from my slingshot just long enough for Bill Boyd to put him out of action with a more formidable weapon.

In the first chapter of this book, Bill Cline tells how in 1966, his then-six-year-old daughter asked him, "What's a serial, Daddy?" Her question made him realize that if his own daughter knew nothing about his favorite subject, there must be many others in the same boat.

Strangely, I was asked this same question in September 1991 by a 28-year-old man during a panel I was conducting at the Atlanta Film and Memorabilia Fair, a festival honoring the stars of serials. The young man had paid to attend, yet he had never seen a motion picture serial. We all assumed that the nearest thing to a filmed serial he had ever seen was watching "Dallas" and other soap operas on television.

As Bill Cline so aptly says it here, the serials were successful because of the expertise of the people involved—from the production team who could turn out a fine product on a short shooting schedule with a limited budget to the actors they hired who could do it right on the first take. For that reason you saw seasoned veteran performers who were stars in earlier days and talented newcomers working their way up and most happy to be seen in serials.

Where again will you see the likes of Ralph Byrd as Dick Tracy, Larry "Buster" Crabbe as Flash Gordon and Buck Rogers, Kirk Alyn as the original Superman, or my dear friend Tom Tyler who was so believable as my alter ego in *Adventures of Captain Marvel.*

Through the years many women have left an indelible mark on serials, and the title "Serial Queen" has been bestowed on many. From the indestructible Pearl White in her *Perils of Pauline* series, followed by such lovelies as Allene Ray, Louise Lorraine, and Eileen Sedgwick. In later years the mantle was worn by beauties like Linda Stirling, the Tiger Woman; Frances Gifford, the first Nyoka; and the gorgeous Kay Aldridge, who continued in that role. Then young charmers like Peggy Stewart; Jean Rogers; and Noel Neill, the original Lois Lane, took their place in the hearts of the viewers.

As crafty and shady as Larry Hagman was while playing J.R. in the long-running television series *Dallas*, he was angelic compared to Henry Brandon as the heinous Dr. Fu Manchu or Charles Middleton as the evil Ming the Merciless in the Flash Gordon serials or even Harry Worth, who turned out to be the Scorpion in my best serial, *Adventures of Captain Marvel*. Then throw in everyone's most hated villains: Roy Barcroft, Eduardo Ciannelli, Bob Kortman, J. Carroll Naish, and Charles King, to say nothing of Bela Lugosi, Frank Lackteen, Lionel Atwill, or Fred Kohler, Sr. That group would bring goose flesh to any audience.

I always thought it was the fine supporting players who added such stability to the casts of serials. Among many others, I had the pleasure of working with Jack Mulhall, John Davidson, Kenne Duncan, Carleton Young, Bryant Washburn, Sr., and Jason Robards, Sr. Mulhall, Washburn, and Robards were big stars in the silent days, and Mr. Robards, Sr., has a son doing well in his own right.

In *Adventures of Captain Marvel* the venerable mystic Shazam was played by the respected character actor Nigel De Brulier, who had played Cardinal Richelieu in the silent films *The Three Musketeers* and *The Iron Mask*, starring the great Douglas Fairbanks. With all his expertise and credits, he was happy to accept one day's work in our serial.

Many fine producers and directors won their spurs in the serial days. Probably the single biggest impact on serials was made by Henry MacRae, who headed the program at Universal for years, followed closely by Nat Levine at Mascot and Sam Katzman at Columbia. I had the good fortune to work for that trio, as well as for these action directors in either a serial or a feature film: J. P. McGowan, Clarence Melford, George B. Seitz, Richard Thorpe, Ray Taylor, Alan James, Ford Beebe, Reeves "Breezy" Eason, Spencer Gordon Bennet, and the great team of William Witney and John English. I learned a lot from these masters of the craft.

Behind the cameras there were technicians with equal talents. At Republic the work of Howard and Ted Lydecker in special effects was recognized throughout the industry. The Lydecker brothers could accomplish more, faster, and with less money than their contemporaries in the major studios. Even Steven Spielberg admits he patterned many of the illusions in his *Raiders of the Lost Ark* trilogy on their work.

Now I am doing my best to interest a new generation, my grandchildren, in the serials and the cliffhangers. When my grandchildren come to the house, instead of wanting to watch cartoons on television, they always ask to see a chapter or two of one of my serials.

They have seen me wearing war paint as Uncas in *The Last of the Mohicans* with Harry Carey and as Jackie Cooper's pal Ken in *Scouts to the Rescue*, but their favorite is watching me transform into Captain Marvel, "the world's mightiest mortal," by uttering the magic word, "Shazam!"

One daughter had her children here recently and after viewing a chapter of *Adventures of Captain Marvel,* she said her five-year-old whispered in her ear, "Can Grandpa really fly?" She smiled and answered, "Yes dear, but he can't fly as fast as he used to."

So, settle back and get real comfortable. Make some popcorn and open a Coke, if you wish, because you are about to enjoy the most entertaining book about serials ever written. Please believe me because I was there.

Shazam!!!

Frank Coghlan, Jr.
Summer 1993

PREFACE

Serial (sir'-i-ul) n.
    1. A long story told in parts, or episodes.

Cliffhanger (klif'-hang-ur) n.
    1. A motion picture serial telling a long mystery/adventure story by the showing of one chapter per week that concluded with the hero's life in peril, and possible escape unresolved.
    [Paraphrased from Webster's New World Dictionary.]

In recent years, a number of books have dealt with motion picture sound serials. But this one is different. The purpose of those that have gone before—including my own, *In the Nick of Time* (McFarland, 1984), a reference book—was to inform readers about serials as a type of movie entertainment that was unlike other types, such as short subjects, series films, and especially feature pictures. Those books focused on the technical, the creative, and the production aspects; examined the marketing appeal of the continued pictures; and delved into the success or failure of many of them with the moviegoing public, pointing out how television eventually changed it all, virtually eliminating the cliffhanger serials as a viable draw for theatergoing dollars.

The purpose of this book, on the other hand, is to have some fun trying to figure out what happened with the fans during and since the cliffhanger's heyday: how the public reacted to the serials then, what they think of them now—nearly 40 years after the last one was released—and why.

For several years, I have been writing a column for the monthly collectors' publication *The Big Reel*, which is put out by Donald Key of Madison, North Carolina. The idea of the column, which at the start we temporarily entitled "Serials-ly Speaking," was to comment briefly on some aspect of the serial and see if it would bring any response from readers who were also lovers of old serials. Well, sometimes it did, and sometimes it did not. But, what it did do was become an informal, ongoing expression of one serial lover's views, opinions, and prejudices about sound serials, tempered by the reactions we got from readers who wrote, called, or spoke to me personally at film fairs and conventions and expressed opposing thoughts and ideas. And, despite the play on words that was first intended as a sort of corny joke, the title caught on and became permanent.

After a while, some of the readers began to suggest a compilation of those columns into a book, so they could retain what they had come to consider a unique series of articles. So, that's what we have here: a selection of "Serials-ly Speaking" columns (not in the order in which they were published, incidentally), with a brief commentary on why the particular topic or subject was chosen for each one, and the response it evoked, if any. Though factual material is included it was not the purpose of the columns to serve as reference guides. The idea is to express my views to garnish agreement or stir opposition, rather than to educate—thus, to have some fun.

If you love the old cliffhangers, I hope you will like what I have to say about them. If not: Well, then, just drop me a line....

Chapter 1
"What's a Serial, Daddy?"

There is a time-honored technique used in serials called the "recap," which brings you up to date and prepares you for the current episode by reviewing briefly what went on in previous chapters. Since there is an undeniable connection between my book In the Nick of Time *and this series of columns, the first article included here provides some background on why and how the research for that book was undertaken.*

It is also a personal tribute to three people who gave me what was needed to get started as a writer: material to document what I wanted to say and the confidence it takes to sit down and write it.

The Question and an Unseen Friend
December 1985

Just a few days ago, I learned that Fernando Pedreira is dead—that he died several years ago. I didn't want to learn that. But, I think I knew it already. Inside. I had wanted to hear that he was alive and well. Watching his grandchildren grow in Brazil. Still remembering the silent serials of Allene Ray and Walter Miller and William Desmond and Joe Bonomo. I wanted to tell him about the success of In the Nick of Time, for he shared in its creation. To send him a copy. And hope he would be proud of me for writing it. That would have mattered. But it had been too long since his last letter. And there had been so many letters before, even though some had long gaps between them. After a while you can tell when there won't be any more. And then yours come back marked "No Forwarding Address." So I think I knew. Inside.

Fernando and I never met, but I've never had a friend who was more real to me than he was. Unabashedly, I dedicate this column to him. It is appropriate.

***Undersea Kingdom*—Republic, 1936—the action classic that raised the question, "What's a serial, Daddy?"** *From left:* **C. Montague Shaw, Ray Corrigan, and Lon Chaney, Jr.**

One day in 1966 I walked into the den where my six-year-old daughter, Anita, was sitting on the floor playing with her dolls. On the TV there was a movie that seemed strangely familiar and hauntingly reminiscent. I sat down to watch, and it took only a few minutes to determine that it was a chapter of *Undersea Kingdom,* the 1936 Republic serial that had starred Ray "Crash" Corrigan. It had been ten years since anyone had released a serial, and I was pleasantly jolted by a flow of memories from those days when I had tried so hard (sometimes in vain) to keep up with every episode of some of my favorites. Some things I had not thought of for years flashed across my mind, and I was momentarily drawn back in time to those Saturdays that had meant so much to me growing up.

It felt good. I tried to explain to my little girl what I was feeling: "This is one of the serials I used to enjoy when I was a boy going to the movies," I told her, "And I used to go home afterwards and play it out again in the backyard all the next week with my buddies. Isn't that something?"

Without even looking up, she answered, "What's a serial, Daddy?"

Her question stunned me for a moment. I had assumed everyone knew what serials were, and always would. It had never occurred to me that the passage of so little time would so quickly relegate them to history and the memories of those who had seen and enjoyed them. But, there it was: "What's a serial, Daddy?"

Right then I decided that someone would be telling future generations what a serial was, so I went to the library to see what books were available on the subject. There were none.

I wrote to the Library of Congress in Washington, the public libraries of a dozen major cities such as Los Angeles, New York, Chicago, San Francisco, etc., to see what they had on serials. There was nothing!

Surely the distributors of films for television, the television stations themselves, distributors of 16 millimeter films such as *Blackhawk*, etc., would have something; so I contacted some of them to find out what they had in the way of historical data on the serials they handled. Zilch!

I panicked! The awful but apparently unavoidable truth was that no one seemed to even care about preserving the story of the serials, much less be doing anything about it. Everywhere you went there were books on the movies—every aspect of them it seemed—but nothing on the cliffhangers. There were books devoted to the classic features, the musicals, the westerns, the comedies, the Academy Award winners, the art films, the techniques of movie-making, histories of Hollywood, the love stories, the gangster films, the war pictures—but nothing at all on serials. It was as if people writing books chose to believe they had not existed. And that just wasn't so. Continued pictures had meant too much to too many of us to be thrown out and forgotten.

The least I could do, I concluded, was to compile all the information I could find on this unique and beloved film form, so that for me the serial would not die out of neglect. Since there was so little material available to the average person at that time, this appeared to be a monumental undertaking. But, I reasoned, somebody had to do it.

In the ensuing search for information, one of the things that eventually brought results was placing an ad in Sam Rubin's *Classic Film Collector*, which enjoyed international circulation. The first person to reply wanted to charge me ten dollars an hour to do "'research" at his local library, so that was easy to ignore. Another wanted to sell me his collection of newspaper clippings (mainly on the careers of Chaplin, Valentino, Arbuckle, etc.) for some ridiculous figure. But, one day an envelope came from Tom Osteen in Brevard, North Carolina, who has since passed away. It contained a solid handful of information on cast and credits for a number of Mascot and independent serials which I had not been able to find elsewhere. Tom had kept "diaries" on all the films he had shown in Brevard since starting as a young man, and gave me information he had copied right from the films themselves.

Then I received a letter from Fernando Pedreira in Rio de Janeiro, Brazil. He explained that his primary interest was in silent serials, but he also liked and had a good bit of material on sound serials—and would I be interested in swapping information? That started a correspondence that lasted for a decade, and a friendship that I will always treasure. Right now I have very little on silent serials, because every time I found anything, or could finagle anything, I have sent it to Fernando. When I needed information on sound serials that were being imported and shown on Rio television, here it came along with Fernando's observations on the quality of each one. Any day I might go to the mailbox and there would be, unsolicited, an envelope from Brazil containing, uncannily, just the item of information I needed right then. In one of his letters, he said he was sending me a package of materials by steamship that he hoped I would like. When it arrived some weeks later, the package contained over seventy-five lobby cards on sound serials, ranging from early Republics to late Columbias—a priceless gift from a totally generous friend. They are the cornerstone of my collection.

In addition to all that I gathered from Fernando in the way of serial lore and information, I also learned that he had a wife whom he loved dearly, and daughters who were growing into wives, mothers, nurses, teachers. He was a proud family man, and each letter gave me news of some new family development, as well as some new serial "goodie."

In my years of film collecting and serial studying, I have met several men who are like Fernando Pedreira. For that I am grateful. They offset the unpleasant experiences with the other kind—those who are in collecting only for what they can "hustle."

"What's a serial, Daddy?" For me, that question was the key to a door that, once opened, has brought me the same kind of pleasure and joy I used to experience watching serials—only now in reviewing, renewing and sharing them with people like Fernando Pedreira. And it led me to Bob Malcomson, who gave me the idea that I could write about them and others would read it, an idea I had not dared dream before. So, taking what I had learned from Tom and Fernando, and writing about it as a result of Bob's influence, produced *In the Nick of Time*, which was published by McFarland [in 1984], and is so far "doing very well."

Captain America—Republic, 1943—the most expensive of all the "trash" or "treasure" produced by Republic. *From left:* **Charles Trowbridge, Dick Purcell, and Lorna Gray.**

Now my little girl, who is twenty-five and just recently married—or any other little girl or boy, for that matter—will never again have to wonder, "What's a serial, Daddy?" Thanks, Fernando mi amigo, for helping me to tell her.

After completing In the Nick of Time *and seeing it so well accepted by serial fans, I had the urge to keep finding out and writing about continued pictures, which led me to write the column "Serials-ly Speaking." Since I started writing the column in 1984, many things I have learned about people and their various opinions about the same subject, their insight into things I had not considered before, and their downright enthusiasm about the old cliffhangers, have made it one of the most interesting ventures of my life.*

As a columnist, one of the things I discovered first was the existence of outright artistic prejudice in some people, who profess to love movies, but really mean "only certain kinds, you understand." So, in an early column, I just had to give that a go.

To enjoy serials properly, it is necessary to put them in perspective. For years I had deliberately not mentioned serials and series westerns to people I knew because, generally, the reaction I got was a look of disdain and a haughty, "You don't like that trash, do you?"

Assuming it had happened—and was happening—to other serial lovers, I decided one day to state a case for serials in the column to see what would happen.

Of Trash and Treasure
November 1985

It never ceases to amaze me how some people seem to insist on continuing to miss the point when it comes to discussing serials and series westerns. No matter how many times you repeat that the quality of the films being discussed is purely relative, nor how much you emphasize that all expressions of complimentary endorsement are based on the elementary view of those films within their own context, nor how strongly you state that the appreciations derived from them come from nostalgic and consequential effects, there are still people who—at the mere mention of serials or "B" westerns—will snort and respond haughtily, "Why, that stuff wasn't worth anything. It was just trash!"

What they always mean is that it's "trash" compared to *Gone with the Wind, Casablanca, Going My Way, The Best Years of Our Lives, An American in Paris, The Greatest Story Ever Told, From Here to Eternity* and *Ben-Hur*. And there ain't no argument about that. Compared to those pictures (and countless others that could be named) serials and series westerns *were* trash. But only if you insist on comparing fruit with vegetables and nuts with meat. Comparing serials and westerns with other pictures produced for the sole purpose of providing immediate, familiar, but unpretentious entertainment for people who like their films simple and straightforward, they came off pretty doggone well. It is in that ballpark that boosters of westerns and serials are playing when they write and speak of the virtues of the breed—not the other one. And in that ballpark, a good western or a good serial is a "treasure," rather than "trash."

Now, some of the "graduates" of serials may not like to recall their participation in what the snobs call "trash." I don't think the late George

Tim McCoy starred in the first all-sound serial, *The Indians Are Coming*—Universal, 1930.

Brent was ever too anxious to talk about his role in Mascot's *The Lightning Warrior;* and I've heard that Lloyd Bridges, Jinx Falkenburg and Jennifer Jones are not too crazy about recalling their parts in *Secret Agent X-9, The Lone Ranger Rides Again* and *Dick Tracy's G-Men.* I don't know how Ken "Festus" Curtis felt about *Don Daredevil Rides Again;* nor Leonard "Mr. Spock" Nimoy does about *Zombies of the Stratosphere;* nor Ruth Roman about her role in *Jungle Queen.* And I can't image what Gene Reynolds, producer of the award-winning television show, *Lou Grant,* would have to say about his part in *Junior G-Men of the Air.* But, regardless of their later attitudes, I think every one of them would have to admit that they were glad to be in them at the time, and benefitted from the experience.

On the other side of the coin, there are many highly respected actors who gladly accepted roles in serials—not only because they might have needed the work at the time, but also because they knew that a real actor plays in whatever vehicle is available and respectable, in order to ply his trade—and gave their performances the best effort of which they are capable. In the doing, they helped raise serials above the level of "trash," by *any* comparison. I have yet to meet one of these thespians who would balk at discussing his serial roles, along with any of his others.

Several of these solid-pro character actors came into serials from the silent era. Monte Blue, who is credited with roles in serials from all three companies—Universal, Columbia and Republic—was a romantic leading man in silents, before becoming a top character actor in sound films. Noah Beery, Sr., veteran of serials at Mascot, Republic and Universal, was a top villain in silent films as well as sound ones. A venerable silent film thespian was Tully Marshall, who contributed his considerable talents to two classic Mascot serials, *The Hurricane Express* and *Fighting with Kit Carson.* During the 1920's, at the peak of the silent era, William Farnum was the highest paid actor in Hollywood (a super-star, if you will). His serial credits range from *Fighting with Kit Carson* in 1933 to *Adventures of Red Ryder* in 1940, and number more than half a dozen.

Several actors whose faces appeared in so many major company features during the 1930's and 1940's that it would be difficult to number them all, also graced serials with solid portrayals that lent substance to them. Robert Armstrong (star of the classic *King Kong*) made at least four serials for Universal. Charles Bickford, one of the most respected talents in Hollywood, literally stole the one serial he made at Universal. Joseph Crehan (four for Universal), Douglas Dumbrille (two for Republic, one for Universal), Joseph Girard (one for Mascot, three for Columbia), Howard Hickman (two for Republic), Russell Hicks (two for Republic, two for Universal), Selmer Jackson (one for Republic, one for Columbia), Ralph Morgan (two for Universal, one each for Republic and Columbia) and Herbert Rawlinson (one independent, one for Columbia and seven for Republic) all played senators, governors, judges, lawyers, doctors, businessmen—whatever was needed—in major company features, as well as in serials.

Stanley Andrews played in four serials for Republic, and then became television's "Old Ranger" on *Death Valley Days,* a character loved by two generations of viewers. Abner Biberman was one of the villains (Japanese) in *King of the Mounties* for Republic, and then became a top director of movies and television (*Hawaii Five-0,* for example). And two much-respected British character actors (Miles Mander in Republic's *Daredevils*

Top: James Craig (with Anne Nagel, in *Winners of the West*—Universal, 1940) graduated from serials to leading roles in major films. *Bottom: The Lone Ranger*—Republic, 1938—a prime example of "the magnificent curse," was one of the best western serials made and helped establish Republic Pictures as a viable studio. *From left:* Tex Cooper and Lee Powell.

FLAMING ARROW REVENGE!

TERROR IN THE NIGHT
Chapter 13

OVERLAND WITH KIT CARSON

BILL ELLIOTT

with Iris Meredith · Richard Fiske · Bobby Clack

Screen play by Joseph F. Poland, Morgan B. Cox, Ned Dandy
Directed by SAM NELSON and NORMAN DEMING

A COLUMBIA SERIAL

of the Red Circle and Syril Delevanti in *Red Barry* for Universal) lent their dignified portrayals to the serials.

The presence of these actors gave serials some very memorable scenes. Their influence on other members of the casts (who had yet to make their marks) was also considerable. In the tight-budget, no-nonsense atmosphere of serial production, their professionalism and expertise also helped the directors to save money.

And, what's more important, their performances on screen gave the "trash" they were making a touch of "class." In that regard, these fine actors, along with the stuntmen and highly skilled action specialists they worked with, helped make serials—AS JUDGED ONLY BY WHAT THEY WERE MEANT TO BE!—the entertainment "treasures" that they were.

This was one of the first columns to evoke almost complete agreement from readers. Many of the readers said they had endured the same "snobbish" attitude from people who professed to be "students of the cinema," and they had not known how to answer the charge that serials were trash. One fellow said that he now thought he could answer a couple of his friends because he happened to know that they liked to eat in fast-food restaurants: By comparing serials to fast food (which is basically good food, just not fancy) and "A" features and "art" films to regular restaurant fare (which is also basically good food, just made to appear fancy, so higher prices can be charged), he could point out that his friends did the same thing with food that he did with entertainment. And, to his surprise, the point was made, more often than not. At least, he told me, it made him feel better to know about all the top-quality performers who had worked in serials, which had come as a surprise to some of his friends and helped him make his point.

The response to the article "Of Trash and Treasure" was gratifying because it fortified a column run a couple of months earlier in which I delved a little deeper into the matter of prejudice against westerns and serials. But rather than the prejudice of self-appointed "critics," that one was about the prejudice shown by the film business itself: the movie industry, in general, and the "art" and "awards" sector, in particular.

It had always annoyed me to know how prevalent the practice was to let the financial success of westerns and serials support other types of films that did

Opposite: *Overland with Kit Carson*—Columbia, 1939—is memorable for the outstanding performance by Trevor Bardette as mystery villain Peg-leg.

not show a profit—and then not allow the same westerns and serials to be recognized for whatever quality they did contain.

The Magnificent Curse
September 1985

Several people have told me recently that they saw *Pale Rider* and *Silverado;* that they were, "hey, pretty good"; and that they, "you know, liked them." I was surprised—and not surprised—by their comments.

I was not surprised because I also saw the pictures and liked them. My surprise was at *their* seeming surprise that the films were "hey, pretty good!"—almost as if they had been sure they wouldn't be any good (because, after all, they are westerns, you know), but had gone to see them anyway out of curiosity. I couldn't help thinking back to the time when it was surprising if a western *wasn't* real good. Back to when film makers poured the best of their knowledge, skills and resources into making whatever film they were working on—western or otherwise—as good a picture as it could be. Without even trying hard, I can remember top quality pictures such as *Jesse James, Union Pacific, The Oklahoma Kid, Western Union, Stagecoach, Buffalo Bill, Belle Starr, Tall in the Saddle, Red River, Fort Apache, Shane, High Noon*—and that is just barely scratching the surface. Historically, westerns have been basic to the motion picture form, but the thing we sometimes forget is that they have always run in cycles, and they always come back.

Paradoxically, westerns have given the motion picture industry a shining legacy of talent and tradition, but have received in return—without fail—immediate criticism for any weaknesses, and—with rare exceptions—almost automatic exclusion from praise by the "art" sector of the industry. Over the years that has not made much difference, though, because westerns were always held in high regard by the studio business heads, who knew that they made the money that allowed the so-called "art" pictures— that would lose money—to be made. You could say it has been for the westerns their "magnificent curse."

During the last two decades, when the studios have declined, and most films are now made by independent production companies for release by film companies that are almost companies in name only, there is no voice (or champion) for the westerns, and they have fallen to the wayside or been changed to something not too closely resembling what westerns used to be. (Minor example: 1981's *Legend of the Lone Ranger.*) And to some people, that is the problem in a nutshell. Maybe *Pale Rider* and *Silverado* can change that.

Western serials have also provided a legacy for the industry, and as a result occupy an important place in the history of westerns in movies. The fact that they are rarely recognized for it marks them for inclusion in the "magnificent curse."

The first major serial with sound was *The Indians Are Coming,* a western produced by Universal in 1930. Starring Tim McCoy and Allene Ray, it launched the era of sound serials with a bang, playing in top theatres in big towns as well as small. In the next twenty-six years, more than five dozen western serials were released. Some of them became classics of the serial field just as some of the previously mentioned westerns are classics in the feature field. *The Miracle Rider,* because of Tom Mix's incredible virtuoso performance at an age (55) when most men are thinking of retirement; *The Phantom Empire,* for its bold attempt to do something that hadn't been done before; *The Lone Ranger,* by virtue of its quality, its sheer enjoyment, and its contributions to the mystique of one of the longest-running traditions in American entertainment; *Overland with Kit Carson,* with one of the most brilliant performances of a villain in western pictures; *Riders of Death Valley,* for its scope, cast, and inspired musical score; and *Daredevils of the West,* by reason of its unrelenting, head-knocking, free-swinging action and stunts, are just a few western serials that could be called classics. In 1956, mainly due to the pre-emption of television, the final sound serial was released: Columbia's *Blazing the Overland Trail.* Right!—a western.

Aside from the obvious success of those cliffhangers starring the big western stars of the early 1930's—the ones made by Buck Jones, Tim McCoy, Tom Tyler, Harry Carey, Sr., Tom Mix and Ken Maynard—western serials also opened up new careers—or helped expand those just getting started—of a number of others who became top western stars of the late 1930's and 1940's. It's pretty well known that Johnny Mack Brown, Gene Autry, Robert Livingston, Ray Corrigan, Duncan Renaldo, Bill Elliott, Don Barry, Allan Lane, Clayton Moore and Jock Mahoney all trace their beginnings back to the 12- and 15-chapter continued pictures.

Not so well known is the fact that other actors who achieved prominence in non-western movies and television also got boosts up the ladder by appearing in western serials. Along with their brothers, the "B" western features, the serials were an amazing training ground for young actors who were trying to learn all they could about making pictures. Unlike major features, where emphasis by directors was on the artistic or theatrical perfection of cast and production—necessitating sometimes countless retakes and endless conferences which resulted in a lot of wasted time and talent—the budgets on westerns and serials demanded that everyone do the best he could the first time around, and then move on. So young actors learned how to get it right fast—or else! That's why you can see, in the

DAREDEVILS OF THE WEST

A REPUBLIC SERIAL IN 12 CHAPTERS

with ALLAN LANE · KAY ALDRIDGE

EDDIE ACUFF · WILLIAM HAADE
ROBERT FRAZER · TED ADAMS

John English—Director
Original Screen Play by Ronald Davidson · Basil Dickey
William Lively · Joseph O'Donnell · Joseph Poland

CHAPTER 3   THE KILLER STRIKES

work of crews that worked together for very long, the quality of what comes through on the screen improves with each production, and eventually becomes standard.

Although later known for the same type of roles as his famous father, Lon Chaney, Jr., played the lead in a western serial in 1932. *The Last Frontier* was the only serial ever released by RKO Radio Pictures, and Chaney played a hero known as "The Black Ghost." Later, he also appeared in *Riders of Death Valley* and *Overland Mail* for Universal in 1941 and 1943.

Another famous son of a famous father, Noah Beery, Jr., twice played in western serials with his father—*Fighting with Kit Carson* in 1933 and *Overland Mail* in 1943. In between he also played in *Riders of Death Valley*, as well as several non-western serials.

Western serials produced three of the most handsome romantic leading men of the 1940's, two of the screen's most respected character actors, and one of television's most beloved personalities.

One of the five players suspected of being the masked hero in *The Lone Ranger*, was a young man named George Montgomery Letz. He didn't turn out to be The Lone Ranger, but went from that serial on to become a top star at 20th Century Fox, romancing female stars like Betty Grable and Alice Faye. A handsome young singer named John Carroll played the hero in Republic's western serial *Zorro Rides Again;* then starred in his own musical features at that studio and also at Metro-Goldwyn-Mayer. From a supporting role in *Overland with Kit Carson* at Columbia, and second lead in *Winners of the West* at Universal, James Craig rose to stardom at Metro-Goldwyn-Mayer, where he was even considered as a replacement of the great Clark Gable during his absence in World War II.

Another one of the ranger suspects in *The Lone Ranger* (but also not *the* Lone Ranger) was young Olympic star Herman Brix. Later, using the name Bruce Bennett, he became an outstanding character actor in films such as *Sahara* and *Treasure of the Sierra Madre*. Reed Hadley, possessor of one of radio's most sought-after voices, and narrator of many important motion pictures, as well as being a highly respected character actor in many major films of the 1940's and 1950's, played the title role in the 1939 Republic serial *Zorro's Fighting Legion,* one of the most memorable of all western serials because of its action, its remarkable stunts, and Hadley's commanding screen presence.

Milburn Stone played a heavy in *The Royal Mounted Rides Again* for Universal in 1945, after playing the hero in two of their non-western serials—*The Great Alaskan Mystery* and *The Master Key*. For the next decade he played a variety of supporting roles in major features, leading

Opposite: *Daredevils of the West*—Republic, 1943—acclaimed for its fast action and amazing stunt work.

Flash Gordon—Universal, 1936—owed part of its amazing success to an outstanding musical background score arranged by Charles Previn and Hans J. Salter. Larry (Buster) Crabbe (*center*) played Flash.

roles in minor features and character parts on television. A first-quality actor who could always be counted on to deliver, he never met that moment of destiny until the producers of a proposed television series to be based on the successful radio drama *Gunsmoke* picked him to play the part of Doc Adams, a role done on radio by veteran actor Howard McNear. From then to now, as *Gunsmoke* became an instant TV hit, grew to become an institution, and lives on almost as a show business legend, the character of Doc, along with Matt, Miss Kitty, Chester, and Festus, has become a part of all of us. And there are many who say it was Doc, as played by Milburn Stone, who gave *Gunsmoke* its "heart," that indefinable quality that causes us to raise one series—or movie—above the others. Whether or not that is true, he certainly did his part.

Back in the serial days, it would not have been possible to look at these people and know what they would all become. None of us have that prophetic gift. And now, it is impossible for some of us to watch what they became and not think of their beginnings—when they were jumping up and down on those horses, slinging those fists in mock combat, and firing those blank-filled guns with such earnest vigor.

In a way, that may be our own magnificent curse.

As time went on, some western features began to receive the long-overdue recognition they deserved, when landmark films, such as Duel in the Sun, Broken Arrow, High Noon, *and* Shane, *displayed such quality and substance that they could not be ignored any longer. These films proved to Hollywood's "art" connoisseurs—literally rammed it down their throats, actually—that a good story, told well, with superior performances, and properly presented technically, could be successful even though it was a western.*

But alas, it was too late for the serials. By the time these great motion pictures came along, television was already beginning to grind up the cliffhangers and blow them away. So we have to try and recall the time before television to appreciate fully the western serials that were part of the "magnificent curse."

There were many ways we could be attracted to and held by the cliffhangers. The most obvious, of course, was the cliffhanger itself: How would the hero escape the jaws of death at the end of a given episode? But, before reaching that point, how could the theater exhibitor get us interested in the first place?

One way was so basic that it was almost too obvious, so it was often overlooked, but most of the exhibitors eventually figured it out: quite simply, "the proof of the pudding is in the eating."

The Captive-ated Audience
February 1987

Eleven excruciating weeks had finally gone by, and you had seen your current hero go through every danger imaginable to try and bring to justice the despicable villain who had seemed so indestructible at first. Now, after escaping every diabolical trap the bad guys had set for him, and outwitting the evil mastermind at every turn (even if by luck some of the times), the final chapter was coming up and the hero would get the job done; and we would all breathe a sigh of relief; and go home satisfied that all was right with the world. Right?

Wrong!

Back then the theatres had it figured out so that wouldn't happen. While they had you in the theatre, they reasoned, something had to be done to entice you to come back. It was clearly unthinkable to let off the hook so easily someone who had just undergone eleven weeks of worry and frustration over the fate of the hero and his friends, and helping them squeek out of the most deadly cliffhangers conceivable. So, while they had you there, they started the next serial to get you hooked on it. And nobody I know objected to it. For many of us, it was our first encounter as children with the magic word, "Bonus!"

A reminder of this practice came to my attention again in a very unusual way last week, along with some other very interesting tidbits of nostalgia. As we all have experienced, you never know what you're going to run into when you get a lead on a piece of material concerning movie and theatres from the 1930's and 1940's.

Max Brown is a printer in Concord, North Carolina—owner of the town's oldest and most respected printing shop. He's also a fellow Lions Club member and one of my most cherished friends. Unsuccessfully, he tried for years to get me to join the "Spebs"—S.P.E.B.S.Q.S.A.—whose full name is the *Society for the Preservation and Encouragement of Barber Shop Quartet Singing in America*. Mary, his wife, plays the piano for our Lions Club singing; and Max and I alternate as chairman of the music committee—meaning we swap off leading the guys when we group-sing. Max also knows about my love of old movies—especially serials—and bought one of the first copies of *In the Nick of Time*.

When I got home from work one evening last week, Edna said, "Call Max. He's excited!"

So I jumped into my car and drove to the printing shop. When Max is excited, he "don't go home early." When I got there, sure enough: he was still there, and he really was excited and showed me why. He had found a piece of nostalgia that blew both our minds.

In the basement, at the bottom of an old box that had contained a couple of tired old press motors for years, there was a little 4-page tabloid titled *The Merchants Movie News*, which was dated May 18, 1933. This little paper was put out every week by the Paramount Theatre, and contained ads for the local merchants, along with articles about the current films about to play at the Paramount. It was distributed free and included people's names (apparently taken from the telephone book) in the ads. If your name appeared in an ad, you could take the paper to the theatre and be admitted free to one show.

It contained ads for the pictures playing that week, as well as the mer-

Opposite: The Lone Ranger Rides Again — **Republic, 1939 — benefited from an exciting original musical score by William Lava, whose serial scores have become classics.**

chant ads, and had a complete schedule of the theatre's films. Here is the line-up for that week in May, 1933:

> Friday–Saturday, May 19–20:
> JAMES CAGNEY IN PICTURE SNATCHERS
> LAST CHAPTER SERIAL CLANCY OF THE MOUNTED
> FIRST CHAPTER SERIAL THE LAST FRONTIER
> Monday–Tuesday, May 22–23:
> KING KONG
> Melody Novelty   News
> Wednesday, May 24:
> Jimmy Durante–Buster Keaton in
> WHAT! NO BEER
> Betty Boop Cartoon   Special
> Thursday, May 25:
> 15¢ Bargain Day!
> Al Jolson in
> HALLELUJAH!, I'M A BUM!

There were separate little articles on each picture, stating that *Picture Snatchers* shows Jimmy Cagney's new method "of making his ladies behave," that *King Kong* should win "without a moment's indecision" the choice as the most "unusual picture of the year," that Buster Keaton and Jimmy Durante "turn 4-percent beer into 100-percent laughs" in *What! No Beer,* their latest Metro-Goldwyn-Mayer vehicle, and that for *Hallelujah, I'm a Bum,* Al Jolson "corralled a cast of Hollywood comedians the like of which has never been seen in one production unit," including Harry Langdon, Chester Conklin, Frank Morgan, Tammany Young, Bert Roach and Victor Potel.

As a lover of serials, the overlap of *Clancy of the Mounted* by *The Last Frontier* was what gained my immediate attention. Just a little while ago, I acquired a chapter of *The Last Frontier,* the only serial produced by RKO Radio pictures. Since it came before my time, and since Concord had only two theatres then, I never really knew whether it even played our town or not. Well, this little tabloid, *The Merchants Movie News,* answered that question for me. And it also reminded me of why I enjoyed growing up in Concord and going to the movies there. Back then, the whole town loved its theatres, and everybody enjoyed going to them, because—unlike a lot of moviegoing today—it was a joyous, fun thing to do. And the whole community was involved.

Now, that just might be the simple key to what's missing in our entertainment world today. At a frantic, super rock star concert, at one of those multi-room complex "screens," or especially at home with a TV or a VCR, doesn't entertainment seem "lonely" today? Perhaps we need to—somehow—learn to "captive-ate" an audience again.

Well, the proof of the pudding was sure enough in the eating. For the audience, having gotten a taste of the new serial, the rest was a foregone conclusion, if the new serial was any good at all. And the producers always made sure that the first three chapters were the best of the lot, the reason being that those were the episodes that were "trade screened" for exhibitors who were deciding whether to book each new serial. If the exhibitors liked the first three chapters, then it was presumed that the other nine would be of the same caliber. And what worked for exhibitors also worked for fans.

"What's a serial, Daddy?"

Well, sweetheart, they're trash, they're treasure, they're a curse, they're a blessing, they're suspense, they're relief, they're action and adventure, and they're excitement and thrills. They're deliciously nostalgic, and they're still alive today—at least the concept is.

And, when at their peak, they were simply wonderful! One of the main reasons they were so wonderful was the great music that came with them. In serials there was never a dull moment—even when a dull moment came—because the music always kept you in a spirit of high adventure and sometimes was the best part of the whole thing.

The Echo-ing Sound of Adventure
February 1985

One of the everlasting delights of the Saturday morning serials in the 1930's and 1940's was the background music. More than in most features (western or otherwise), the action and suspense in serials was brought up to and maintained a fever pitch by the use of rousing, provocative and rhythmic—almost contagious—passages of stirring music. The chases, fist fights, gun battles and physical stunts were honed to the edge of pure excitement by the driving and relentless beat of music it would have been impossible to ignore. (As a related example, try listening to John Philip Sousa's "Stars and Stripes For-ever" without feeling a stirring in your bones. You just can't do it.) And, even in the slower, plot-developing or mystery-surrounded sequences, the music they used gave you the appropriate feeling of anxiety, suspicion or dread that the scene was trying to convey. From the opening credits to the closing card of each chapter, the viewer was almost never left alone without music to enhance what was being seen and heard. To a serial fan of that era, hearing a few familiar

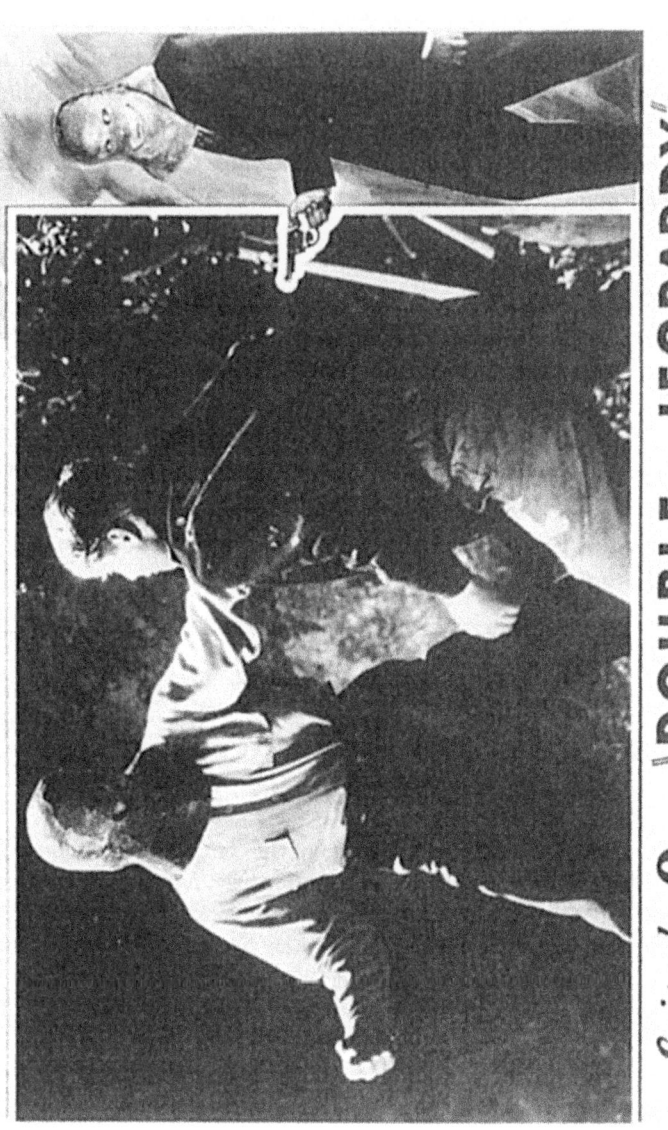

notes from the score of a fondly-recalled cliffhanger will set the juices flowing, and make him wish for more.

Some of the really good serials were made even better by excellent musical scores. Several not-that-good productions were made to appear very good by the use of exciting background music. A few that would have been pretty sad without it, were even salvaged to some extent by the use of good musical support. And almost none (well, maybe a couple) were ever diminished in any way by their music scores. So, music and its use in cliffhangers had much more to do with our entertainment than we might have thought.

The musical director was the person responsible for the proper selection and use of music to support the technicians' and actors' efforts on film. They reviewed the finished product and scored each scene and sequence with an appropriate passage of music either from an original score, from published classics, or from combinations of the two. They then conducted the studio orchestra in recording the passages selected to synchronize with the film as it was being shown; and the resulting mixture of sounds, words and music became the soundtrack. There were outstanding men of music assigned to this job at each of the three main serial-producing companies; and their work is forever woven into the fabric of the motion picture sound serial.

At Universal's peak in the late 1930's, the music was provided by Charles Previn and Frank Skinner; and in the 1940's by eminent composer Hans J. Salter on several releases. All three were respected composers and top-flight musical directors of that studio's best feature films, as well as the serials. The distinctive themes they used in *Flash Gordon* in 1936 were used again many times, not only in the two Flash Gordon sequels, but in other serials as well. During that time, several other unique passages were developed and seemingly catalogued for use in current serials then in progress to fit certain requirements—such as different types of action or mystery sequences, or as themes for certain characters in the plot (hero, villain, etc.) as they appeared on the screen.

One of the most lively and exciting scores of all Universal serials was the one for 1940's *Winners of the West*, which starred Dick Foran and James Craig. In the course of its thirteen chapters, nearly all of the standard passages, several of the *Flash Gordon* excerpts, and a central theme of original music by Frank Skinner, were all used to make it highly memorable. For the 1941 super-serial *Riders of Death Valley*, Skinner and Previn incorporated the haunting theme of Felix Mendelssohn's

Opposite: Mysterious Doctor Satan—Republic, 1940—**One of the best musical scores for an action film ever written came from Cy Feuer, who later became a top Broadway producer.**

"The Hebrides Overture: Fingal's Cave" and the well-known Universal passages into what has become perhaps the most famous of all their serial scores. It is difficult to find a western/serial fan who, having seen *Riders of Death Valley*, does not remark in effect, "And, man! Do you remember that music?" It is a good example of a serial that is made to appear better than it actually is by the exciting music score. Throughout the last decade of Universal serials, the succinct use of the classics, in combination with previously developed "standard" passages, and original writings by Skinner, Previn and Salter, provided a string of melodic and "hum-able" music backgrounds: The Flash Gordon trio, *Jungle Jim*, *Wild West Days*, *Flaming Frontiers*, the Green Hornet duo, *Winners of the West*, *Sea Raiders*, *Sky Raiders*, *Riders of Death Valley*, the Don Winslow pair, *Gangbusters*, *Overland Mail*, etc.

At Columbia Pictures, the music directors were Abe Meyer (one of the most respected talents in the music business), Lee Zahler and Mischa Bakaleinikoff. During Meyer's tenure, he provided the music for *Secret of Treasure Island*, parts of which have become some of the most copied background music ever, showing up as action and mood music in the series westerns of nearly every independent producer of that era, as well as in Columbia's for years thereafter. As Previn and Skinner had done at Universal, Zahler recorded score after score during the early 1940's using a combination of classical music (leaning heavily toward Wagner and Liszt) and original passages of his own. His successor after 1947, Bakaleinikoff, continued the practice, providing what is known to serial buffs as the "Columbia sound," right up to 1956 and *Blazing the Overland Trail*.

A mixture of the classics and original passages also made up a good part of Republic Pictures' music scores in the beginning, and for the first decade of their serials. Notably different were the scores of William Lava. His five serial scores at Republic were not taken from the classics, but were almost entirely original, and were five of the most outstanding scores in the studio's history. They are all examples of making good serials even better. Beginning with *Hawk of the Wilderness* in 1938, there followed *The Lone Ranger Rides Again*, *Daredevils of the Red Circle*, *Dick Tracy's G-Men* and *Zorro's Fighting Legion*. The latter is thought by some to be the very best score ever written for a serial. Cy Feuer, who followed Lava as music director, wrote original scores (*Drums of Fu Manchu*, *Mysterious Doctor Satan*, *King of the Royal Mounted*, *Adventures of Captain Marvel*, *Jungle Girl*, etc.) and also interspersed his own writing with other works ("Oh, Susanna" for

Opposite: *King of the Texas Rangers*—Republic, 1941—Combining his own music with "Slingin' Sammy" Baugh's school song (Texas Christian University), Cy Feuer created an unforgettable score.

Adventures of Red Ryder, "(Come) to the Bower" for *King of the Texas Rangers,* etc.) to produce some of Republic's most memorable music for cliffhangers. Their successors—Mort Glickman, Joseph Dubin, Richard Cherwin, Stanley Wilson and Dale Butts—continued the fine tradition and gave serial fans many hours of thrilling sound.

During the latter days of serials in the 1950's—when shortcuts, stock shots and process scenes were in obvious use—the background score was often the only thing that made the finished product bearable; and even then it was a hard job to ask a piece of music to do. In some cases it just couldn't be done. But in the "golden years," the marriage of good action and dialogue with thrilling music gave us many moments to remember and savor. If the eyes are the "windows to the soul," then the ears must be the "doors to the heart."

What's a serial, Daddy?

To your father, my dear Anita, they were what opened the doors and windows to my heart and soul when I was a boy. They teased my eyes to see all the other things I encountered around me—the faces of beautiful people, the grandeur of nature's wonders, and all the art people are capable of creating—and they pricked my ears to hear what so many others never do: the singing of birds and the rustle of grass, the magnificent music of genius composers, and the gentle laughter of a little girl.

There are many things that can trigger a person's perceptions, and it can happen at any age. I always felt lucky that it happened to me as a boy, and it was serials that did it—for, that way, I could enjoy it my whole life long and could know, as the days went by, that I was playing out the serial of life.

Chapter 2

"Didn't You Used to Be Don 'Red' Barry?"

It almost goes without saying that the serials were what they were because of the people who made them. That's true of anything you want to discuss. So, when the serials ceased to be and the people who made them went on to other things, why did they not just fade away and become distant memories of other times? Why have they continued to come back and influence—almost haunt—moviemakers and movie watchers of later times? And why is the cliffhanger technique still at work today throughout the entertainment business—in movies, radio, television, and even (believe it or not) in television commercials?

Because it is the essence of life itself. Every day—in one way or another—we are left to wonder about the next. And therein lies the magnet: Stories that leave something for tomorrow have always appealed to our natural curiosity about the future.

The last motion picture serial was released in 1956, which was nearly 40 years ago. But the people who acted in and directed them during the 2+ decades before that year had endeared themselves to serial fans as few stars of major films did—by going out to hundreds of small towns, where the westerns and serials had been most popular, and making personal appearances in the late 1940s and early 1950s. Most of these small towns had never been visited by a major celebrity, but a great many of them could boast visits by the western stars and serial heroes, who not only put on shows at the local theaters, but went outside the theaters between shows and met their fans one on one.

The town where I grew up was no exception, and it triggered one article that was pure nostalgia about those times.

ADVENTURES OF RED RYDER

FROM THE FAMOUS NEA NEWSPAPER CARTOON

A Republic SERIAL IN 12 CHAPTERS

Chapter 2 HORSEMEN OF DEATH

The Circuit Riders
April 1986

Quite frankly, I'm in a nostalgic mood; so this one is going to be a "name-dropping" piece. I'm warning you up front, just in case you want to skip this entry. Some people don't like name-dropping pieces. But, if you don't mind a little reminiscing about the days when the cowboys came to town in person, read on.

During the 1940s, when most of the western stars traveled throughout the Southeast making personal appearances on what was known as the "Kemp Circuit," my headquarters was at the Paramount Theatre in Concord, North Carolina. It was called "Kemp time" because the booker for most of the tours was T. D. Kemp, owner of Southern Attractions, Inc., in Charlotte, and brother of popular orchestra leader, Hal Kemp. His bookings—Concord, N.C., overnight to Bluefield, West Virginia, then overnight to Spartanburg, S.C., and again overnight to Hagerstown, Maryland, for example—were legendary among the stage show folk; and to this day can get a knowing reaction from such veterans of the "circuit" as Pee Wee King, Cal Shrum, Lash LaRue and Sunset Carson.

All of the stars that played the circuit came through Concord, and we at the Paramount met and worked with them all. Afterwards, we retained memories and stories of our encounters with them, and we still remember them today. Some of my favorites center around the visiting celebrities who had made serials, since they were kind of special to me—even a little more special than the others. Thinking back on some of the days when they were in town recalls some fond moments with several, and belies some rumored characteristics of several others.

For example, I have heard some pretty unkind things said about the late Don "Red" Barry since I became a collector—stories of his supposed selfishness, or arrogance, or shortness with fans. But the day he was in Concord, I happened to step out the stage door into the alley beside the theatre during the afternoon, and there was "Red Ryder," surrounded by a half-dozen or so kids. He was grinning and talking to them, and patiently answering their questions. Didn't seem too short, too arrogant or too selfish to me. And the kids were loving it.

Allan Lane, they say, was a pure-tee tyrant on his movie sets: wouldn't let anybody else wear dungarees because he wanted to be the only one

Opposite: Don "Red" Barry *(third from left)* was one of the most popular of the circuit riders making personal appearances in the late 1940s, despite his reputation for brashness and arrogance.

Ralph Byrd *(right)* surprised everybody in town with his outgoing, enthusiastic personality as a circuit rider, after portraying the "all-business" Dick Tracy in four serials. Here, he is shown with Harry Lang *(left)* and Ted Pearson *(center)* in *Dick Tracy's G-Men*—Republic, 1939.

wearing them. Pretty rough on co-workers, they say, because he always wanted things done his way. Real "stuck-up" sorehead, they say. Took himself too serious. You know. But when he visited Concord, the star of *King of the Royal Mounted, King of the Mounties, Daredevils of the West* and *The Tiger Woman* was a pleasant, jovial man. The people who saw his personal appearances on stage, and those who met him personally, thought he was a pretty nice guy. He readily shared stories of his personal experiences and movie roles with anyone who asked him. Probably would have made a pretty good Film Fair guest if he had lived long enough. Stuck-up? Guess he had us all fooled that day.

Ralph Byrd, who played Dick Tracy in four of the best serials I ever saw, was one of the friendliest, most open, out-going people who ever came along on "Kemp time." After seeing him perform so expertly as the

Opposite: **Allan Lane *(right)*, here struggling with Anthony Warde, was another circuit rider who belied a reputation for egoism by being an open, friendly visitor to small towns.**

great fictional detective on the screen, it was disarming to find him such an ingratiating, anxious-to-please movie personality.

Johnny Mack Brown had been the first celebrity I ever met. His handsome, athletic good looks were even more pronounced in person than on the screen. Star of five serials—*Fighting with Kit Carson, Rustlers of Red Dog, Wild West Days, Flaming Frontiers,* and *The Oregon Trail*—plus countless western features, he came to town during the time he was moving over from Universal to Monogram; and his wide grin and deep Southern drawl charmed everybody he met.

One of the most memorable days of my life was spent on a slow Monday in January, 1949. George "Gabby" Hayes was booked for a one-day stand and he had called on Sunday night from Spartanburg, South Carolina, to ask the time of the first show Monday, and how far it was from Spartanburg to Concord. I had told him about ninety miles, and he had said,

"Good. That'll take me an hour or so."

I repeated that it was about ninety miles, not sixty, and he had said, "Right. I heard."

The first show was set for 1:00 P.M., I had told him; so we were all gathered in front of the theatre at 12:30 to see if he would make it. At 12:45, up roared a Lincoln Continental convertible, and out stepped the familiar-looking old veteran of the serial "The Lost City," and more westerns than one man could recall. Dusting off his tailored western-style suit, he smiled and said,

"Woulda' got here sooner, but traffic was sorter heavy—heh, heh, heh!"

The rest of that day I was privileged to spend all the time between shows in one of the little dressing rooms backstage—just "Gabby" and me with our feet propped up on the dressing table—listening to a "living legend" spin his yarns about film making with the greats.

And I take a lot of ribbing about being a hopeless Wild Bill Elliott fan; but I really don't mind. Elliott starred in three serials—*The Great Adventures of Wild Bill Hickok, Overland with Kit Carson* and *The Valley of Vanishing Men*—as well as becoming one of the biggest and most popular western stars of the 1940s and 1950s. While he was in town, I had the rare treat of having the star himself tutor me on the proper handling of his matched pair of beautiful six-shooters, which—as most people know—were worn gun butts outward in specially tooled holsters. As I stood in the office of the theatre, wearing that famous gunbelt, Wild Bill himself coached me in how to draw, handle, twirl and return the guns the way he did in his movies. When I didn't get it just right, his gentle, understanding chuckle would put me immediately at ease, and he would say patiently, "That's okay. Here, try it again—this way."

One of the all-time favorite 1940s circuit riders was Johnny Mack Brown.

Being subject to the folly of the young, I seldom ever asked for an autograph or tried to get one of the stars to pose with me for a picture. I figured it would last forever. But in reality it lasted for just a short time. Funny, though: When you're in a nostalgic mood, the memory serves almost as well, anyway.

Well, if you stayed with me this far, thanks for indulging me on a revisit with the Riders of the "Kemp Circuit."

Another all-time favorite circuit rider was Wild Bill Elliott.

Opposite: George "Gabby" Hayes *(second from left in the inset)* was one of the most beloved of the circuit riders. Only a few of us even remember that he appeared in this one serial.

In retrospect, it sometimes seems unreal that all those people actually came to our town. All you had to do was wait, and most of them came along sooner or later. It was many years later before someone figured out that a variation of that idea might work for a later generation. They reasoned that if they got a bunch of the people together who had made western movies and serials in those bygone days, then the people who loved to watch them then—and meet them when they came to town—would come to see them and meet them again, just like a reunion of old friends with a mutual interest. But, a new generation who knew them from television and 16-millimeter print showings would come to meet them, too.

In 1972, a group of film collectors in the Memphis, Tennessee, area banded together and staged the first of a long line of Western Film Fairs, conventions for western and serial fans who could come and congregate for three or four days, watch 16-millimeter print showings of old western movies, and complete 12- to 15-chapter serials at one sitting. There were also visiting guests from Hollywood who had taken part in filming the serials and westerns that were being shown — people like Tex Ritter, Lash LaRue, and Max Terhune—who did as they had done before when visiting the small towns: shake hands, sign autographs, pose for photos, and chat one on one with fans who were thrilled once more to be meeting their favorite stars personally. It was a big success and made news nationally. The resulting publicity sparked a new flame in people all over the country who had thought they were the only ones who remembered. The Western Film Fair moved to St. Louis for a couple of years, and then, in 1980, a committee of film collectors, headed by Wayne Short and Bob Thompson, picked up the ball that was about to be dropped and moved the fair to Charlotte, where it has been held ever since (except for three times in Raleigh, North Carolina). A nonprofit organization, the Western Film Preservation Society, Inc., was formed to promote and manage the annual events. Film collectors in Raleigh formed the Raleigh division of the society and were the ones who staged the event in 1984, 1989, and 1990. For me, being a part of these events in Charlotte and Raleigh has been a little like reliving those days in the middle and late 1940s when "the cowboys" rode into town doing "Kemp time." I didn't feel a bit ashamed to plug one of the film fairs in the column, as follows:

From the Horse's Mouth
June 1985

If you want to get information first-hand, directly from the people who were there when the serials were made, who are themselves part of the fabric of the cliffhanger tradition, and who are more than eager to talk to you about those wonderful old action films, then The Western Film Fair is where you need to be in July. In Charlotte since 1980—except for last summer when it was in Raleigh—The Western Film Fair over the years has made sure to provide serial lovers with guests who are alumni of those beloved cliffhangers and will tell you stories you could hear no other way. Heroes, heroines, villains and stuntmen have all come our way via the Film Fair, and have made our lives richer for the meetings. And they're still coming....

There was Victor Jory, the renowned actor who included in his lists of credits not only a memorable role in the classic *Gone with the Wind*, but the leading role in two Columbia serials—*The Shadow* and *The Green Archer*. Of them he said,

"*The Shadow* was a pretty good picture. We had a lot of fun doing it, and it came out all right. But we weren't so lucky with the other one *(The Green Archer);* it didn't make much sense."

Nevertheless, there are those of us who enjoyed it anyway, Victor.

Rod Cameron sat through several chapters of *Secret Service in Darkest Africa* at the Film Fair and recalled how swiftly they had worked at Republic to move from one set-up to another, to make the best use of the time they had to work in.

"I didn't remember doing some of those things shown in the fight scenes we just saw," he said, "I thought they had the stuntman—what was his name? [Tom Steele, someone volunteered]—doing all those things."

Viewing of the subsequent chapters showed that Cameron had, indeed, done more himself in the fight scenes than was normally done by the lead actor in a serial. Tom Steele had done all of the really dangerous things, of course, but Cameron was personally involved in a surprisingly large amount of the fight footage.

The stories coming from stuntman-star Jock Mahoney while in Charlotte have been endless. And I daresay they are somewhere still a-coming. And the next time you see him, there probably will be yet some more to come. Jock has been a treasure house of good serial stories.

Everybody remembers with great fondness the good old bad guys like Charlie King, Jack Ingram, George Chesebro, Stan Jolley, Bud Osborne, Al Ferguson and Stan Price. We too often think of them as just that—good

***Gunfighters of the Northwest*—Columbia, 1953. Jock Mahoney's *(left)* stories at Charlotte's Western Film Fair kept everybody entertained, coming—as they did—from "the horse's mouth."**

old bad guys—and not much more. But to Nell O'Day, who played alongside them in Columbia's *Perils of the Royal Mounted*, they were the REAL professionals of the westerns and serials.

"The directors simply told them what they wanted to get on film, and those men just instinctively gave it to them," she said while in Charlotte.

Dorothy Gulliver told Fair-goers of knowing a different John Wayne than most of us would suspect. She was his leading lady in Mascot's 12-chapter serial *Shadow of the Eagle* in 1932, and spoke of him as a quiet, almost shy young man—not like some of the "Duke" stories we have heard over the years from others. It was during the filming of that same serial that Wayne and the great Yakima Canutt first met; and Yak had a story to tell us serial buffs about that:

It seems that members of the crew told Yak that Wayne was a "spy" for the head office, so he better watch out for him; and told Wayne the same thing about Canutt.

"We spent most of our time dodging each other, till we finally got mad and had a showdown. We've been friends ever since," rasped the legendary stuntman.

Top, left: Victor Jory, famous for his serial role in *The Shadow*—Columbia, 1940—was an informative guest at Western Film Fairs for as long as he lived. *Top, right:* Unfortunately, western and serial badman Charlie King died several years before the film fairs began. When fans fantasize about "what if...," he leads the list of those they would have most liked to meet. *Bottom:* Always placing high on the list of "what if..." guests for film fairs are "good old bad guys" George Chesebro *(left)* and Bud Osborne *(right)*.

One testimonial to the high regard in which Yakima Canutt is held by those who have worked with him came from Jean Carmen, who as Julia Thayer played the Rider of the Stallion in Republic's 12-chapter classic *The Painted Stallion*. At the showing of that serial in Charlotte, she addressed the audience during each reel change and gave background stories and anecdotes about its filming back in 1937. She had been selected to portray the Rider because of her horsemanship, and did most of the riding called for in the filming — except, she specifically recalled, when the script called for the Rider and the Stallion to leap across a wide gorge.

"When you see those scenes," she smiled coyly, "that was Mr. Canutt. He was the only one they knew could do it. Why, when Mr. Canutt mounted a horse, it almost seemed to take wings!"

Miss Carmen had brought to Charlotte with her an ankle-length feather head dress that was supposed to have been worn by the Rider in the serial; but, since it obscured too much of her, they changed it to a much shorter, shoulder-length one.

"And they gave me this long one as a souvenir, which I have kept ever since," she beamed, "Isn't it beautiful?" And in truth, it was.

Beautiful leading lady Jennifer Holt was featured in two serials — *Adventures of the Flying Cadets* at Universal, and Columbia's *Hop Harrigan* — and vivacious Peggy Stewart made four — Republic's *The Phantom Rider* in 1945 and *Son of Zorro* in 1947; and Columbia's *Tex Granger* (1948) and *Cody of the Pony Express* (1950). They both have charmed Film Fairgoers at Charlotte.

John Crawford played good and bad guys in at least nine serials for both Columbia and Republic; and Terry Frost played in at least a dozen — and they both had many good stories to tell about the "Sam Katzman days." Tommy Farrell played sidekick to Buster Crabbe in Columbia's *Pirates of the High Seas* in 1950, and nearly flipped out when he confirmed, by comparing their serial credits, that he and John Crawford had made one together.

"You see, Johnny, there it is!" he exclaimed, pointing at a copy of *In the Nick of Time, — Son of Geronimo!* "1952! Farrell there; and Crawford there. I *knew* we did one together!"

George Montgomery talked about his role as one of the five young rangers in the classic Republic serial *The Lone Ranger* in Charlotte; Joe Sawyer recalled his part in Universal's *Raiders of Ghost City* in 1944; and Lash LaRue will admit to making *The Master Key* for Universal in 1945, but does not like to be reminded that he was billed as Alfred Larue at the

Opposite: **Jennifer Holt *(left)* is requested as a Western Film Fair return guest more than almost anyone else. Fans love her charm and never-fading beauty.**

time. All three moved on to bigger things, but they each remembered the serial they did, and would share the memory with you at the least suggestion. And if you want to hear some stories, ask Oliver Drake—actor, writer, composer, director, producer—about his work in serials. He wrote *Undersea Kingdom* when Republic was brand new, and *Riders of Death Valley* when Universal wanted to do a "Million-Dollar Serial," but a lot of the stories he has shared in Charlotte are about those serials he worked on without official credits.

And the beat goes on!

This year—July 11, 12 and 13 at the Radisson Plaza Hotel in Charlotte—there will be James Craig, who made *Flying G-Men* and *Overland with Kit Carson* for Columbia and *Winners of the West* for Universal before rising to stardom as a romantic leading man at Metro-Goldwyn-Mayer; Shirley Patterson, who played "Linda Paige" in Columbia's 1943 *Batman* before becoming a leading lady in westerns and features; Pierce Lyden, who played a henchman in a number of Columbia serials, as well as in countless westerns at Columbia, Republic and Monogram; and House Peters, Jr., who will be there to talk about his work in Universal's *Adventures of Frank Merriwell*, Columbia's *Batman and Robin* (1949), and his leading role as Tris Coffin's right-hand man in Republic's serial classic *King of the Rocketmen*.

In addition to being able to meet and talk to these folks who were there when it happened, you will also be able to see samplers of some outstanding serial chapters, and complete showings of *Winners of the West, King of the Rocketmen, Dick Tracy* (Republic, 1937) and *The Secret Code* (Columbia, 1942), which have been confirmed so far—with another cliffhanger to be selected from several other titles in the works at this writing.

And that's just the serial part. We haven't even mentioned the "main event"—the westerns!

So, after all is said and done—if you're a serial or western fan—you need to be in Charlotte next month. I hope you will be; and I'll see you there.

Needless to say, it must have worked. As usual, the Western Film Fair was well attended, and a good time was had by all.

There has always been one sad element to the Western Film Fairs, however, and that is that no one thought to start them before so many of the western and serial favorites passed on. It seems that someone is always making the remark that it's a shame that "so-and-so" could never visit a film fair. And, strangely, most of the actors named were the ones who played the bad guys. For some reason, the fans regret not having the chance to meet certain screen villains.

The "What-If" Time Warp
September 1986

When you stop to think about it, a fantastic thing has happened in the past fifteen years.

Since the first serial and western fan conventions in the early 1970s—and up to the most recent Western Film Fair this past July—people who were little kids back in the hey day of the cliffhangers and horse operas have been able to meet and get to know personally some of the stars and players they used to thrill to on the movie screens each Saturday. Back then we never dreamed we would ever see any of those people in person—much less actually *meet* them. Then, when it began to happen, the old films and our memories of them took on a new dimension: we were able to watch them again with the players sitting there in the room, answering our questions and explaining scenes we had always wondered about. If we had ever dreamed of meeting and talking to our favorites, the film conventions have been a dream come true for many of us.

To a devout serial fan, it still seems unreal to say that we have had conversations with the likes of Jock Mahoney, "Crash" Corrigan, Kirk Alyn, Buster Crabbe, Bob Livingston, George Letz, Frank Coghlan, Clayton Moore, Victor Jory, Don Barry, and Rod Cameron. These are the men who helped shape our young lives with their displays of bravery and derring-do.

And, believe it or not, many of us now have personal memories to treasure that involve those men that played the heroes, as well as some who played the bad guys: Tris Coffin, Terry Frost, George J. Lewis, Pierce Lyden, Yakima Canutt, Marshall Reed, John Crawford—and on and on.

Furthermore, in addition to the great Yak Canutt and Jock Mahoney, serial fans have heard first-hand from other stars of the stunting profession such as George De Normand, Tom Steele, and the legendary David Sharpe, describing exactly how they conceived, planned, prepared and executed some of the breathtaking scenes we recall from childhood.

We have been privileged to fall in love again with the beautiful leading ladies of serials and westerns. First we loved their celluloid images, now the ladies themselves, thanks to meeting them at Film Fairs. Who could meet and not fall in love with Peggy Stewart? And the vivacious Nell O'Day? Can you forget how Nyoka Kay Aldridge thrilled the fans at St. Louis? The gorgeous Joan Woodbury, serialdom's "Brenda Starr," was as beautiful as ever there. The remarkable, bird-like charm of Jean Carmen, Republic's very first female serial hero billed as Julia Thayer; the lovely and unforgettable Jennifer Holt. The enduring personality of Dorothy

Gulliver; the courage and grit of Iris Meredith. And, more recently, the regal beauty and grace of Shirley Patterson.

A dream come true is just about the only way to sum up the phenomenon of the Film Fairs. Certainly not many of us would have expected to meet so many of our heroes in person back when we were kids watching them on the screen. But since it has happened, it has created a new fantasy that we sometimes hear talked about among fans of westerns and serials. A fantasy that would involve a "What-if... time warp."

It goes like this: What if ... the fan conventions had started about fifteen years before they did? Or, What if ... time could be controlled so as to bring back some of the people who had passed on before the early seventies? And, What if ... some of those people could be brought in as convention guests? What would it be like to talk to them as we have these others? And, if the "what-if's" were to be granted, who would we choose to return?

At first you might think this is merely conjecture. But I have heard that "What-if..." a surprisingly large number of times at the various conventions. And it is interesting to suppose just what it would be like.

For example, what if Ralph Byrd could have attended a film convention? There is no way he could, for he died very young—in 1952 at the age of 43—and no one had as yet even thought of having fan conventions. But, if he could, just think of the stories he could tell from his days at Mascot, the four fantastic Dick Tracy serials at Republic, his work at Universal, as a featured player for Cecil B. DeMille, his roles in the RKO Dick Tracy features, his starring roles in action films for Lippert, and the ill-fated Tracy TV series. Having met him in the late 1940s when he was on a personal appearance tour, I can attest that he would have been a great Film Fair guest.

The same is true of the other heroes of serials like Warren Hull, Kane Richmond, Tom Tyler and Duncan Renaldo. And western stars who made serials such as Buck Jones, Johnny Mack Brown and Wild Bill Elliott. Their stories about serials or westerns would be legion.

But the "What-if's..." I have heard the most have been, interestingly enough, not about the stars or the leading players, but the "bad guys." That tough-talking, swaggering, hard-riding, shot glass-drinking, saloon-fighting gang of ne'er-do-wells who always caused trouble for the heroes, and who always got their come-uppance before the film was over. For some reason, they are the ones that fans always mention when they say "What-if...."

What if ... Bud Osborne could come to a Film Fair? Bud was in the first sound serial *(The Indians Are Coming)* and the last one *(Blazing the Overland Trail)*, and most of the western ones in between. Just think of the stories.

And how would you like to be able to talk to Jack Ingram? If it had not been for Jack (who loved sailing on his time off, and sometimes rented his ranch out for movie location shooting), Columbia's serial department would have had to hire at least three other guys. Jack did everything at Columbia.

George Chesebro. A person who calls himself a serial or western fan and does not know who George Chesebro was, is flying under false colors. Just to see the man sneer in person would be a treat.

Equally at home under one of the biggest hats in western movies, or in a saloon-keeper's black suit, or deep inside the armor of one of "Ming, the Merciless's" troops, or in the famous disguise of the Frankenstein monster, or behind the friendly moustache of "Sam, the bartender" in *Gunsmoke*, Glenn Strange must have had a wealth of tall stories to tell. And I have it from those who knew him that it didn't take too much to get him started.

One of the most under-rated actors in westerns was Ernie Adams. But the fans all remembered him, and that's what mattered. A stalwart from silent movie days up to his death in 1947, the sad-faced little thespian would also have had some stories to tell.

Anybody who ever saw the Charles Starrett westerns would want to meet Dick Curtis. He was Charlie's perennial nemesis. So much so that all the good work he did in so many other westerns and serials is often overlooked because of what he was best known for. But, as anyone who has been to them knows, the Film Fair is where you can really find out what happened in an actor's career.

Smooth-talking I. Stanford Jolley; kindly (or deadly, depending on the role) old Edmund Cobb; and rough-sounding Kenne Duncan would have been terrific on the guest panels or in personal conversations along the aisles in the dealers' room. Each one could tell you many tales of their experiences in cliffhangers and soap operas.

Of all the people who worked in serials and westerns, the two that are most mentioned as candidates for the "What-if . . . time warp" are Charles King and Roy Barcroft. Above all the rest, most serial and western fans feel that if any two could be brought back as guests at a film fan convention, it should be these two. Barcroft's impact on Republic serials was overwhelming (as well as his impact on their westerns). And Charlie King's impact on series westerns was nothing short of phenomenal (as well as his impact on Columbia serials). Every fan knows these two, and to a man agree that they were the absolute leaders as bad guys. To meet them personally would be as much as a serial or western fan could ever hope for.

Charles King's career stretched all the way from silent films to the 1950s. He played in serials for practically everybody who made them, and portrayed the outlaw in westerns with just about every major western star

of the entire period. You can imagine what stories he could have told. And I'm told by those that knew him that he, too, would uncork them at the slightest hint or provocation.

Most of the people who have come to the film conventions that ever worked with Roy Barcroft have said the same thing about him: He was a thorough professional and a joy to work with. A big, gruff bully on the screen in most of his film appearances, they say he was a gentle, good-humored man off screen. When the time came to do business, however, he was a very conscientious and accomplished actor. His career spanned from the late 1930s in bit parts in Universal and Republic serials up to the late 1960s in character parts for TV shows like *Gunsmoke* and *Bonanza*. His greatest fame was between 1943 and 1953 as Republic's ace serial and western villain. Just think of the experiences he could recall.

All of these "bad guys" would probably be surprised at how popular they would be with fans of the old serials and westerns if they could come back as guests at a Western Film Fair. But I have a hunch that Barcroft might be a little bit astounded to learn of the great respect his work is now being held in; and Charlie King might be more than a little touched to find out how much his fans have come to love him.

Without a "What-if..." time warp, though, I guess they'll never know.

Oh, well, no use crying about it; it just wasn't meant to be. Fortunately, not a lot of time is wasted on what might have been, since most people who attend Western Film Fairs seem satisfied with being able to meet and talk to the ones who can come. The fans seem to recognize that the film fairs are a phenomenon that should be enjoyed while it is possible, just as the "Kemp-Circuit" tours were, 40-plus years ago.

Just as in all things, there have been feasts and famines for serial lovers at the Western Film Fairs. A couple of times no serial actors have attended (except for Alfred "Lash" LaRue, who appeared in one serial and comes to every film fair), and other times almost everyone was a serial veteran. In one column I reminisced about one such year with a great deal of pleasure:

Opposite: The late Roy Barcroft, dean of the bad guys in the westerns and serials, tops any list of would-be guests for film conventions in a "what-if" situation.

The Cliffhanger Revisited
October 1987

Serials were well represented at the Charlotte Western Film Fair this year. There were no less than six guests this time who had been featured in one or more serials. In a way it kind of made up for that one year when we "goofed" and didn't have any. Also, the guests that were here represented a cross-section of the characters that inhabited serials—a hero, a heroine, a villain, a child star, a top stuntwoman, and a featured player who became a star. And their activities in serials ranged from 1937 to 1956—nearly the entire span of the sound serial era. Indeed, this was a vintage year.

The actor who played a serial hero was Richard Martin, who headed the cast of Universal's *Mysterious Mr. M* in 1946. His co-star was Dennis Moore, and the cast included people like Pamela Blake, Virginia Brissac, Edmund MacDonald, Danny Morton, Byron Foulger and Jack Ingram. This serial had the dubious distinction of being the last chapterplay released by Universal—August, 1946. Martin was better known as the character known as "Chito Rafferty," the part–Mexican, part–Irish sidekick in many Tim Holt westerns at RKO in the late 1940s.

During his appearance on the Panel of Stars at the Film Fair, Martin related an incident that occurred when he was a teenager in the 1930s, involving a movie luminary we all knew of. As a helper on a milk delivery truck, he and the truck's driver made a run every day past a house in the Bronson Canyon area of Los Angeles. At intervals, they noticed a man outside one of the houses doing a very strange thing—trimming his hedge with a long bullwhip. Curiosity, he said, finally got the best of them, so they stopped one day and asked the guy why he was doing that. His reply was that he was keeping in practice with the bullwhip for his job, which was working in the movies. When they questioned him further, he explained that he was a stuntman and used a whip a lot. His name: Yakima Canutt.

The serial heroine, who was making a return trip to Charlotte, was Jean Carmen—also known as Julia Thayer. In addition to portraying the mysterious Indian girl who rode the pinto stallion and warned the wagon train pioneers of impending danger in Republic's *The Painted Stallion,* she also had played the leading lady in many westerns with The Three Mesquiteers, Fred Scott, and other top western stars in the 1930s. For many years, she has produced and starred in movies in Europe, and had one—*The Pawn*—honored with an award at the Cannes Film Festival.

Our visiting villain was veteran serial heavy Pierce Lyden. Featured in more westerns and serials than you could count (and uncredited in some of them), Pierce started menacing the good guys at Columbia as early as 1941, and continued to do so for several decades. Two of the serials he appeared in—*The Sea Hound* and *Blackhawk*—were shown at the Film Fair, and Pierce sat in on both, as well as several westerns he was featured in.

Evelyn Finley, one of the greatest stuntwomen in Hollywood, was there, as lovely as ever. Her single serial credit, *Perils of the Wilderness*, was released by Columbia in 1956, and she was billed by another name, Eve Anderson, for that one time only. Her own personal life, however, contained more thrills and spills than any Sam Katzman serial, and she was very gracious about discussing any of her stunts and assignments with her legion of fans.

Of course, Lash LaRue, who has been a star guest at every Charlotte Western Film Fair so far, is the featured player who went on to become a star. In 1945 he appeared in Universal's *The Master Key* in a featured role, billed as Alfred LaRue. But, shortly after that, he won a part in an Eddie Dean western and made such an impact on the western fans that he was starred in a series of his own, with Al "Fuzzy" St. John as his sidekick. Those westerns starring the "King of the Bullwhip" have become classics of what are known as "B" westerns.

Sammy McKim was 12 years old when he played Kit Carson as a boy in *The Painted Stallion,* in 1937. In addition to roles in westerns at Republic for the next couple of years, he went on to be featured in four other serials. In 1938 he played in *The Great Adventures of Wild Bill Hickok* for Columbia and in Republic's classic *The Lone Ranger.* And in 1939 he was featured in *Dick Tracy's G-Men* for Republic, and had a key role in Columbia's *The Flying G-Men.* So great was his impact that Republic considered making a series of westerns starring Sammy as a boy western star; but, because of financial disagreements, no contract was ever completed and the series was not produced.

Following World War II, Sam appeared in several small roles at Republic and 20th Century–Fox, and worked in the art department at Fox. An accomplished artist, his career evolved to the Walt Disney studio, where he spent 32 years as an artist and illustrator, working on some of Disney's greatest effort at Disneyland in California, and Walt Disney World in Florida. Sam retired in January of this year at a very young age of 62, and came to Charlotte with his lovely wife, Dorothy.

It was interesting for me to note that both Jean Carmen and Sammy McKim sat through all 12 chapters of *The Painted Stallion*—and it was the second time in recent years for each of them.

It is obvious that they, too—like all of us serial fans for many years—know a good thing when they see it.

In talking to the people who made the serials, I always found it refreshing to hear them talk about other actors you might have met during the theater-tour days or at earlier film fairs. It was a lot like hearing about old friends, even though you knew that realistically they were not actually friends of yours; they only seemed so.

And, I guess that's the charm of meeting the people in person who made the films you liked so much. Whether you know each other or not, there is the feeling that you shared something in common with them. And a lot of them—it is obvious to see—feel just the same way.

Chapter 3

"Sure, I Can Do It... Do What?"

One of the most fascinating things about meeting the people who were involved in the production of serials is that you can learn a lot if you will only listen. The stories some of those actors recall are perhaps being told just to make a point the actors want to make—and they do. However, they also contain background and "throw-away" information that may be intended to frame the story, but that also provides valuable insight for someone who wants to know more about how the films were made. Hearing someone complain about some slight problem he had on the set, for example, gives you some understanding of what the casts and crews went through to get their proposed stuff on film.

It is sometimes strange to hear that your screen heroes had everyday problems making movies—just like everyday people do in their jobs—and even stranger to learn that they are often only all too human as well. However, it is never strange to learn that there were those who instinctively knew how to make things work—who led the way in discovering new ways to make movies more exciting and more fun for us. And it is reassuring to know about the people who could put it all together and bring it to life.

The Way You Do It, Making Movies
April 1988

One of the greatest of all serial heroines was Helen Holmes, who made some of the earliest cliffhangers of the movies. She, along with Helen Gibson, Mary Fuller, Grace Cunard and the great Pearl White, were the leading ladies who established the serial as a distinct form of movie entertainment in its first several years of existence. As the form evolved from

that of a series of complete episodes to the open-ended chapters, incomplete and continued from week to week, these ladies—along with leading men such as Ben Wilson, Creighton Hale, Tom Santschi and Francis Ford (John's brother)—gave the new form its life and direction. As they perfected it, the serial form stayed basically the same throughout its entire life.

In 1914 Helen Holmes starred in perhaps the longest series/serial ever made. *The Hazards of Helen*, produced by Kalem Productions and released by Pathé, was started in theatres in November, 1914, and ran for 119 episodes. In October, 1915, Miss Holmes left Kalem to go to Universal, and the role of "Helen" in *The Hazards...* was continued by Helen Gibson (wife of cowboy star "Hoot") until the end of the series, which finally ran for over two years.

Recently, with a group of friends, I enjoyed watching Episode Nine of that great classic, titled *The Leap from the Water Tower*. Helen Holmes and a group of heavies were all over a moving train—running, dodging, fighting, and hanging over the sides—and it was obvious there were no stuntmen doing it, just the actors themselves. When the tense moment came for the brave railroad girl to drop from the water tower on to the moving train, it was Helen Holmes herself who did it. By today's standards, it seems remarkable to contemplate such a thing.

But in 1914 no one thought that was unusual. It was just the way you did it, making movies. No big deal. The plucky Miss Holmes performed dozens of equally risky feats—some, even more risky—during the filming of *Hazards*. As her director, J. P. McGowan, was quoted as saying on a number of occasions, "It's all in a day's work."

Famous western star Lash LaRue, while attending the Western Film Fair in Charlotte, and sitting on panels there and elsewhere, has said many times regarding the use of stuntmen,

"At P.R.C. we couldn't afford to hire them, so we had to do those things ourselves. It ain't because we wanted to; we just had to."

That's just the way you did it, making movies.

In 1932 a young rodeo and former silent western star met a rising young player on the set of a Mascot serial being produced by Nat Levine. Yakima Canutt, one of the greatest rodeo performers of all time, met young John Wayne while making *The Shadow of the Eagle*, and the stunt profession as we know it today was born. They, along with such innovators as Richard Talmadge and Alan Pomeroy, developed techniques and

Opposite: Pirate Treasure—Universal, 1934—featured **Richard Talmadge** *(in midair)*, who followed the tradition of Helen Holmes, Pearl White, Helen Gibson, and Joe Bonomo as an action stunt pioneer and innovator, doing things "the way you do it—making movies."

devices to enable trained professional stuntmen to substitute for the actors in scenes involving risk or dangers, so that the actors would not be injured by accident, and also the action would look more credible on the screen. These techniques became the accepted way to do things in subsequent film production. In only a few years, it was just the way you did it, making movies.

For the next decade, it was difficult to determine whether you were seeing John Carroll or Reed Hadley—or Yakima Canutt—as "Zorro"; Tom Tyler or Kane Richmond—or David Sharpe—as "Captain Marvel" and "Spy Smasher"; and Dick Purcell or Roy Barcroft—or Dale Van Sickel—as "Captain America" and "Captain Mephisto." With skillful editing and expert direction, it was made to appear that one person, the actor, was doing all that was seen on the screen. Even today, purists still debate where certain editing cuts or actual switches were made in various scenes.

It's kind of funny, though, how something can go to the extreme—even this. And I became more aware of it just the other night. From a time when the principle players did all the action scenes themselves, things went full-circle to a time when none of them did—and the person who did remained totally anonymous.

I was watching *The Masked Marvel,* a Republic serial released in 1943. The hero was a masked crimefighter who was supposed to be in reality one of four young investigators played by Rod Bacon, Bill Healy, Richard Clarke and David Bacon. All handsome young men, and all bearing a physical resemblance to the masked hero, none of them ever did any of the action scenes—even the actor who was supposed to *be* "The Masked Marvel." All of the hero's scenes—plus the stunt work for each of the investigators when they became involved in the plot—were done by professional stuntman Tom Steele.

The curious thing is that Steele received absolutely no billing in the serial at all, even though he also played a heavy in several episodes. The reason is that Republic at first entertained the idea of billing him at the top of the cast and then—for fear the public might react in the wrong way—took his name off the top as the lead actor. The only thing is, they failed to put it back in anywhere else.

Oh well, that's just the way you do things, making movies.

In addition to doing research, there is no better way to learn how movies were put together than to hear it from those who were there. And it is intriguing to find out that sometimes they weren't done the way you thought they were, but the way you do it—making movies.

Tom Steele *(left)* grapples with ace stuntman Eddie Parker in this classic 1943 action serial and was the featured hero for 12 episodes, with no mention of his name in the credits. Sometimes, "that's the way it is, making movies," he said.

Most of us view the making of motion pictures with an innate romanticism. With rare exceptions, when moviemakers themselves have depicted the production of movies on the screen, a minimum of the human side has been shown. Mainly what you see is the set; the camera, with a busy cameraman fussing with lenses; the actors, being theatrical; and a dapperly dressed director, who gives his instructions to the actors and technicians in "fatherly" tones and calls out "Cut!" when something looks good or goes badly. All businesslike. And, essentially, that may be the way it is. But, you learn from those who were there, that it is not all there is.

In making movies—especially serials—you find out that things may or may not be what they seem—that, sometimes, human beings can be overzealous in their efforts to find work and can get involved in something for which they are not equipped or prepared, and the result is not so businesslike. That thought got me going one day.

Gentle Deception
August 1985

When the long-awaited call came that included the inevitable question, "Can you do a certain job?" the anxious actor's answer always had to be, "Sure I can. When do you want me to report?" Even though you couldn't do the thing being asked, to give any other answer meant they would call someone else; and you always needed the work; so, sure you could.

That sort of reply is a thread that runs through the stories and conversations of most of the actors and actresses of the 1930s and 1940s who come to Film Fairs and conventions. They all have stories about themselves—or others—that reflect the eagerness that actors had to get work—any work—even to the point of not sticking strictly to the truth about their qualifications or capabilities. But it was never meant as a lie or to harmfully deceive anyone. It just meant that they had to quickly become good at something they had never done before—sort of a capsule illustration of the old cliches "to have greatness thrust upon you" or "rising to the occasion."

An immediate example that comes to mind is the story Lash LaRue tells of how he became "Lash" instead of "Alfred" LaRue in the movies. As the latter, he was under contract to Universal and had appeared with Milburn Stone and Dennis Moore in the 1945 serial *The Master Key*. When P.R.C.. needed an actor to play a "bad-good guy" in an Eddie Dean western they were preparing, the call went out for a young man who could not only act the part, but could also handle a bullwhip. When LaRue was interviewed and asked the key question, "Can you handle a whip?" his answer was, "Sure, I can. How long a whip do you want me to handle?" Well, he got the part; and, as Lash tells it, he nearly beat himself to death learning how to use a bullwhip—but he learned. And, as they say, the rest is history.

Eddie Dean also has a story to tell along that line: One day in the early 1940s, when he was doing supporting parts and musical numbers in westerns with Hopalong Cassidy and other stars, he received a call from the producer of a new Johnny Mack Brown western asking him if he had a trio that could sing in the picture. "Sure, I do. When do you want us?" he asked. "This afternoon," came the reply. Well, Eddie had never performed in a trio before, he says; but, by that afternoon, he and two friends of his were the trio the studio wanted, and no one was the wiser. The intervening hours of rehearsal at his house were kind of hectic, though, he recalls with a grin.

Someone has asked western singer and champion yodeler Carolina Cotton how she learned to yodel, or if she had always known how. Her answer was that she didn't know anything about it until one day during a rehearsal when she was asked if she could do a certain song with yodeling in it, and her reply was, "Sure, I can. Why not?" Only after she got started did she find out that she could. From there to world's champion yodeler "Ain't bad."

When Universal was putting together a cast for their 1935 serial *Adventures of Frank Merriwell*, the producer, Henry MacRae, decided to use the sons—"juniors," if you will—of famous actors, as fellow team members of hero Frank Merriwell, who was played by Don Briggs. He lined up Jean Hersholt, Jr., Wallace Reid, Jr., and Bryant Washburn, Jr.— among others. Young House Peters, Jr., had not received a call yet, but wanted to be in that serial. So, he climbed the fence at Universal and joined in with the other "juniors," just as if he had also been called. When asked if he were one of the "juniors," that had been called, he answered, "Sure, I am," and it was no lie: his father was a very famous star of the silent screen. His bluff worked, and he became the "heavy" team mate who always expressed doubts about the hero's motives and intentions—a substantial featured part.

The stories get pretty hairy when they get around to people saying they could do certain things in action scenes and involving livestock when they really couldn't. In that kind of movie-making (as serials were), there is an element of danger involved that makes it very risky for an amateur to pretend professionalism. One of the potentially dangerous incidents of that nature is related by veteran bad man Pierce Lyden about a young actor he knew and Lyden's old friend, serial director Spencer G. Bennet. Early in that young actor's career, Bennet hired him to play in *Perils of the Wilderness,* the 15-chapter serial he was filming for Sam Katzman and Columbia Pictures on location at Big Bear country in California. When the actor was asked if he could ride a horse, his answer was the usual, "Sure, I can. When do I report?" So, he got the job and was assigned to be a bad guy alongside Lyden, who was an expert horseman.

In one of their first scenes together, Lyden recalls, the two of them were to ride up and around a formation of rocks, stop at a designated spot in medium range of the camera, speak several lines of dialogue, and then ride on out of range. Well, everything worked all right up to a point: The two men mounted their horses, rode around the rock formation, and Lyden came to a stop—but the other guy kept right on going. He could stay on the horse, but he didn't know how to stop it. The crew had to scramble to keep from being run over. After several unsuccessful attempts to get it right, Bennet switched the positions of Lyden and the other actor and told Lyden to head him into the rocks—or something—

but get him stopped at the proper place. Lyden did that and the shot worked.

"It was typical of good old Spence," recalls Lyden with a smile. "It never occurred to him to fire the guy and replace him."

According to Pierce Lyden, in all of the more than two dozen serials Spencer Bennet directed for Columbia, it was a rare thing for the veteran director to fire anybody—even when it was obvioius that the person was not working out, or had misrepresented himself.

"He was probably my favorite director of all," offers Lyden, "and was one terrific man. Spence wanted everybody to work who wanted to work. It's a little surprising he didn't get more cons worked on him than he did."

And, could all the other directors always spot a phony?

Sure, they could!

In their anxiety to stay employed, some actors would agree to almost anything. That's why they would quickly respond, "Sure, I can do it," without even knowing what the job was going to be. Practically every visiting guest from Hollywood I have ever met has a story to illustrate that human trait in actors, and it has come as somewhat of a surprise to learn how many careers (such as LaRue's) were launched that way.

In one area of filmmaking, however, this was almost never done. It could be fatal to dash in to it unqualified or unprepared, so it became the exclusive province of that small group of specialists known as "stuntmen," who were trained and organized for it and who risked their lives and safety to perform hazardous physical feats for the actors. The stuntmen performed unheralded, but their work became the visual centerpieces for each serial. The cliffhanger would have been nothing without them, but, with them, it became a thing of wonder.

As in any field of endeavor, one person led the way: the starter, the innovator, the designer, the mechanic, the executor, the critic, the analyst, or the perfector—the best. Many others in the profession became good enough to excel in one or two areas—maybe becoming almost as good—but none became good enough to succeed him. Eventually, even the official motion picture industry had to acknowledge his accomplishments and his worth.

Opposite: Pierce Lyden *(left)* related an experience with a young actor named John Mitchum (Robert's brother), who indulged in "gentle deception," with almost disastrous results.

The King of the Hill
March 1986

On that September day in 1914 when he rode out of Colfax, Washington, headed for Walla Walla and the Pioneer Frontier Days Rodeo, he was not yet 19 years old. His main goal was to win first prize in the saddle-bronc riding event; and, having already ridden just about all the horses the Whitman County Fair had to offer, he allowed himself the luxury of high hopes. There was no way of knowing at that time that he would not only accomplish that immediate task, but go on to perform many others and eventually become much more than his mind could even conceive. His name was Enos Edward Canutt, and he was taking the first step toward becoming a legend in his own lifetime.

A couple of months ago, that young man turned 90. Now he is internationally known as "Yakima" Canutt, and is recognized as the greatest movie stuntman who ever lived—bar none. He is credited by many students, devotees and historians of the motion picture with having actually created the stunt profession as we know it in American films. I have yet to meet a serious challenger of that contention. His credits as actor, stuntman, stunt coordinator, second-unit director and director reach from *Equus* in 1976 all the way back to *The Girl Who Dared* in 1920, and include every type of film from serials and "B" westerns—in some of which he played an Indian (with a western drawl)—to the classic feature *Ben Hur*, for which he staged the greatest chariot race of all time.

In the early 1930s, while working for Nat Levine making Mascot serials, Canutt and young actor John Wayne, along with the troupe of veteran screen heavies who also worked at Mascot, began changing the "job" of stunt-doubling for the leading players into a "profession." Almost an "art." Their choreography of screen fights elevated that bit of visual action from a hodge-podge of flailing elbows and limbs to a finely designed pattern of coordinated physical motion between the actors that allowed the audience to comprehend and almost become a part of what they could see happening. The result gave the moviegoer a sense of participation that had been lacking.

The same concept was adapted to action stunts of other kinds as time went on. Canutt was a master at performing a dangerous feat with such deliberate, fluid motion that it almost looked easy. At least, the viewer could understand exactly what he was trying to do and how he was doing it. The reason, of course, is that nothing—not even the tiniest split-second detail—was left to chance. Canutt planned and timed every motion he was going to make before a man moved, a horse walked, a wagon rolled, or the

Doubling for someone in an action scene one moment and playing a small part in the next was all in a day's work for the "king" of the stuntmen, Yakima Canutt (*third from the left* in this scene from *Mysterious Doctor Satan*—Republic, 1940).

camera started. He then, deliberately and painstakingly, carried out the plan to the letter. The result was, in a word, perfection. His leaps from a horse to a moving vehicle, from one vehicle to another, to the ground from a vehicle as if shot from it, over the head of a stumbling horse, and (his masterpiece) a drop from the tongue of a stagecoach to the ground under running horses, all were performed many times, and always completely without injury to any animal involved, or to any actor who followed Canutt's very explicit directions.

Always, he has said, his primary concern in designing a stunt was to get the action on film, but without anyone getting hurt. That's why there was so much planning involved before anything happened. If anything was to go wrong, he figured, let it go wrong on paper, not on the set. In his book, *Stunt Man* (Walker & Co., 1979), by Canutt and his old friend Oliver Drake, the incident is related in which his own son, Joe Canutt, while doubling for Charlton Heston in the *Ben Hur* race, changed his positions on the chariot just slightly from his dad's instructions, and nearly wound up with a broken arm.

Yakima Canutt, King of the Hill.

In the middle 1930s, Mascot and several other small companies merged with Consolidated Film Industries, a film processing company, and became Republic Pictures. One of that new company's brightest stars would be John Wayne; but, one of its most valuable assets would be Yakima Canutt. His expertise and unexcelled professionalism at making action scenes come alive on the screen became the standard at Republic. Following that standard, the new company became the leader in making budget action films (primarily westerns) and the undisputed champion in the serial field, which was founded on that kind of action. For many years it prospered by turning out action pictures that still hold up by comparison today; and, during that time, Yakima Canutt directed a good many of them, while influencing all of them.

During the 1950s, Canutt moved his experience and expertise to the

Walt Disney Studio and continued to provide direction for many films for theatrical and television release. Following this and his classic chariot race for *Ben Hur* in 1959, he could almost "write his own ticket" as an action director in Hollywood. On April 10, 1967, the Academy of Motion Picture Arts and Sciences gave him a special award for his contributions to the motion picture industry—the only time it had chosen to so honor a member of the stunting profession.

Not too many people get to reach the venerable age of 90. Fewer still get to realize most of the dreams and ambitions they had for themselves when they were young. And only a select handful can say that they really reached the pinnacle of their chosen profession during a lifetime—and thus became "King of the Hill," as it were. So, when a man does all these things—as Enos Edward Yakima Canutt has done—I think it's pretty safe to say he is a legend in his own lifetime.

At the absolute least: to any true lover of westerns and serials, he is.

It was because of men like Yakima Canutt that serials were as good as they were. Whether you think of serials as "trash" or "treasure," the stuntmen made them something to behold. And the music men made them something to remember.

The person who usually asked the question, "Can you do such and such a thing?" so that actors could quickly say, "Sure, I can," was the director. It was his responsibility to put all the various resources together and come up with a finished product. There were a number of good directors, but the passing of one of the best several years ago triggered a tribute to him and his work.

"Directed by Spencer G. Bennet..."
December 1987

It's kinda funny how often you start out to do one thing and wind up doing something else. Life keeps dropping things in your path that divert you away from your original goal. But, often what you find is that the new thing really works in with the other thing, and you still arrive at the same destination, or conclusion. This article is an example of how that works.

As most collectors know by now, the 1948 Columbia serial *Superman* was recently released on videocassettes, and the reaction has been varied. There was general elation at first that this long-withheld chapterplay was

finally being made available to serial fans. Then there was mixed emotion when the tapes finally came out: praise for the high quality of the reproduction, but disappointment that the openings and closings had been edited out of all but the first episode on each of the two cassettes. Also, when some critics saw it for the first time, there were some negative reviews about the production itself (mainly based on thoughtless comparisons with the multi-million dollar state-of-the-art epics that came nearly 30 years later), and these upset some serial purists who had kept a revered memory of the 1948 production in their hearts. Altogether, the release of this serial has caused more controversy with serial fans than anything has in a long time—at least since the release of *Raiders of the Lost Ark* and the discussion of its kinship to the cliffhangers of the 1930s and 1940s.

This article was to have been about that controversy—examining the plus and minus factors of the *Superman* cassettes themselves, as well as the pros and cons of the reaction to them. What had not already been written down on notes was being mulled over in my mind, until I picked up a copy of the Myrtle Beach, South Carolina, *Sun News* on October 10th and read that Spencer Gordon Bennet had died at the age of 94. That news immediately changed the direction of this article.

It just so happens that Spencer G. Bennet, along with Thomas Carr, directed *Superman* for Sam Katzman and Columbia Pictures in 1948. It also happens that Spencer G. Bennet was—next to Ray Taylor—the most prolific director of serials in the entire sound era, after having been one of the leading directors of silent serials in the 1920s. His sound serial credits reached from *The Last Frontier* for RKO Radio in 1932 to *Blazing the Overland Trail* at Columbia in 1956, which was the last serial ever made. Included are some of the all-time favorites of many of us, and many that are considered classics of the genre. By any standard, Spencer G. Bennet has a place among the top three or four serial directors of all time.

That being the case, the arguments pro and con concerning the *Superman* videocassettes took on a new perspective. To me, it didn't seem quite so important any longer whether the opening credits of each and every chapter were on the tape or not. Nor how Katzman's use of animation to show Superman's flight compared to Salkind's computer-operated matte system. Nor even how it compared with Republic's use of rigging and rear-projection to make Captain Marvel and Rocketman fly. It certainly no longer seemed as important as before how each of the three actors that had played Superman—Kirk Alyn, George Reeves and Christopher Reeve—had interpreted the Clark Kent persona.

The important thing suddenly seemed to be that we now have it for

Opposite: **Of all the serials Spencer G. Bennet directed for Columbia, his best-known production was the film version of this classic comic strip.**

Top: The Purple Monster Strikes—Republic, 1945—was the eighth of 13 serials Spencer G. Bennet directed for Republic and is remembered by serial fans as the prototype for the science fiction films of the 1950s. *Bottom: Congo Bill*—Columbia, 1948—Don McGuire, who played the hero in this serial directed by Spencer G. Bennet, later became a director himself, primarily in television.

what it's worth—to see and enjoy. That it is one more example of the kind of work done by the old "masters of the shoestring." That it still points up how amazing it was—and is—that men like Bennet—and Bill Witney, and Ray Taylor, and Jim Horne, and Sam Katzman, and Nat Levine—could take so little in the way of financing and come up with anything at all—much less anything good or entertaining—but so consistently did. And what seemed even more important was that the end result of the knowledge, experience, expertise and craftsmanship of these men were films that were, from a purely entertainment standpoint, very often as good—or better—than those upon which millions are spent today. It makes one wonder what those guys could have produced with the money to spend that today's film-makers have. Or, conversely, what today's guys would be turning out if they didn't have such vast sums of money to work with.

As a very young man, Spencer Bennet worked as a stuntman in silent movies before becoming a second-unit director under Bertram Millhauser at Pathé in 1920. He then served as assistant to the great George B. Seitz during the early 1920s, working on some of Pathé's greatest thrillers starring Pearl White, Charles Hutchinson, Allene Ray and Edna Murphy. His experience with Millhauser and Seitz prepared him to become one of the all-time great action directors, whose career spanned the entire serial era and extended into television.

The first release to credit him as director was Pathé's *Play Ball*, released in July 1925, starring Allene Ray and Walter Miller. It was the beginning of a 30-year career in serials that is unsurpassed by any other person. Until Pathé's demise in 1929, Bennet directed every serial starring Allene Ray and Walter Miller, which are considered by many students of silent films as classics, even today.

In the first decade of the sound era, Bennet directed mostly features and westerns for several studios, but he helped the new Columbia serial unit get off the ground in 1937 by directing *The Mysterious Pilot,* starring Captain Frank Hawkes. He then returned to Columbia in 1942 to direct *The Secret Code* and *The Valley of Vanishing Men*. From August 1943 (with *Secret Service in Darkest Africa*) until July 1947 (directing *The Black Widow*), Bennet continued the tradition of quality begun by William Witney and John English by directing all but two of Republic's serials—*The Crimson Ghost* and *Jesse James Rides Again*. During this time, he created what have become some of Republic's most memorable successes: *The Masked Marvel, The Tiger Woman, Zorro's Black Whip, Manhunt of Mystery Island, The Purple Monster Strikes, The Phantom Rider*, etc., and was directly instrumental in helping select Linda Stirling for the role of *The Tiger Woman*, which gave her a permanent place in the hearts of serial fans.

In late 1947, Sam Katzman hired Bennet to direct his serials at

UNDER MERCURY'S SINISTER SPELL!

JUNGLE DEADFALL
Chapter 13

MYSTERIOUS ISLAND
CAPTAIN HARDING'S FABULOUS ADVENTURES

with RICHARD CRANE as Captain Harding
Hugh PROSSER, Bernard HAMILTON as Neb
Marshall REED, Karen RANDLE, Ralph HODGES as Bert
as Rulu
as Pencroft
and GEORGE H PLYMPTON
Screen Play by LEWIS CLAY, ROYAL K. COLE after the novel by JULES VERNE
Story "L'ILE MYSTERIEUSE" · Directed by SPENCER BENNET
Produced by SAM KATZMAN · A COLUMBIA SUPER SERIAL

"*Directed by Spencer G. Bennet...*" 69

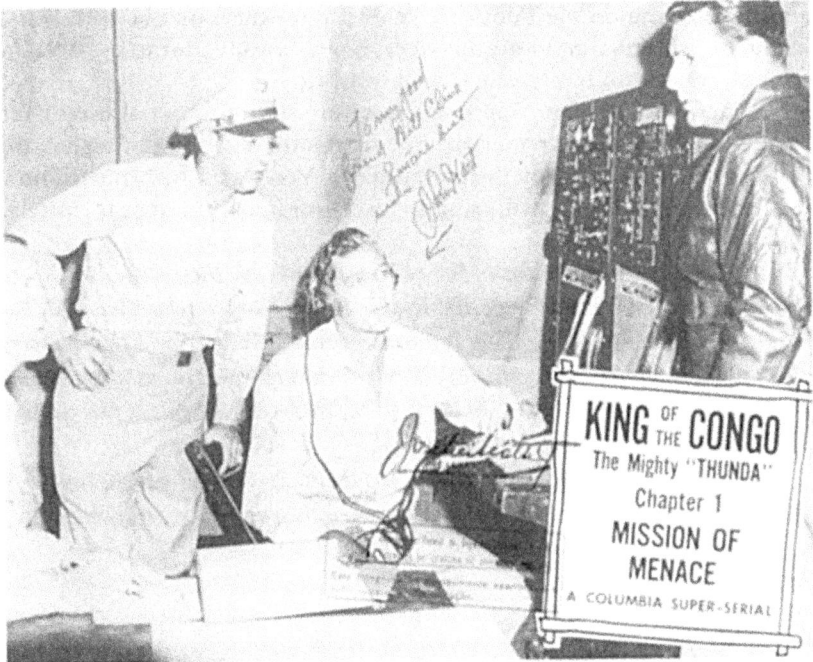

Buster Crabbe's final serial, *King of the Congo*—Columbia, 1952—was directed by Spencer G. Bennet and included in the cast John Hart *(center)*, who played the Lone Ranger on television for one year.

Columbia, beginning with *Brick Bradford*. From then until the end of the serial era in 1956, Spencer Gordon Bennet directed every serial released by Columbia except one. For a fan of Sam Katzman's Columbia serials— and they are many—this achievement includes the *Superman* serials, *Congo Bill*, *Bruce Gentry*, *Batman and Robin*, *The Adventures of Sir Galahad*, all three Jock Mahoneys, two Buster Crabbes, *Mysterious Island*, *Captain Video*, *Blackhawk*, *Son of Geronimo*, and the last three serials ever released: *Adventures of Captain Africa*, *Perils of the Wilderness* and *Blazing the Overland Trail*.

Without much fear of contradiction, it is easy to say that anyone who likes serials has enjoyed the work of Spencer Gordon Bennet—not just once, but many, many times. With so much to his credit, it would be difficult to find anyone in this collecting game who had not seen at least some of his work. So, we all owe Spencer Bennet a great debt of gratitude,

Opposite: **Spencer G. Bennet translated to the screen stories from classic literature, as well as from comic strips and radio shows.** *Mysterious Island*—**Columbia, 1951—is an example.**

and the recognition I am not sure he ever fully knew that he had. What he did has meant a lot to us; therefore, he has meant a lot to us. And, in farewell, we say to him again: Thank you, sir.

When you get your *Superman* cassettes—if you don't already have them—watch them and remember Spencer Gordon Bennet and all he gave us. And in so doing, enjoy them even more. You might be surprised how the little negative things will fall into place—or maybe disappear entirely.

Spencer Bennet was one of the best serial directors there was. But, there were also Bob Hill, Ford Beebe, B. Reeves Eason, Ray Taylor, and William Witney and John English. There is a consensus that Witney and English were tops, with Spencer Bennet and Ray Taylor running close. Be that as it may, these were the men who knew how to forge the different elements of filmmaking into a completed motion picture chapterplay.

When given a tough assignment in serial making and the nagging question arose, "Can you do this?" these were the men who could say, truthfully,

"Sure, I can!"

Chapter 4

"Do It As Well As You Can, But Do It Only Once!"

The most remarkable thing about serials may well be that so much was put on the screen for so little expense. In a recent television interview, a director of major motion pictures for a large Hollywood studio told his interviewer how amazed he was that small studios like Republic could work as efficiently as they did. He recalled an incident when he had gone on location to film scenes for a multi-million-dollar spectacular and encountered a Republic crew shooting a scene on the next hill.

The Republic director told him they were going to roll a covered wagon down the hill; turn it over at a certain point; and have it come to a stop, bottom side up, at a designated spot. The major studio director was confused, he related, because they only had one wagon.

"Where are your backups?" he inquired of the Republic director and was told there were none.

To his utter amazement, the man recalled, they "slated" the scene; started the camera and action; and the wagon began to roll, turned and tumbled, continued on down the hill, and then flipped over, bottom side up—right on top of the marked spot.

The electricians struck the set, the prop men packed the gear, the crew got into the vehicles, and they all left to go to another setup. The man said he was dumbfounded. For that scene in his picture, they would have been there at least two days and used a dozen wagons, and, chances are, the result would not have been a bit better. He wanted to know how they had accomplished it in one take. The answer was total calculation and preparation. And a certain measure of luck.

"You do it as well as you can," some of the visitors to the Western Film Fair have told us, "but you do it only once!"

Therein lies the secret of the serials.

CHAPTER 4
THE BRIDGE OF DISASTER!

A UNIVERSAL CHAPTER-PLAY

OVERLAND MAIL

Masters of the Shoestring
September 1988

As they rounded the turn one more time, racing at breakneck speed, the drivers whipped their horses in mad frenzy, trying to get that last, final burst of energy from animals that had already given more than should be expected of them. Manipulating the reins as a puppeteer might do his wires trying to give life to his puppets, each driver frantically tried to transmit his own flashing thoughts through them and into the bodies of the horses. They lurched, careened, swerved and dodged each other, weaving in and out of the pack, trying to find through the thundering stampede that exact but elusive direct path to victory. As miscalculations were made, or collisions took place, some drivers suddenly found themselves thrown through the air, and their horses veering crazily off to the side—victims of the mad race to the finish line.

To further complicate matters, one of the drivers had equipped his vehicle with vicious, razor-sharp, cutting blades attached to, and protruding from, each of his wheel hubs. As he moved up alongside another vehicle—wheel to wheel—the rotating blades would slip into the spokes of the other vehicle's wheels and chew them up like match sticks. The result was a terrific crash, another driver thrown bodily out of the race, and one less competitor to deal with. Coldbloodedly, he had put a couple out of the race already.

And, now the vehicle with the deadly blades was moving in on the hero...

If this scene sounds a little like a cliffhanger in a western serial, it should not be too surprising. The vehicles could be stagecoaches, and the cutting blades could be any number of devilish devices thought up by the villains who inhabited the serials. Certainly, the frantic action, the fierce determination of the drivers, and the thundering thrills of racing toward a finish line were elements present in many a good serial race. And, most of all, the man responsible for this scene was a veteran of more serial action than there could ever be made an account record of. But, the scene was not a serial cliffhanger. It is the chariot race in Metro-Goldwyn-Mayer's *Ben Hur*, one of the most outstanding classic features of all time.

For directing the picture *Ben Hur*, William Wyler won the 1959

Opposite: "You do it as well as you can, but you do it only once." That was the credo of serial makers. The secret was planning every move to the split second and then using action experts to carry out the "gag," as it was called.

Academy Award; but the man totally responsible for the chariot race was old friend Yakima Canutt, who had acted in, or done stunt work for, or supervised second units of, or co-directed, serials for every company that had made them, all the way back to silent film days. Wyler, recognizing Canutt's unparallelled expertise as the man who "invented" the stunt profession, turned over to him the job of planning, preparing, producing and directing the key scene of the whole picture. Not only did the entire production hinge on the chariot-race scene, but it became the picture's most memorable sequence—its "trademark," if you will. Mainly because of it—but also because of all the other work he had done to establish his mark on motion pictures—Canutt was presented a special Academy Award in 1967.

In just a few weeks from now, it will be a year since a great serial director, Spencer G. Bennet, passed away. In briefly summarizing his career right after that happened, this column touched on the question of what guys like him and Ray Taylor, Bill Witney, James Horne, Sam Katzman and Nat Levine—with all their knowledge, experience and craftsmanship—could have produced with the money to spend that major filmmakers have. The question was left unanswered because it seems sort of obvious to those of us who love serials what the answer would be. And serial veteran Yakima Canutt being given the opportunity—and the money—to show us for sure, simply proves it: What they could have produced would have been great! Because what they did produce—on "shoestrings" and tightly limited budgets—was pretty darn good.

There was a stagecoach race in *Adventures of Red Ryder,* directed by William Witney in 1940. And, while making no attempt whatever to compare that with the *Ben Hur* chariot race, it was a pretty exciting sequence. It had to be made exciting using a combination of clips from an actual stagecoach race staged with stunt specialists, close-ups of hero Don Barry in front of a process screen urging off-screen horses to faster paces, and medium shots of a single stagecoach passing under a tree limb, where one of the bad guys waited to lasso Don and pull him from the coach, which was the cliffhanger. Under Witney's expert guidance—and with the aid of a stirring musical background that kept the audience fired up—the scene probably gave to small kids nearly as much of a thrill as *Ben Hur's* chariot race did for sophisticated grown-ups.

In Universal's *Gang Busters,* directed by Ray Taylor in 1942, there is a scene in which bad guy George J. Lewis is running from the law and kidnaps heroine Irene Hervey as a hostage. As they approach a roadblock, Lewis forces her to get out on the car's running board to act as a shield

Opposite: **Crashing a stagecoach directly in the path of stampeding cattle, while the coach horses race away to safety, was all in a day's work.**

against police bullets. Already wounded, he tries to drive the car, but is blocked at every turn by police cars. Finally turning on to a bridge over a highway, Lewis loses control and the car goes over the bridge and crashes on to the highway below. Just before the car goes out of control, co-hero Robert Armstrong pulls up alongside Lewis's car and the heroine transfers to Armstrong's police car and safety. As conceived and executed by Taylor, it was a very exciting cliffhanger and take-out (rescue), but had to be accomplished using a mixture of location traffic shots, a process screen for Hervey's close shots, and a quick switch to a double-exposure special-effects shot of the car crashing on the highway. With money and time to set it all up ideally, it could have been one of the classic scenes in serials.

For his cliffhanger at the end of Chapter One of *Mystery Mountain,* the 1934 Mascot serial starring Ken Maynard, producer Nat Levine had one stagecoach chasing another stagecoach to stop a valuable piece of evidence from reaching the proper authorities. Heroine Verna Hillie was aboard one of the coaches. Just as the second coach overtakes the first one, they both round a dangerous mountain curve and one of them—presumably the one containing Hillie—gets bumped and veers off the road over the embankment. It's an exciting scene, but done so quickly and edited so fuzzily that the actual crash scene becomes a mass of dust and confusion. Unless it was planned that way—in order to throw off the audience's perception until the following week—it appears to be one of those scenes that could only be shot once (due to budget limitations) and didn't quite come off right. With more time, and more money, it could have been honed into a vividly memorable sequence.

There are any number of other examples that could be used, but the point would not be any better made. As exciting and thrilling as serial action was made to be by experts like Canutt, Taylor, Witney, Levine and Bennet, the real appreciation comes in knowing that it was created by these craftsmen who got it on film at a minimum cost. And there is a certain poignancy in knowing that, with more time and more money, these same men could have given us miracles.

Because, one of them did...

The proficiency and expertise of many of the people who helped produce serials and westerns within restricted budgets often helped them move up to more important filmmaking. Their know-how would come to the attention of people like the major studio director quoted earlier, and they would be offered lucrative work by the big film companies. Television especially benefited from knowledge and experience these people had, and a great many of them became important figures in television production.

This also held true for the stuntmen, even though most of the good ones continued to work in serials and westerns—as well as in television and major films—because the money for their services was good.

Because of his resemblance to several leading superstars, one veteran stuntman of serials and westerns became so busy working in major films that he eventually enjoyed the reputation of being one of the top stuntmen in demand by the leading studios in Hollywood. He could rarely find the time to work in cliffhangers, but he did so as often as possible. Also an actor, it was only in serials and westerns that he was allowed to play parts because the major companies did not want his face seen in the pictures featuring the stars for whom he also doubled. It would have been confusing to the public, they feared.

An Unsung Hero
November 1984

Now, we all know what unsung heroes are: They're the people in any endeavor who get in there and work their tails off; and move the work along; and make the progress that counts; and finally get the job done. And then they stand back and watch someone else get the credit and take the bows. They're everywhere—in every phase of life, in every profession—and in serials they called them stuntmen.

Ted Mapes was an unsung hero, and he died September 9th, at the age of 82.

And, boy, was he a stuntman!

Starting in 1935, when he began to stunt-double for Columbia's newest western star, Mapes fought, rode, jumped, leaped, fell, dived, rolled, ran, scrambled, boxed, wrestled and brawled for over 30 years, for such action stars as Herman Brix and Bill Elliott in serials, and Gary Cooper, John Wayne and James Stewart in "A" pictures, stretching from *Sergeant York* in 1941 to *Bandolero* in 1968.

And he was an actor, too!

But, unfortunately, it was the fate of Ted Mapes also to be an "unsung" actor. At least three times, he just missed out on gaining the "brass ring."

The first was in 1935, when director Ford Beebe persuaded him to move over to Columbia from Mascot. Mapes had been a "grip boss" since 1929 (and was "head grip" on Tom Mix's only serial, *The Miracle Rider*, and Gene Autry's first starring film, the serial *The Phantom Empire*). Before that, he had been raised on a ranch near St. Edward, Kansas; had grown up an expert on livestock; and had become a top-flight horseman

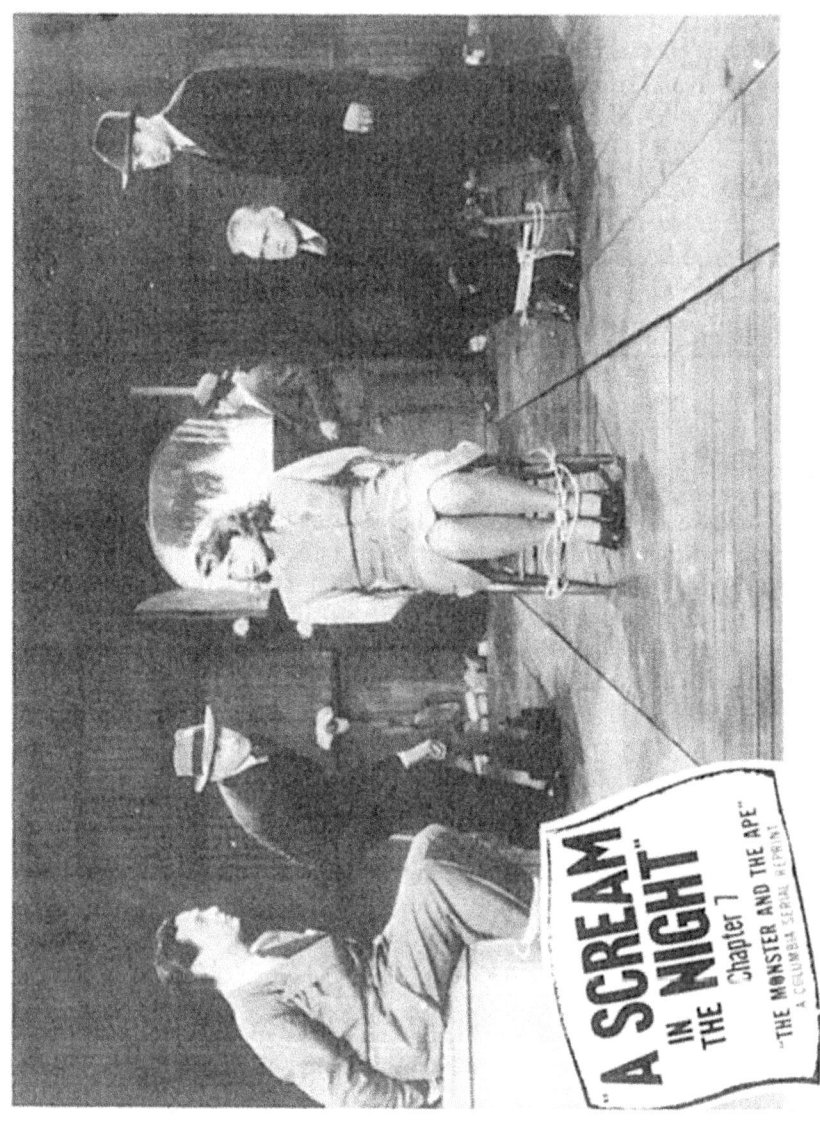

and rider. After going to California, he had driven trucks for an oil field and a van and storage company; was in first-class physical condition. Beebe reportedly told Mapes that the new guy signed for Columbia's western series—a "pretty boy" from New England—couldn't possibly make it as a western star; and, after the first few pictures, would probably be replaced by Mapes if he would come on over to Columbia and be ready. Well, the guy from New England was Charles Starrett, who not only made it, but remained a star for the next 20 years. And Mapes stayed on and doubled him for nine of them.

Next, he applied—and was strongly considered—for the leading role when Republic was planning *The Lone Ranger* as a 15-chapter serial production in 1937; but the part went instead to Lee Powell. So, Ted Mapes became the stunt-double for Herman Brix in *Hawk of the Wilderness* and *Daredevils of the Red Circle;* doubled Bill Elliott in *The Great Adventures of Wild Bill Hickok;* played G-Man Ted Murchison in *Dick Tracy's G-Men,* and a pioneer named Merritt in *The Lone Ranger Rides Again.*

Then, in 1940, Mapes was all set for the title role in Republic's proposed 12-chapter serial, *Adventures of Red Ryder.* But, with only 48 hours left until shooting was scheduled to start, the decision was made to re-cast the leading role with Don Barry, whom Republic president Herbert J. Yates wanted to groom for stardom; and Mapes lost out again.

So, instead of a leading role—and possible stardom—he took the part of "Black," one of "Wade Garson's" henchmen, in *King of the Royal Mounted;* played a seaman in *Adventures of Captain Marvel;* and was the keeper-of-the-door at the outlaws' hideout in *The Valley of Vanishing Men,* before signing on as Gary Cooper's stunt-double in *Sergeant York*—beginning an association that continued for 17 pictures, up to Cooper's death in 1961. He also continued to appear in many "B" westerns in small, medium and large parts—both billed and unbilled. Just to name a few: *In Old Cheyenne* and *Red River Valley* with Rogers; *Royal Mounted Patrol* and *Riders of the Badlands* with Starrett; *Tonto Basin Outlaws* and *Thunder River Feud* with the Range Busters; *Prairie Gunsmoke* and *Vengeance of the West* with Elliott and Ritter; *Gauchos of Eldorado* with The Three Mesquiteers; *Home in Wyomin'* with autry; and *Below the Border* with The Rough Riders.

During the time he doubled Cooper, Mapes continued to play parts in serials, such as *Black Arrow, The Monster and the Ape, The Black Widow, Daughter of Don Q* and *Tex Granger* (as Smith Ballew's stunt-double).

In 1950, Mapes was signed to stunt-double for James Stewart in the

Opposite: **Typical of the unsung hero, in this scene stuntman Ted Mapes, playing a minor part, stands in the rear next to the open furnace, while the principal actors hold the forefront.** *From left:* **Robert Lowrey, George MacReady, Carole Mathews, Ralph Morgan, and Anthony Warde.**

20th Century–Fox classic western, *Broken Arrow*. He then continued doing the same job for the lanky star from Pennsylvania until *Bandolero* in 1968, after which he stepped away from the camera and became an advisor for the American Humane Association. In that capacity, he worked behind the scenes on all pictures being filmed using live animals in any way. His background as a rancher, livestock expert, horseman, grip, stuntman and actor qualified him eminently, and he did that job for several years. In the early 1970s, he rejoined his old friend, Bill Witney, Republic's ace serial director, and worked with him on the television series "The Cowboys."

Within the past couple of years, at my good friend and fellow Film Fair associate, Larry Reed's, suggestion and urging, several attempts have been made to persuade Ted Mapes to come to the Western Film Fair as a guest; but, unfortunately, he was not able to make it on either occasion. With his experience in serials and westerns (both "B" and "A"), he would have been a terrific guest. But, alas, once again—in the Mapes tradition—we fans just barely missed the "brass ring"; and it's our loss.

Some time ago, when he was being paid tribute on television for his many years in movies, James Stewart singled out Ted Mapes for special recognition; and, as Mapes rose from the audience and stood tall and erect, grinning broadly, Stewart announced to the world that this was the man who had made him look good for so many years in those great action movies he had made. For just one shining moment—to the rest of the world—one of our unsung heroes of serials and westerns was proudly and deservedly "sung!"

Thanks, Mr. Stewart. We needed that.

One of the best-known and most accomplished of the serial stuntmen who was also an actor was David Sharpe. Sharpe's involvement, like Ted Mapes's, involved training the stars he doubled, as well as standing in for them in action scenes. One of his assignments at Universal studios in the late 1940s was to instruct major star Douglas Fairbanks, Jr., in the art of fencing. As an unsung hero, he also created two of serialdom's most memorable heroes.

In 1941, Republic brought to the serial screen what is generally thought of as the best-produced serial ever made, Adventures of Captain Marvel. *As part of the deal Republic made for the rights to that serial with Fawcett Publications, it also acquired the screen rights to another famous comic strip hero, and the following year Republic released the classic action serial named for that character:* Spy Smasher. *In both these outstanding productions, the title character and main hero was played in fast-action and high-risk scenes by David Sharpe.*

An interesting note on these two serials is that both had double heroes, and

Sharpe did stuntwork for the whole crowd. In Adventures of Captain Marvel, actor Frank Coghlan, Jr., played Billy Batson, who could shout the magic word, "Shazam!" and after an all-enveloping cloud of smoke dissipated, became the superhero, Captain Marvel, who was played by actor Tom Tyler. In Spy Smasher, actor Kane Richmond played Alan Armstrong, who donned a special outfit and fought as the hero, Spy Smasher, and Alan's twin brother, Jack, took Alan's place as Spy Smasher in Chapter 11, sacrificing his life for his brother. At times during the course of the two serials, David Sharpe doubled Coghlan, Tyler, and Richmond as both brothers.

These were only two of a total of a dozen or so serials that Republic produced from 1937 to 1944 that were based on comic strips. Throughout the life of sound serials, quite a few were made by the three companies that made serials—Columbia, Republic, and Universal—and, as in so many other things connected with serials, it didn't stop there. As we approached the 1990s, the movie companies were still doing it.

Coming Back Like a Song
June 1989

What goes around, comes around:
Every few years it seems, Hollywood gets a renewed interest in a form of entertainment that has remained consistently popular with the American public since the early part of the century—comic strips. The movies first took notice and did films based on famous newspaper strips in the middle 1930s; and serial makers were no exception. The first serial based on a popular comic strip was Universal's *Tailspin Tommy*, released in 1934. Since then there have been more than four dozen made, the final one being *Blackhawk*, released by Columbia in 1952. Naturally, the serials were based on the adventure comic strips—those which could be transferred to the screen with all the slam-bang action you might imagine they would have if brought to life. The more humorous or dramatic strips were better adaptable to feature films, and many of them were made into excellent movies.

In the late 1970's, there was a great deal of excitement when it was announced that a multi-million dollar production was underway of one of the comics' most successful strips ever—*Superman*. It became one of the biggest grossing movies of all time, and was followed very soon by costly productions of other such popular strips as *Flash Gordon, Buck Rogers*, and *The Lone Ranger*. Subsequently, television followed up with their own made-for-TV movies based on strips like *Wonder Woman* and *Captain*

Tom Tyler, former western star, portrayed one of America's favorite comic strip heroes when the strip was adapted to the serial screen: *Captain Marvel* for Republic.

America, and offered series based on the *Buck Rogers* movie and the *Wonder Woman* TV movie. Nothing happened as a result of the *Lone Ranger* movie.

Prior to that time, it had been the mid–1960s when a surge of interest had occurred following the all-in-one-evening showings of the 1943 Columbia serial, *Batman*, in theatres around the country. ABC-TV then developed the now infamous series "Batman" that starred Adam West and Burt Ward as the "dynamic duo"; and 20th Century–Fox made a theatrical movie feature to follow up that did very well at boxoffices around the country. Behind *Batman* in that era came also the ABC-TV series "The Green Hornet" (which was primarily a radio serial, as well as a comic strip), and a large-scale Broadway musical based on *Superman*. All of this

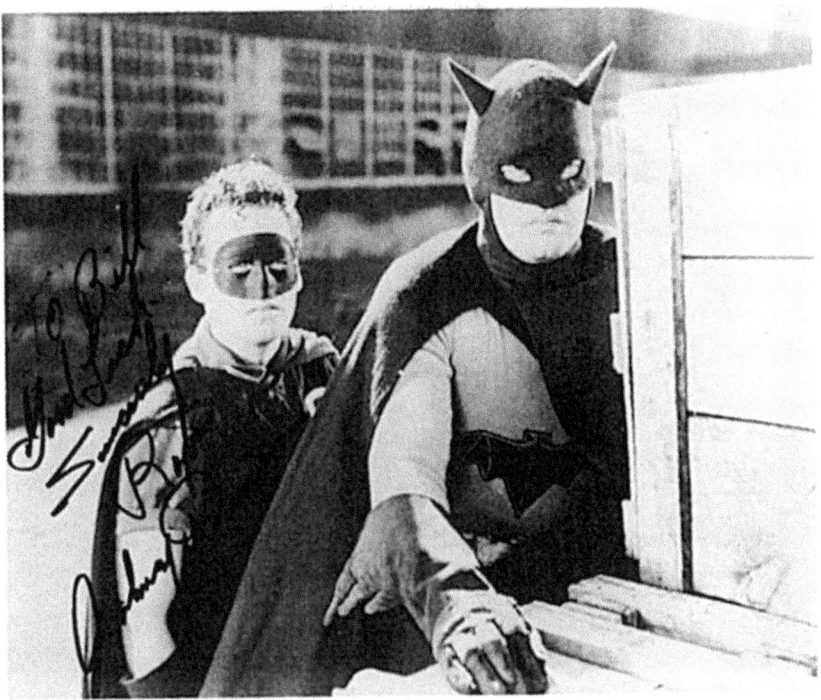

Johnny Duncan *(left)* as Robin, and Robert Lowery *(right)*, as the Caped Crusader, in *Batman and Robin*—Columbia, 1949. From 1945 to 1952, Columbia released no fewer than 10 serials based on comic book heroes.

eventually led to other projects based on what they were then calling "pop art," including a disappointing large-screen movie based on the closely-related pulp novel character, *Doc Savage—Man of Bronze* in 1975.

Upcoming this year—as everyone must know by now—is the latest big-screen adaptation of Bob Kane's great Detective Comics strip, "Batman." As you read this, theatres are advertising the opening date of the multi-million dollar Warner Bros. production starring Michael Keaton and Jack Nicholson. Coming later this year, we are promised, will be the long-awaited Warren Beatty rendition of Chester Gould's classic comic strip, *Dick Tracy,* and the eventual release of the Brooke Shields starrer, *Brenda Starr—Reporter* (and, although comic strips only as a result of being characters in classic literature first, there are also the recent TV-movie featuring Edgar Rice Burroughs' famous jungle man, *Tarzan;* a new big-screen movie about "Hopalong Cassidy" and his rangeland colleagues in *The Great Bar 20;* and yet another adventure with the swashbuckling heroes immortalized by Alexander Dumas as *The Three Musketeers*).

And, to kick it all off is the movie that opened the last week in May

Don Winslow of the Navy—Universal, 1941—became one of Universal's most successful serials when, shortly after its release, America entered World War II. Walter Sande *(left)* played Red Pennington, and Don Terry *(right)* was Winslow.

that was inspired by the comic strips and movie serials—*Indiana Jones and the Last Crusade.* Playing in hundreds of theatres all across America right now, this is the third picture in a trilogy that was conceived in the minds of its producers as the successor and heir apparent to the cliffhangers of the 1930s and 1940s, many of which themselves were little more than transplanted comic strips. So, it seems that in this one area of entertainment, we haven't grown up too much, but our toys have just gotten to be more expensive. What used to cost us a dime and thrilled the pants off of us as kids, now costs us $4.00 to $4.50 (and even more in larger cities), and reminds us of what used to be.

After Universal released *Tailspin Tommy* back in 1934, and saw young audiences take it to their hearts, they couldn't wait to get its sequel into release. Exactly 12 months later, they released *Tailspin Tommy in the Great Air Mystery,* and then in succession at least one comic strip every six to ten months for the next seven years, up to *Don Winslow of the Coast Guard* in December 1942. Along the way, there were great Universal chapterplays based on such strips as *Flash Gordon* (three serials), *Ace Drummond, Jungle*

Jim, Secret Agent X-9 (two), *Radio Patrol, Tim Tyler's Luck, Red Barry, Buck Rogers, The Green Hornet* (two) and *Adventures of Smilin' Jack*.

Republic Pictures entered the comic strip scene in 1937, with serials based on great comic strips like *Dick Tracy* (four serials), *The Lone Ranger* (from radio and the comics—two serials), *Red Ryder, King of the Royal Mounted* (two), *Captain Marvel, Spy Smasher* and *Captain America*.

In their second year of serial production, Columbia launched *Mandrake the Magician*, which was followed by a long line of comic strip cliffhangers: *Terry and the Pirates, The Shadow* (radio and the comics), *Captain Midnight* (radio and comics), *Batman* (two), *The Phantom, Brenda Starr, Hop Harrigan, Jack Armstrong, The Vigilante, Brick Bradford, Tex Granger, Superman* (two), *Bruce Gentry, Thunda, King of the Congo* and *Blackhawk*.

Most of these great action films were produced on budgets that wouldn't even pay the salary of a middle-echelon executive on today's *Batman, Dick Tracy* or *Indiana Jones*, but they trained a small army of filmmakers who went into TV production in the early 1950s and helped get off the ground a fledgling medium that today controls the minds and actions of much of the "civilized" world. During the first decade of television, there was a great deal of evidence to be seen from the budget-production days, and many of the old series classics still stand up alongside today's state-of-the-arts-created stuff. Largely because of the people who came out of low-budget movie making. (It kind of makes you wonder about what things will be like 20 years from now, doesn't it?—when the recent pioneers of television will be then-obsolete "hardware.")

Well, I'm looking forward to seeing *The Last Crusade* (hope it's better than *Temple of Doom!*), the new *Batman* (hope it's better than Fox's *Batman—1966*), *Dick Tracy* (hope it's better than *Reds*), and new *Brenda Starr—Reporter* (hope it's better than *Sahara*), and *The Great Bar 20* (hope it's better than *Legend of the Lone Ranger*). In the meantime, I've got 16 millimeter and videotapes of *Captain Marvel, Doctor Satan, Spider's Web, Valley of Vanishing Men, Drums of Fu Manchu, Daredevils of the Red Circle, Gang Busters, Zorro's Fighting Legion, Winners of the West, Secret of Treasure Island* and *Adventures of Red Ryder* handy, just in case.

And I feel one coming on right now.

Although these later adaptations were not serials, but features, the influence of the cliffhangers could clearly be seen in them. The only thing that seemed to be missing was the old enthusiasm that the serial makers put into their productions. The visitors to the film fairs, who had helped make them, explained that one reason for a lot of the enthusiasm was the admonition to "do it as well as

Tom Tyler portrayed another of America's favorite comic strip heroes in *The Phantom* for Columbia.

you can, but do it only once." When the cameras rolled and the man yelled, "Action!" he, by damn, meant "Action!"

No stuntman was more capable of projecting action than Tom Steele. And no actor was more capable of instilling a scene with enthusiasm or fervor than veteran thespian Tom London. But, an article fusing the two of them and their

Blackhawk—Columbia, 1952—starred Kirk Alyn, who had already become known to serial fans—for all time—as Superman.

careers into a single vein probably never would have occurred to me, except for things happening exactly as they did. The resulting tribute to the two Toms wound up as almost a surprise to me. But, thank goodness, it seemed to be well received.

Tom-Tom: Anonymous But Not Unknown
January 1991

Well, it happened again! Starting out to write about one subject, I am winding up with something very different. The change in direction seemed like a logical move under the circumstances; but, as usual, you will be the judge.

I had planned to focus attention this time on the serials' veteran character actor, Tom London, and briefly examine his lengthy and prolific career as a talented, many-faceted performer who served as a dependable

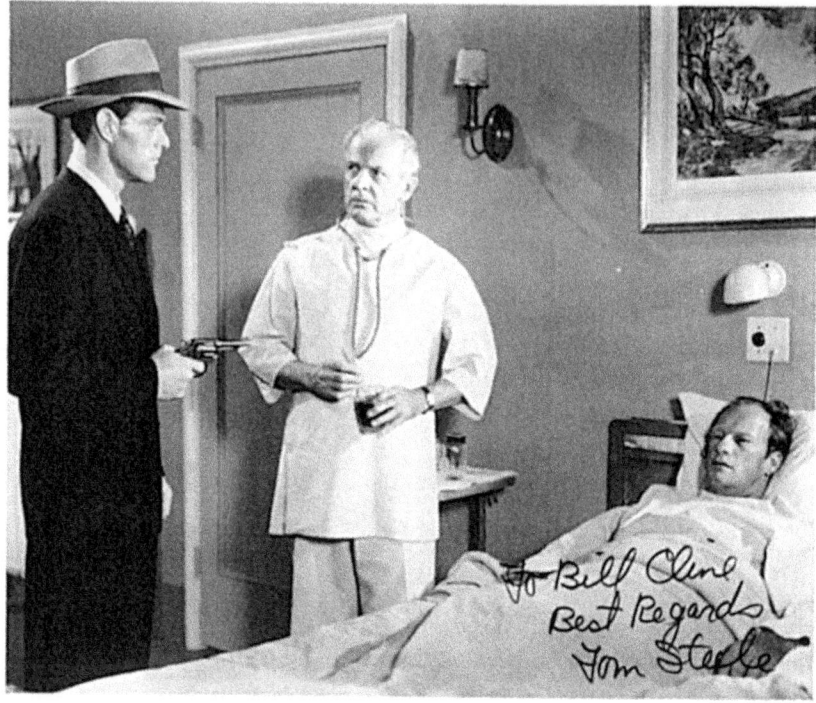

The Masked Marvel—Republic, 1943—Tom Steele *(left)* in the stuntman's tradition, was "anonymous but not unknown." In this scene he portrays a heavy who has the drop on "Doctor" Forbes Murray and "patient" Stubby Krueger, who was himself a fine stuntman.

standby for almost any kind of role that might come up. But, barely started on that, I suddenly received the news that Tom Steele, one of the all-time great stuntmen, had just passed away, and it brought back a flood of memories regarding his work in serials.

While remembering Tom Steele, and with the career of Tom London so much on my mind, it started becoming apparent how much of a parallel there was between the contributions of the two men—not so much in what they did, but in how they did it. And, since it was my great privilege to have met both men, my new direction was set. The focus then became: Tom and Tom—two of the industry's most reliable "stand-bys" in action movies, and two prime reasons for the success of Republic serials.

Born in 1882, Tom London started life with the name Leonard Clapham. His first movie role was in the very first movie, *The Great Train Robbery*, playing the locomotive engineer on the train that was held up by the bandits. That was in 1903, and his final movie role was in 1962 in the Randolph Scott–Joel McCrea feature, *Ride the High Country*. During the

Zorro's Black Whip—Republic, 1944. Linda Stirling *(right)* looks on as George J. Lewis aids the fallen Tom London *(left)*, a veteran actor who was, like the stuntmen, "anonymous but not unknown."

intervening 59 years—as Leonard Clapham in silent movies, then as Tom London in sound films—he appeared in more movies than any other actor in American films, a fact duly recorded in several record books. His roles included practically every type of person an American male can be—heroes and villains, comics and cynics, fathers and sons, paragons and politicians, well-to-do's and ne'er-do-wells, preachers and sinners, gamblers and reformers, ranchers and rustlers, bankers and thieves, sheriffs and outlaws—all of these. Whenever an actor was needed to step in and do a character that was vitally necessary to the plot—and do it with great professional credibility—Tom London was there, ready and able. He salvaged many a scene that otherwise might have "missed the mark" entirely. But, except for a short series of silent films in which he played the hero, London always played supporting roles, backing up—or opposing—the leading man. His face was known by every moviegoer, but very few knew his name. The glory went to the people he supported.

In the late 1940s, he came to the Paramount Theatre in Concord on a personal appearance tour, billed as "The Sheriff of Western Movies." To promote the event, we arranged to meet him at the city limit with an open convertible and give him a police escort into town to the theatre, accompanied by the mayor and the chief of police. To open the first show, he was to be welcomed officially by the mayor, and made honorary Police Chief of our town.

Everything went great until the mayor stepped up to the microphone to welcome "Sheriff" London to Concord and make him honorary Chief. Instead of remarking that people who may not know his name as an actor would still recognize him because of all his screen appearances over the years, "his honor" got his words twisted around and blurted out to the amused but good-natured London,

"Well, uh, Mr. London, I might not recognize your face, but you sure-as-shootin' would recognize mine!"

He didn't understand until later why everybody was laughing when he proudly pinned the Chief's badge on the smiling actor.

Later that day, I asked Tom London how many movies he had actually appeared in. He grinned that wide London grin and replied in that familiar, husky voice,

"Well, I really don't know. For instance, how many pairs of socks have you ever worn? All I know is, I get up and go to work every day; I stand where they tell me to stand; say what they tell me to say; and do what they tell me to do. And then I go on back home. It's a great life."

Everybody in town enjoyed having Tom London for a visit that day. He came out between shows and visited with fans in the lobby and out on the sidewalk in front of the theatre, answering questions, signing autographs, and posing for pictures with them. He seemed to enjoy it as much as they did. And, thanks to the alert action of one of the theatre employees, he was even saved from having his career ended—or at least severely interfered with—while he was there:

Just before each stage show began, the backstage crew would "fly" (or raise out of sight) the movie screen, to make more room for the stage presentation; then "land" (or lower) it back in place for the film program to resume. Although counter-balanced, it was still pretty heavy, so had to be flown and landed very carefully. Right after one of the stage shows that day, crew member Lewis Hinson had just started to land the heavy screen when Tom London—unaware that it was being lowered—suddenly bent over to pick up something from the stage floor and inadvertently placed his head, neck and shoulders directly under the descending screen. Luckily, Lew saw immediately what had happened and threw his full weight downward on the rope and stopped the screen just above London's head. The actor straightened up and walked into the wings without a scratch. When the screen finally came to rest on the stage floor, Hinson nearly fainted.

After that, every time I saw Tom London up on that screen, I couldn't help but breathe a sigh of relief that he didn't get hurt in our theatre, and I would smile at the memory of meeting one of the nicest people in "show business" who ever came our way.

Very much like him in almost every way was the other "Tom"—Tom Steele. Just as Tom London stood ready to play any part needed for the plot of a film, Tom Steele stood ready and able to step in for an actor and perform any physical activity needed for an action scene. Horseback riding, jumping, diving, fighting, brawling, tumbling or whatever—he was an expert at all of it—his work made the actors he doubled look even better to moviegoers than they ever would have themselves. And, like Tom London, the glory went to the people he supported, while Tom Steele remained anonymous. However, just as Tom London acquitted himself very well in the action department when the need arose, Tom Steele was not a bad actor either, and could step in and do a character when that was required. There were even times when stuntman Steele would double actor London in a knock-down-drag-out fight scene.

Before changing it to Steele, the name of the tall, lanky Scotsman was Thomas Skeoch. His father, a construction consulting engineer, brought his family to New York from Scotland when Tom was only two years old. From there they moved to San Francisco, where Tom's dad worked for U.S. Steel and helped to rebuild and remodel a lot of the damage done by the great earthquake. There, near Torrance and Palo Alto, Tom grew up and completed his education.

In his early twenties, Tom went to Los Angeles to try and get work in movies. His first job was a bit in *Lone Star Ranger* at Fox, in which he played a young man at a dance who cut in on George O'Brien and Sue Carol and danced the "bunnyhug" with Miss Carol, following which he scuffled with O'Brien and took a tumble down some stairs. After a few other jobs, and a near-miss at becoming a leading player at Selznick Releasing (a young fellow named George Duryea got the nod instead, and the studio changed his name to Tom Keene), he met up again with George DeNormand, a stuntman friend of his, who got him a job doing stunt work in the Errol Flynn swashbuckler, *Captain Blood*, for Warner Bros.

Realizing he was not going to make it as an actor, young Tom settled down to becoming the best stuntman he could be. At Universal in the middle 1930s, he was thrown in with eight other young stuntmen, and the nine of them began calling themselves "The Cousins." All nine could do any stunt that might be needed; but, as in any profession, each was also a specialist in one area or another. Former circus performers David Sharpe, Loren Riebe, Jimmy Fawcett and Ken Terrell were acrobats, and could make any piece of action seem more lively by their swift, sure movements. Bud Wolfe, Louis Tomei (who had driven racers at Indianapolis) and Carey Loftin were experts with cars, and could maneuver them into doing

***Trader Tom of the China Seas*—Republic, 1954—had stuntman Tom Steele *(left)* playing a featured role (as an Oriental hit man). Here he struggles with hero Harry Lauter.**

anything that automobiles were capable of doing. Eddie Parker and Tom Steele were superior horsemen, as well as being two of the most outstanding fight men in the business. During the late 1930s, the Cousins worked in such serials as *Flash Gordon* (Tom Steele doubled Charles Middleton as "Ming, the Merciless"), *Radio Patrol, Red Barry, The Green Hornet, Buck Rogers* and *Junior G-Men.*

While working mainly in Universal serials, the Cousins also did stunt work over at Republic Pictures, absorbing even more of their craft from other experts there like George DeNormand, Ted Mapes, Duke Green, Fred Graham, and the maestro himself, Yakima Canutt. By the early 1940s, they had practically settled at Republic and there became the nucleus of a stuntman team the likes of which had never been seen before, and has never since been equalled. With Yakima Canutt as their "ramrod," they turned out a string of serials and westerns that have become classics, taken each in its own right or all taken together. When Canutt was elevated to the status of director, Tom Steele succeeded him as "ramrod," and Republic's stunt team continued to amaze the otherwise blasé film industry. During that time, Tom's most outstanding mark upon the serials was his portrayal of the title hero in Republic's *The Masked Marvel* in 1943.

In July 1974, Tom Steele went to Houstoncon 74 in Texas as an unannounced guest, to replace Frank Coghlan, Jr., who was unable to attend at the last minute. Never having been to a film convention, and not knowing what to expect, he asked old friend George DeNormand to go with him. It was there I met them both, along with ace stuntman Dave Sharpe and Jock Mahoney, and actors Kirk Alyn and Billy Benedict. Needless to say, I was very pleased. I had never expected to meet so many of my serial heroes all at once—and that at my first film convention.

All of these men were excellent guests, full of good stories and anecdotes and anxious to share them. Dave Sharpe was a fountain of information on serial making; Jock Mahoney had one tale after another about making the Durango Kid westerns at Columbia; and George DeNormand kept us constantly entertained with humorous yarns about filming all movies in general and serials in particular. But, Tom Steele was very quiet at first, and didn't have much to say. It was as if he were still trying to be anonymous and remain in the background, just as good stuntmen always did. Eventually, though, he began to understand what we were all there for, and began to loosen up. It was then that we were able to get the benefit of his years of experience in making serials.

Regarding *The Masked Marvel*, I asked him if they had really believed that the public would not recognize him as the man behind the mask and doing all the stunts, as well as being the "Marvel" in plot scenes.

"Yes, we really believed you would not know me," he explained. "We had no reason at that time to think that you would know who I was."

I pointed out that *The Masked Marvel* had followed *Secret Service in Darkest Africa* that year, and that every real serial fan knew who the guy was that had doubled Rod Cameron in that.

"But, you see," he said, "Rod's body frame and style of movement were so similar to mine, we didn't think anybody would notice the difference in that one, either."

"Besides," he went on, "Rod did so much of his own fighting in that serial that I didn't have that much to do."

It surprised me that anyone in the film business could be that modest. But, then I thought of Max Terhune, whom I had met in 1948 and heard say, "I never liked to see myself on the screen, because I always know I should have done better"; of Ray Whitley, who stood in the office of the Paramount a couple of years earlier and told me, "I ought to feel guilty about being in movies, for the Lord has allowed me to be paid for doing what I love the most"; of George "Gabby" Hayes, who confided to me in 1949 that he never understood why he was allowed to survive as an actor because, "I don't know how to act; I just rant and rave like my grandpa did." And of Tom London, who "just did his work each day and then went on back home."

In a 1984 interview for *Serial World*, film writer Peter Bosch asked the action film veteran how he would like people to remember Tom Steele. The answer was a simple one. He said,

"Not as a great stuntman. Just as an everyday good American boy."

Well, Thomas Skeoch Tom Steele, I hope you won't mind a great deal if those of us who enjoyed your work so much will remember you both ways.

In summarizing the lives and careers of Tom London and Tom Steele, you could almost say that their stories typify nearly everyone who helped make serials what they were. You could almost erase their names and leave the names, places, and dates blank, to be filled in by every other aspiring actor who ever dreamed of going to Hollywood and becoming a star—and then settled for something else.

It was people like them who always threw everything they had into a scene—be it a setup shot for a serial or a serious plot-development scene in a major feature—and the result on the screen was better for it. By learning day by day in serials to "do it the best they could, but do it only once," they learned to do everything else the same way.

And, you know, having met both men—and many of the others just like them—and having seen the results of that philosophy on the screen—and in them as persons—that "ain't a bad way to be."

Chapter 5

"Imagine, Kid, by Labor Day You'll Be a Star!"

Professionally, serials were many things to many people. For many actors, they provided a stepping stone to bigger things in films. For some, they were a temporary involvement along the way and became just a credit in a long list of credits. For several, they touched their careers and branded them for the rest of their lives. For many others, serials and westerns were "what they did"—they were all in a day's work. And for a select few, they even led to major stardom. It was almost a sure thing that you couldn't go for three months being seen every Saturday without people at least finding out who you were.

Since serials and "B" westerns were so much alike in producing action and thrills, it was the natural thing for a studio to employ actors who it wanted to groom for its westerns as players in its serials. The training the actors received in these serials would be invaluable and the publicity, immeasurable. In talking to many of the visiting guests at film fairs, the suspected truth of that became reality.

The Cowboys and the Cliffhangers
March 1985

All of the really great cowboy stars made at least one serial during their careers. And all but a small handful of the near-great ones listed at least one "continued" among their credits. For some, the cliffhangers were vital parts of on-going successful careers; for one a farewell to a legendary screen era; and for several they were the beginnings—the "boost" that launched careers that might otherwise have taken years to establish, or may not have happened at all. The several near-great cowboy stars who

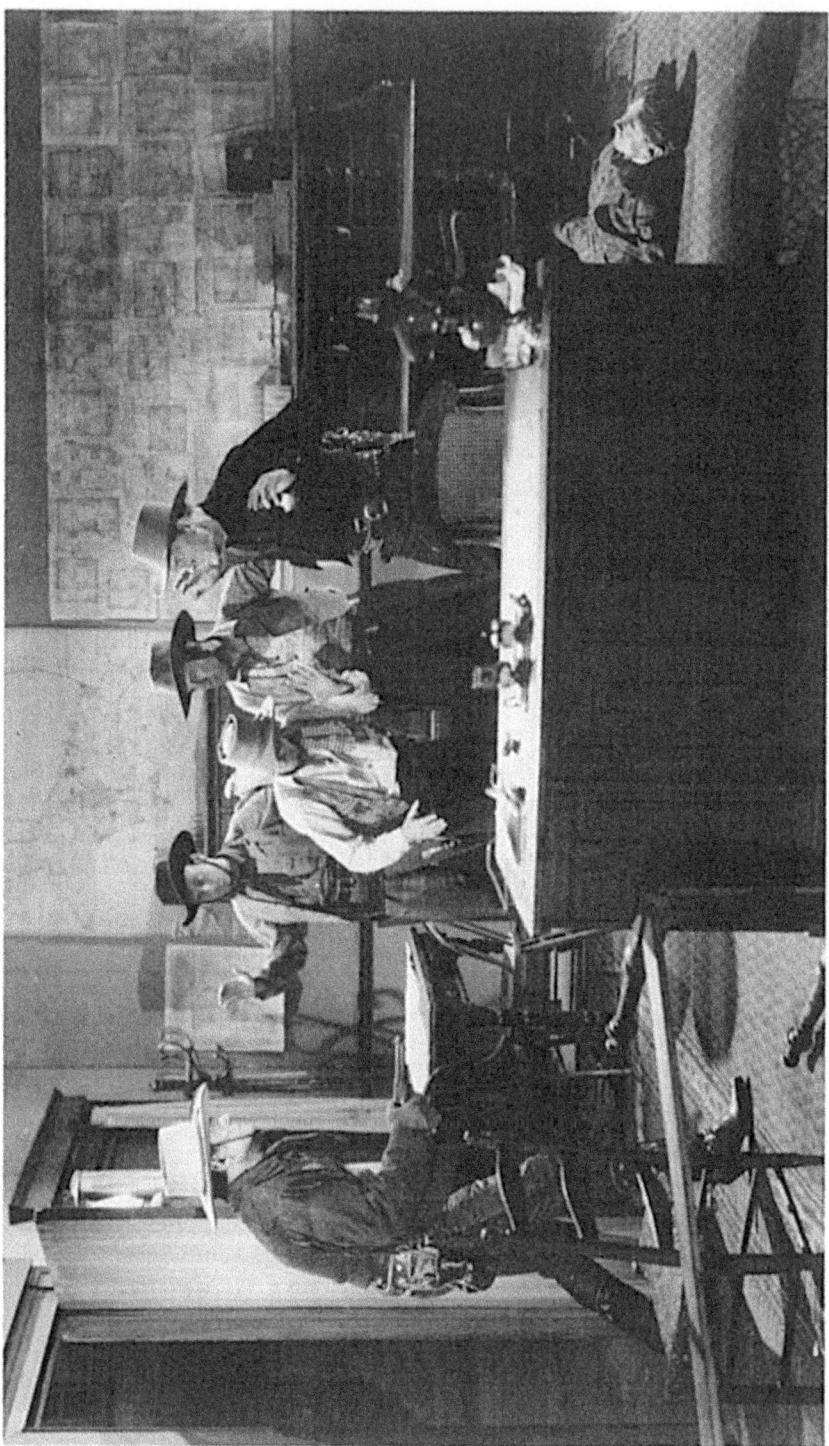

did not appear in any serials had their careers launched and sustained for various reasons—to answer the need for singing cowboys to compete in a new market; to fill a gap caused by contract negotiations and reportedly "keep the star in line"; or to provide specific requirements for new series that producers were committed to—and were therefore not beneficiaries of the 12 to 15 weeks of exposure such appearances would have afforded. But the ones that were being groomed for western stardom by the studios that also made serials, did get the advantage of the serial's weekly exposure—and it helped.

Buck Jones, possibly the most beloved of all the really great western stars (whose following today is almost of "cult" proportions), starred in six sound serials from 1933 to 1941: *Gordon of Ghost City, The Red Rider, The Phantom Rider, The Roaring West, White Eagle* and *Riders of Death Valley.* The very first sound serial in 1930, *The Indians Are Coming,* starred the great Colonel Tim McCoy, who followed up with *Heroes of the Flames* the next year. Ken Maynard, undeniably the greatest horseman of all the screen cowboys, starred in *Mystery Mountain* while he was still one of the most popular and well-liked western stars on the screen. Battling Bob Steele took time out in 1933 to film a non-western 12-chapter thriller titled *Mystery Squadron;* and the legendary Hoot Gibson co-starred in *The Painted Stallion* in 1937. For Tom Mix, perhaps the greatest cowboy star of all, *The Miracle Rider* in 1935 was the swan song of a brilliant career that spanned both the silent and sound eras. Gene Autry's long and astronomical career was boosted into orbit by his leading role in *The Phantom Empire* in 1935 for Mascot's Nat Levine. Less than two years before that, Levine had launched another western great in a 12-chapter serial titled *Fighting with Kit Carson.* Former All-American football star, Johnny Mack Brown, was the hero, and it started his career as a top western star that lasted for more than 20 years. During the first five years, he starred in four more serials at Universal: *Rustlers of Red Dog, Wild West Days, Flaming Frontiers* and *The Oregon Trail.* It happened again in 1938, when one of the great western stars was launched by his role in a serial. Gordon Elliott played the title role in Columbia's *The Great Adventures of Wild Bill Hickok,* and thereafter was always known as "Wild Bill" Elliott. Through series westerns at Columbia, then at Republic, and in major productions at Republic—billed as William Elliott—he was still known to his fans as "Wild Bill." After his first serial, he made two more for Columbia: *Overland with Kit Carson* and *The Valley of Vanishing Men.*

Many of the near-great western stars also began in serials, as did

Opposite: White Eagle—**Columbia, 1940—featured the great western star Buck Jones** *(left),* **who led the cast in five serials for Universal and this one for Columbia.**

Autry, Brown and Elliott; and then moved into leading parts in series westerns. They became well-known stars with western fans, even though they never became one of the really great western stars. In 1936, Ray Corrigan played "Crash" Corrigan in Republic's *Undersea Kingdom,* and a tall, good-looking actor named John King played "Ace" in Universal's *Ace Drummond.* Five years later, they were "Crash" and "Dusty" and were nationally-known—along with Max Terhune as "Alibi"—as The Range Busters, stars of a series of westerns produced by Monogram. During those five years, Corrigan and Terhune had instigated and sustained one of the highest-quality series of westerns ever made at Republic studios—The Three Mesquiteers. Corrigan had also appeared in the serial, *The Vigilantes Are Coming,* and had the leading role in *The Painted Stallion.* The third Mesquiteer was Robert Livingston, who was featured as "The Eagle" in *The Vigilantes Are Coming* and played the title role in *The Lone Ranger Rides Again,* a 1939 serial. After the departure from the Mesquiteer series of Corrigan and Terhune, one of the stars who played "Stony Brooke" was Tom Tyler, himself a western star of the 1930s and hero of seven serials: *Phantom of the West, Battling with Buffalo Bill, Jungle Mystery, Clancy of the Mounted, Phantom of the Air, Adventures of Captain Marvel* and *The Phantom.* In 1940, Donald Barry played the title role in Republic's *Adventures of Red Ryder,* and was thereafter known as Don "Red" Barry. Buster Crabbe, one of the really great *serial* stars, became a western star at P.R.C. in the early 1940s, but always insisted—right up to his death—that the success of those westerns was due to the popularity of his sidekick, Al "Fuzzy" St. John. From four serials in the early 1940s—*King of the Royal Mounted, King of the Mounties, Daredevils of the West* and *The Tiger Woman*—Allan Lane went on to western stardom as "Red Ryder" and as "Rocky" Lane. And from two other serials—*G-Men Vs. the Black Dragon* and *Secret Service in Darkest Africa*—Rod Cameron graduated to series western stardom at Universal, before an even bigger career in features at Universal, Republic and Allied Artists. Before being selected to play the famous character *The Lone Ranger* on television, Clayton Moore had racked up leading roles in six serials—*Perils of Nyoka, Jesse James Rides Again, G-Men Never Forget, Adventures of Frank and Jesse James* and *Ghost of Zorro* as the hero, and *The Crimson Ghost* as a heavy—with four more to come after he started playing the "masked rider"—*Son of Geronimo, Jungle Drums of Africa* and *Gunfighters of the Northwest* as heroes, and *Radar Men from the Moon* as a heavy.

Opposite: Johnny Mack Brown *(left)* was another great western star with major cliffhanger involvement. He appeared in his first serial for Nat Levine at Mascot, *Fighting with Kit Carson* and then did four for Universal during the next nine years.

Serials played a large part in the early careers of western stars Ray "Crash" Corrigan *(center)* and Robert Livingston *(right)*, seen here with Max "Lullaby" Terhune as the Three Mesquiteers.

The very first celebrity I ever met was Johnny Mack Brown in 1943, when he toured the small Southern towns during the time he was moving over from Universal to Monogram. Needless to say, he was very impressive in person. The most recent ones were John Crawford, Dorothy Gulliver, Charles Starrett and Yakima Canutt last summer in Raleigh. During that 41-year period, the most knowledgeable, most professional and most conscientious veterans of western movies it was my pleasure to meet were practically all—with the outstanding exception of Tex Ritter, who was "somebody special"—people who had also played in the serials. I'm not putting that forward as meaning anything in particular—but, ain't it interesting?

Not all serials were westerns, of course. But, even those that were not bore a close resemblance to westerns because of the basic, straightforward premise used in their creation—good versus evil, with little gray area. Knowing that the audiences for both kinds of films were either children or unsophisticated adults, the people who wrote them kept everything pretty well defined, so that the focus would stay on the action, thrills, and entertainment. Consequently, serials and westerns were brothers and sisters, children of the same parents. And the same actors, directors, and technicians were involved in the production of both. It was only natural for there to be a preponderance of western actors appearing regularly in serials and for these actors to appear in them many times.

As in all things, however, there were even exceptions to the rule that once you played in a serial, you would likely continue to do so. The records contain a number of examples of actors appearing in a serial only once and—despite gaining the recognition and popularity that comes to a person seen week after week for three or four months—never being seen in one again.

Some, appeared only once because they were hired for one job, did it, and then moved on to other jobs—away from the serial studios. For some others, it was a matter of finding out that they did not like the rough-and-tumble, daily grind of "doing it as well as you can, but doing it only once." And, for a few, it was simply a case of not wanting to become identified with serials—products of "poverty row" film companies—for career reasons, but doing one job in them frankly because "one has to eat."

For whatever reason, a few actors appeared only once in a serial, but became—for all time—a part of the cliffhanger tradition. This was, however, the exception rather than the rule.

One-Shot Winners
July 1986

Of course, the perfect example is Frances Gifford.

Playing the leading role of "Nyoka Gordon," she appeared in only one serial—*Jungle Girl,* from Republic in 1941—but made such an impact

Frances Gifford starred in one serial only—*Jungle Girl*—Republic, 1941—but because of her impact in that serial, she will always be an integral part of cliffhanger lore.

on audiences as that character that she became forever thereafter a major part of the cliffhanger legend. To this day, no one who can recall the days of Saturday matinees and the anticipation of waiting for the next chapter, speaks of them without fondly recalling the memory of the lovely "Nyoka." The beautiful Miss Gifford could have made a dozen serials, but would be no better—nor more lovingly—remembered than she is for that single one.

Ann Rutherford played in one serial, *The Fighting Marines*—Mascot, 1935—and then went on to major roles in feature pictures.

This happened several times with beautiful leading ladies in serials—just as it did a couple of times with leading men. So strong was the impression made in one role that she is always remembered for it, and is always a key person in discussions of landmark serials. One such lovely heroine is scheduled to be a guest this month at the Western Film Fair in Charlotte, which is set for July 10, 11 and 12 at the Radisson Plaza Hotel. Two others have been guests previously at the Film Fair, and have brought interesting stories of their singular ventures into the fascinating world of cliffhanging.

A number of other well-known actresses graced the serial screen with their presence in single-shot appearances—some memorable and some not—and then moved on to other things. So their serial credits are not what one usually thinks of when their names come up. They are better known and remembered for their work in features and other media. But each played a part in some important or classical serial, and are thus still considered "one-shot winners."

Ann Rutherford, for example, played in Mascot's *The Fighting Marines* in 1935, but is best remembered as one of Mickey Rooney's girlfriends in the Andy Hardy series, and as a top romantic leading lady at Metro-Goldwyn-Mayer. Jinx Falkenburg (without the "burg") was the female lead in Republic's 1939 serial *The Lone Ranger Rides Again,* but is better known as a musical-comedy star in Columbia "B"-musicals, as a top fashion model, and as the star of a radio show in New York in later years. The beautiful but ill-fated Carole Landis, who was at the peak of stardom at the time of her untimely death, had portrayed "Blanche Granville"—who was also the mysterious benefactor known as "The Red Circle"—in Republic's *Daredevils of the Red Circle* in 1939. That same year, another young actress named Phyllis Isley made her only serial appearance in *Dick Tracy's G-Men* for Republic, but later gained top stardom and the coveted Academy Award for her role in 20th Century–Fox's *The Song of Bernadette* as Jennifer Jones. Another beautiful model who played in only one serial was Marguerite Chapman, who was the fiancée of the hero's twin brother in Republic's *Spy Smasher* in 1942. And from the role of a strange and enigmatic young woman who appeared mysteriously to aid hero Edward Norris and his side-kick Eddie Quillan in time of trouble in Universal's *Jungle Queen* in 1945, Ruth Roman rose to top stardom and became one of Hollywood's most sought-after talents in the 1950s and 1960s.

Outstanding horsewoman Nell O'Day, who co-starred in numerous westerns at Universal with Johnny Mack Brown and others, plunged into her one serial role at Columbia, when she portrayed the heroine in *Perils of the Royal Mounted* in 1942. Another great horsewoman and all-around stunt expert, Evelyn Finley, was the heroine when Columbia re-used a lot of the stock footage from *Perils of the Royal Mounted* 13 years later when they made *Perils of the Wilderness.* To match the stock footage, Miss Finley's hair was dyed blonde like Miss O'Day's; and, for some reason, her name was billed as Eve Anderson, rather than Evelyn Finley. Both of these lovely ladies have visited the Western Film Fair and captivated serial and western fans with their grace and charm.

Another visitor to the Charlotte Fair with a unique role in the serial legend was Jean Carmen, also known as Julia Thayer. Billed as the latter, she was Republic's first female heroine in a serial, and it was her only cliffhanger appearance. In 1937, she became for all time a part of serial lore as the "Rider of the Stallion" in Republic's *The Painted Stallion.* Portraying a mysterious Indian girl who seemed to come from nowhere to warn the good guys at crucial moments, she saved them and hero "Crash" Corrigan

Shirley Patterson's solo appearance was in *Batman*—**Columbia, 1943— but, like Gifford and Rutherford, she has become a part of serial history because of that role.**

on several occasions, and has never been forgotten when classic serials are being discussed.

All of which brings us to the present:

Scheduled as a guest at this year's Western Film Fair in Charlotte is the beautiful actress Shirley Patterson. Although well-known as a leading lady in westerns (co-star of several with Eddie Dean, who is also scheduled to be a guest again this year) and in features during the 1940s, Miss Patterson will always be remembered by serial fans as "Linda Paige," the caped crusader's lady fair in *Batman*, Columbia's 1943 classic super-serial. As the only character in the cast playing it straight—Lewis Wilson was "Bruce," who was also the "Batman," who was also at times disguised as an underworld character; Douglas Croft was "Dick," who was also "Robin," who was also a little "flaky" at times; and J. Carroll Naish was "Doctor Daka," who was a scenery-chewing Japanese spy, who also looked Italian, who sounded like "Tweetie Pie" at times, and who was played by an Irishman—it was a real challenge for her to even be noticed at all, much less remembered. But it is nearly impossible to recall that serial without conjuring up a vision of the lovely "Linda Paige," so frequently being threatened by the slinky "Doctor Daka" in his insinuating tone.

There is at least one serial lover who always wished Shirley Patterson had made more than one serial. But, in the true tradition of the "one-shot winners," he also has never forgotten the one that she did make.

Perhaps—in the finest sense of the cliché—the truth of this situation is that, with these lovely ladies and the cliffhangers, in order to be a winner, "once was enough."

A lot can be said about the effect certain things have in the long run. Some of these "one-shot winners" might just as well have never made a serial—it made no difference in their careers. For some others, working in one may have even hampered or hurt a career or two. But, the worst it did for several of them—like Jinx Falkenburg, Phyllis Isley, and Lloyd Bridges (not mentioned in the article, but a veteran of one serial at Universal in 1945, Secret Agent X-9*)—was to give them a credit that they have chosen to try and deny over the years, or at least to ignore. And that's OK, too, for in the words of another cliché, "different strokes for different folks."*

One question that is sometimes asked of a former celebrity—or even one who is still active, but whose current work is not known to the asker—is, "Didn't you used to be so-and-so?"

At a convention in St. Louis many years ago, I heard that question asked of a man who was still doing a lot of acting in television shows, as well as in movies. A young man looked at one of the guests and inquired, "Didn't you used to be Don 'Red' Barry?" The obvious answer, of course, was given in good humor by the former great western star, who said, "Why, yes I was. And from all reports, I still am."

Don "Red" Barry was one of three famous western stars who retained the names of characters they played in serials as part of their official noms de plume for the rest of their careers. "Red" came from Barry's title role in Republic's Adventures of Red Ryder *in 1940. Ray "Crash" Corrigan's name came from* Undersea Kingdom, *a 1936 Republic release in which he played the hero whose*

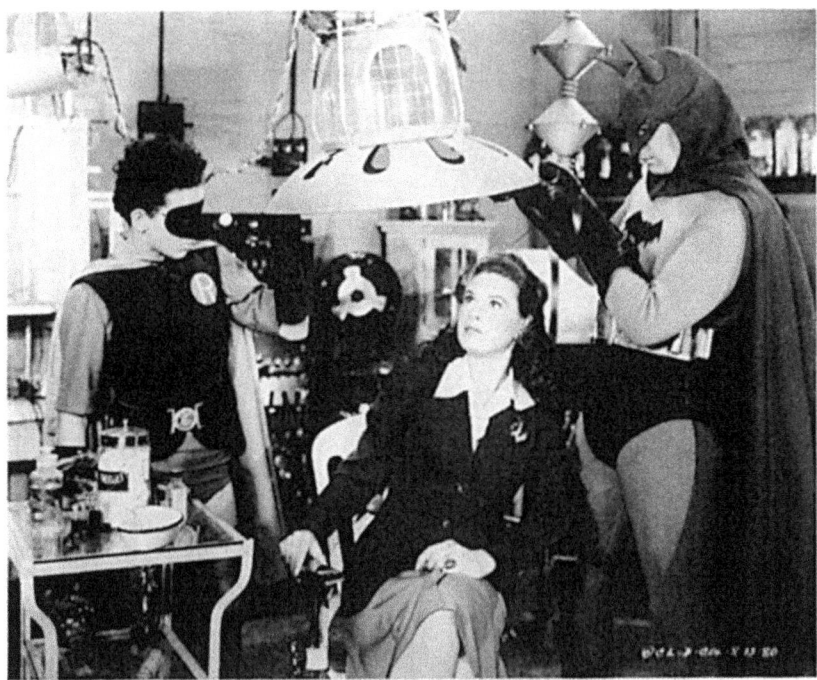

Batman—Columbia, 1943—featured Lewis Wilson *(right)*, as Batman, and Douglas Croft *(left)*, as Robin, who have arrived in the nick of time to rescue Shirley Patterson, as Linda Paige, from Dr. Daka's hypnotic device.

name was "Crash Corrigan" (which rhymes with "Flash Gordon"). Before that, his name had been Ray Benard.

And then there was Gordon Elliott:

The Man Who Became Wild Bill...
August 1987

One of my favorite western stars was Wild Bill Elliott. Who could ever forget that manful stride; that long-legged mounting of a saddle; that laconic grin when he pronounced as how he was a "peaceable man"; and that fighting style with the deadly earnest downward chop that showed how "un-peaceable" he could be when riled; those beautiful matched six-shooters he wore backwards, and his deft handling of them when trouble

came; his gallantry to the ladies; his patient, good-natured dealings with his bumbling sidekicks; and his gentle but compelling way with the kids? It was a real pleasure to watch him work.

Through the years I have known that the name "Wild Bill" came from the character he played in his first serial in Columbia, *The Great Adventures of Wild Bill Hickok,* but I had never seen that serial in its entirety before, and did not realize how much of the rest we know about him also came from there. Recently, thanks to my friend Tommy Hildreth and his friend Brent Smith, I secured a videotape of the serial and have now seen it all the way through for the first time. It was a rewarding experience.

From Wild Bill's friendly patter with chatterbox Roscoe Ates and bug-eyed Monte Collins; to his brotherly association with young Sammy McKim and Dickie Jones as they set up the boys' auxilliary called "The Flaming Arrows"; to his courtly, dignified scenes with Carole Wayne, who played the daughter of the cattle drive's organizer Monte Blue, forced by the death of her father to take over the mission of getting the herd to Abilene; to his face-to-face shoot-outs with Dick Cramer (in the Abilene saloon) and Eddy Waller (after throwing their guns on the ground between them to force his hand); the actor first known as Gordon Elliott developed and presented a character that had solid impact and would become almost a legendary part of the western movie scene for years to come. And it was all born in *The Great Adventures of Wild Bill Hickok.* If you are an Elliott fan, you should get a copy of this great serial, as well as Wild Bill's other two for Columbia, *Overland with Kit Carson* from 1939 and *The Valley of Vanishing Men* from 1942.

In all three of these Columbia serials, as well as the "Wild Bill" feature series at Columbia, the brief series with "Gabby" Hayes, and the "Red Ryders" at Republic, Bill Elliott played the same character he had created in *The Great Adventures of Wild Bill Hickok,* sharpening and developing it as he went along. Until achieving stardom in major features, it had been only in the eight-picture series in which he co-starred with Tex Ritter at Columbia in 1941 and 1942 that he portrayed characters differing to any extent from "Wild Bill." In one of these, *Vengeance of the West,* he even went so far as to play Mexican bandit Joaquin Murietta, who was being closely pursued by a Ranger captain named Lake, portrayed by Ritter. This series stands as testimony to the versatility and acting ability of both Elliott and Ritter.

The last decade of Bill Elliott's career saw him starring in major action features for Republic and later Allied Artists. At first billed as William

Opposite: **Exposure in a 15-chapter serial not only opened up a career for one actor, but gave him a new name that stayed with him for the rest of his life.**

Elliott at Republic for these, and then again as "Wild Bill" at Allied Artists, the man who reminded many people of the former silent star, William S. Hart, concluded his career—after nearly 20 years—starring in several non-western action pictures in the mid–1950s.

During that final decade came a role for William Elliott that first appeared to be a complete departure from all that he had done as "Wild Bill." In *Hellfire* for Republic in 1947, he played a crooked gambler whose life was saved when an itinerant preacher (played by by H. B. Warner) took a bullet meant for him in a saloon fight and died in his arms. Before expiring, however, the preacher's dream of one day building a real church was transferred to the bewildered gambler, who then became a man driven by the obsession to build that church at any cost. In so doing, he vowed not to cause violence to anyone else and to "turn the other cheek" if the occasion arose—which it often did. Not very much like "Wild Bill," until the whole film is run and you realize that the very weaknesses seen in him by other characters in the picture (especially lady outlaw Marie Windsor) were the strengths he had gained through his faith and commitment that would eventually enable him to build the preacher's church. In all that, his character, Zebulon Smith, became a whole lot like the "Wild Bill" of earlier days.

Altogether, Gordon Bill "Wild Bill" William Elliott gave us some fine motion pictures and many great movie scenes to thrill to and enjoy, following that first serial in 1938. And a real fan of his should see it to fully understand where "Wild Bill" came from and how he came to be.

Well done, Mistuh Bill!

There were other actors who became permanently identified with characters they played in serials, but Barry, Corrigan, and Elliott were the only ones to carry the names with them. Buster Crabbe was always known as Flash Gordon, even though he played many other parts—including five other comic strip (or radio) characters who were transferred to the screen. Kirk Alyn was always Superman, although he also played the comic strip character Blackhawk in a serial and another actor played Superman when the strip was produced for television. Tom Tyler was always Captain Marvel, even though he also played The Phantom; and Allan Lane would have been remembered always as Sergeant King, of the Royal Mounted if he hadn't gone on to become a leading star in series westerns. Of course, the actor who was most closely identified with the character he portrayed in four Republic serials was Ralph Byrd, who was always—until his untimely death—known and remembered as Dick Tracy. But

Opposite: Bill Elliott's second serial cast him as frontiersman Kit Carson, but he was still known to everyone as "the man who became Wild Bill."

none of these actors was forever tagged, as were Barry, Corrigan, and Elliott, with the actual names of the characters.

The actresses in serials also created some memorable roles, with which they will always be associated. But none of them carried their characters' names with them into the rest of their careers. Linda Stirling will always be remembered best as the Tiger Woman, and Joan Woodbury made her mark in serials in the title role of Columbia's Brenda Starr, Reporter, but neither was tagged by the names. The best-known female character in sound serials was played by two actresses, and both left indelible marks, but neither retained the name exclusively, either. Nyoka—first played by Frances Gifford in Jungle Girl, and then by Kay Aldridge in Perils of Nyoka—was the heroine's name that came to mean to sound serials what Pauline (from Pearl White's portrayal in Perils of Pauline) had meant to silent serials. But, outstanding characterizations of female heroes, such as Nyoka, Brenda Starr, and the Tiger Woman, were rare in sound serials. Mostly, the leading ladies had a far less active role to play.

Nevertheless, some of them were dearly remembered for the parts they played in the cliffhangers and "horse operas." And, seeing them week after week led to feelings of real affection for them. When it became possible to meet them in person, it was a genuine treat.

A Triple Treasure
October 1988

How can a man be in love with three women at the same time? And how could he ask his wife to understand?

It's easy when the three women are Jennifer Holt, Phyllis Coates and Evelyn Finley. And when his wife knows that he has loved these women all of his life—even before he met her and she became Number One.

Attending the Western Film Fair in Charlotte this year were five people who had made serials in the 1940s and 1950s. For a veteran serial-lover like me, that was a pretty good representation of the cliffhangers, and served as a fair bonus to an already generous return on the investment of time and expense made by any western or serial fan who decided to come.

Two of the five people were men—Lash LaRue, who was featured in Universal's 1945 serial *The Master Key* under his other name of Alfred LaRue; and Walter Reed, who played the hero in two Republic serials: *Flying Disc Man from Mars* in 1950, and *Government Agents Vs. The Phantom Legion* in 1951. It is always great to see Lash, who went on to become a bona fide Living Legend among stars of series westerns. And it was a genuine treat to confirm that Walter Reed—as was always suspected—is just one helluva nice man, in addition to being one of the best character actors of the past three decades. (Many of us were surprised to learn that the famous singing star of radio and television, "Smiling" Jack Smith, is Walter's big brother.) Both of these men are examples of the calibre of professional that came out of a tough school of movie serial production.

But, it was the three women named above who touched the heart of this old serial-lover. Because of their vast experience as leading ladies to many of Hollywood's most outstanding western stars, they have always been regarded as some of our favorite people in those great old series westerns that we all love so much. Without them, the daring exploits of the cowboy heroes would not have meant as much. The leading ladies in westerns symbolized the underlying need of the American frontiersman to push westward and try to settle the new frontier peaceably, in order to have a place to marry his true love, establish a home, and raise his family. She was his reason for going to all the trouble; and, without her, there would have been no good reason. These three women typified that western heroine in literally dozens of the films we have come to refer to as "B-westerns"—and did so magnificently.

However, the thing that endeared them so particularly to me was that they each had also been a veteran of the cliffhangers—a serial heroine. That always makes an actor special for me, and draws me to them. Sometimes, though—when they don't want to remember their serial days, or seem reluctant to discuss them—I have to back off and look again. That actor usually has an ego problem (I will mention no names). But, if they enjoy talking about the serial days—or even seem proud of them!—then, that's my kind of guy or gal. And all three of these lovely ladies seemed anxious to recall the cliffhangers.

Evelyn Finley began her movie career doing stunt work on a picture being filmed near her home in New Mexico. She went to Hollywood in the late 1930s and began a career that included both stunt work and acting in films; but, as she tells it, mostly stunt work. Hers was a case of being "typed," not for being a certain type of actor, but for being an expert horse rider and stunt person. Although a very fine actress—and as "cute as a button," a lovely young brunette—she was always being passed over by casting directors who thought of her only as a "stunt girl." When she did get a job as a leading lady, she was always excellent, so it is a shame they didn't use her more often. During the early 1940s, Evelyn played in films with co-stars such as Tex Ritter, Tom Keene, Crash Corrigan, John "Dusty" King, Dave Sharp, Buster Crabbe and Johnny Mack Brown. At that same time, and for many years afterward, she also doubled and did

dangerous stunts for most of Hollywood's leading actresses who appeared in outdoor adventure films.

In 1956, in order to try for a new direction in her career, Evelyn changed her name to Eve Anderson and played "Donna Blane" in Columbia's 15-chapter serial *Perils of the Wilderness,* which co-starred Dennis Moore. But, alas, it didn't work. By that time, producers and directors knew her only too well as the lady who knew all about horses and riding and doing expert stunt work. So, that's what she is known for best. And she is truly the greatest. The only thing she is greater at—and all who have met her will agree, I am sure—is in being one of the kindest, gentlest, most generous and considerate human beings I have ever met. To get to know her—even briefly—makes it impossible not to love her.

Cast in the same mold is the beautiful, vivacious Phyllis Coates. Arriving on the Hollywood scene in 1950 as the leading lady in *Outlaws of Texas,* a Monogram production starring Whip Wilson, the lovely young actress was destined to become widely-known in three areas—as a western leading lady, as a dashing serial queen, and as the TV "girl friend" of Superman, girl reporter "Lois Lane." In westerns, Phyllis co-starred in a number of pictures at Monogram and Republic with stars such as Whip Wilson, Johnny Mack Brown and Allan "Rocky" Lane; and with "Wild Bill" Elliott in *The Longhorn, Fargo, The Maverick* and *Topeka* at Allied Artists. When *Superman* was first produced for television in 1950, she was cast as the first TV "Lois" and soon gained a faithful legion of fans for her bright and witty portrayal of the girl reporter. When she left *Superman* to star in the pilot for a new series, the role of "Lois" was given to Noel Neill, who had played the part in both Columbia serials based on the world-famous comic strip.

In late 1952, Miss Coates was cast as "Carol Bryant," the leading lady to Clayton Moore (as "Alan King") in *Jungle Drums of Africa,* a 12-chapter Republic serial. In 1953, she was again cast in a serial with Moore—this time in Columbia's *Gunfighters of the Northwest,* in which she played *Rita Carvel,* a brave young woman who pretended to be one of the outlaws led by a masked leader, in order to flush out the killer of her brother, who had owned a rich mine in the north woods country. This time, however, her hero was Canadian mountie "Joe Ward," played by Jock Mahoney. The serial for which she is best remembered is the 1955 Republic production *Panther Girl of the Kongo,* in which she starred as "Jean Evans," a Nyoka-type jungle heroine who dodged bad guys and jungle dangers for 12 episodes. Her leading man and helper, "Larry Sanders," was played by Myron Healey.

Opposite: **The Charlotte, N.C., Western Film Fair's "Triple Treasure" of 1988: three beautiful serial leading ladies.** *From left:* **Jennifer Holt, Phyllis Coates, and Evelyn Finley.**

Since those exciting westerns and serials in the 1950s, as well as her portrayal in *Superman,* Phyllis Coates has caused millions of us to believe that she would be just as charming, witty and vivacious in person, if we would ever meet her. Once we did, that expectation was not just realized; it was far exceeded. What a super human being she really is! On "Hello, Henry," a late night telephone talk show heard on radio up and down the East Coast, Miss Coates was invited to appear and talk to fans who would call in. During that show, a young man called to thank her for her help in completing a thesis he had been working on in college a number of years before. He had phoned her in the middle of the day to ask a few questions; and, due to her interest and concern in his project, had wound up talking to her for nearly an hour. She was delighted when he called, saying she remembered the incident well. (By the way, he got an A on the thesis.) You just gotta love a woman like that!

And I've loved Jennifer Holt since 1941. That was the year a new young leading lady named "Jacqueline" Holt appeared in *Stick to Your Guns,* a Hopalong Cassidy western starring William Boyd. The name "Jacqueline" did not stick, but "Jennifer" did, and she went on to play in westerns with more than a dozen of Hollywood's most famous western stars. And — joy of joys for me — she made two serials along the way.

After that first "Hoppy" western in 1941, Jennifer went over to Universal and began co-starring in westerns with Johnny Mack Brown. When Brown teamed up to co-star with Tex Ritter in a series of westerns for Universal, Jennifer Holt was the leading lady in all of them. For the next decade — at Universal, Republic, Monogram, P.R.C., Screen Guild and Eagle Lion — she appeared in over fifty westerns with such stars as Russell Hayden, Eddie Dew, Hoot Gibson, Bob Steele, Richard Arlen, Jimmy Wakely, Eddie Dean, Lash LaRue and Rod Cameron. I have heard it said that if she had been a man, Jennifer Holt could easily have been a top western star.

Well, she was; and her name was "Tim."

Tim Holt, the great star of R.K.O. westerns for nearly 12 years, an accomplished actor acclaimed for his acting in *The Magnificent Ambersons, Hitler's Children, My Darling Clementine* and *The Treasure of the Sierra Madre,* was her brother. Their father was Jack Holt, the great action star of the 1920s and 1930s, who became a beloved character actor in the 1940s. Had Jennifer Holt been a man, she would have easily been a western star like Tim and Jack. As a woman, however, she was a great western leading lady, taking a back-seat to no one.

And, as I said, she made serials. Two of them.

Just about 18 months after the release of the only sound serial her father ever made — Columbia's *Holt of the Secret Service* (the only one to bear the name of its star in the title) — Jennifer appeared in the 13-chapter

Universal thriller *Adventures of the Flying Cadets,* playing "Andre Mason," a young American girl being held captive with her father by Nazi agents and used as pawns in a scheme to secure lost treasure to finance their war effort. The serial included some chapterplay "old-timers" like Robert Armstrong, Eduardo Ciannelli, Charles Trowbridge and Joseph Crehan, but also featured young players Johnny Downs, Bobby Jordan, Ward Wood and Billy Benedict, as well as Jennifer. Although hampered by wartime shortages and restrictions, the Universal serial division still managed to produce a pretty good serial, thanks in no small part to lovely young Jennifer Holt.

In March, 1946, Columbia released a serial based on the very popular comic strip and radio program *Hop Harrigan,* with William Bakewell portraying "Hop." Playing "Gail Nolan," his beautiful landlord—and romantic interest—was the beautiful and romantic Jennifer Holt. It's kind of ironic that the girl who played in so many western features never made a western serial. Both of hers were airplane adventures.

Nevertheless, as "Jacqueline" or "Jennifer," I have loved that mysterious little smile and that mischievous twinkle in her eyes for all these years. And in person she is even more lovely, more gracious, and more charming than on the movie screen. It is a treat just to know her; but to call her a friend is great joy. And I call her my friend.

How can a man be in love with three women at the same time? If they're Evelyn Finley, Phyllis Coates and Jennifer Holt, how could I not be?

Although the leading ladies were not the main activists in the serials, it is true to say that serials would not have been the same without them. As they gave the westerns the reason for their existence, they also provided serials with a purpose. Without them, it would have been just pointless competition.

Just as Allan Lane could have been remembered forever as Sergeant King, Rod Cameron might easily have become known for his only serial character if he had not gone on to become a major film star. In 1943, in what many people think of as the final year of the serials' "Golden Years," Cameron starred in two serials at Republic, playing action ace Rex Bennett in both. G-Men vs. the Black Dragon *was released in January, and* Secret Service in Darkest Africa *followed seven months later.*

By the end of 1943, and 30 weeks' exposure, Rex Bennett had become one of the most popular serial heroes of that day, and moviegoers knew that a new star had been born. Rod Cameron was already under contract to Universal and starring in his own series of westerns. In a flash, it seemed, he was playing opposite stars like Yvonne De Carlo and Ella Raines, and his career was on the

rise. He became one of Hollywood's most popular and best-liked action stars for many years to come.

Rex Bennett Revisited
April 1987

Within the past several weeks, I have had the pleasure of watching again two of the fastest-paced action serials Republic ever made. Both featured the same lanky hero, Rod Cameron, and both were sheer "field days" for the stuntmen. *G-Men vs. the Black Dragon* came out in January 1943, and was followed seven months later by *Secret Service in Darkest Africa*. Between them was the classic western serial *Daredevils of the West*, and they were followed closely by *The Masked Marvel* in November and *Captain America* in December–January. Coming on the heels of 1942's *Spy Smasher, Perils of Nyoka* and *King of the Mounties*, these two Rod Cameron serials hold a place among the last of Republic's greatest "Golden-Age" serials. And, some will say that 1943 was the peak year, never again to be matched by Republic, nor any other serial producer thereafter.

That's not to say there weren't some mighty good serials made after 1943. Fans of the Tiger Woman, or Captain Mephisto, or the Black Whip, or the Purple Monster—not to mention the Scarlet Horseman, Superman or the Rocketman—would argue with you readily about the merits of their favorite cliffhanger in the later days. But, it is generally agreed that after 1943 most productions from all three companies—Columbia, Universal and Republic—did not measure up to the high quality of those "magic" years from 1936 to 1943. Also, most of the serials from 1944 on were less innovative than those in the early years. They kept on doing the things that had been tried and tested and found to please audiences, without attempting too much what was new and risky. Movies in general—and television later—followed the same pattern. Only, with movie features and television, there eventually had to come a return to innovation and experimentation when audiences tired of seeing the same things over and over too much. It didn't happen with serials because they were replaced by TV in the late 1940s and early 1950s, before a return to those things could take place. Television was the new week-to-week teaser for the public that serials had been; and, unfortunately, the cliffhanger would never again see days of greatness.

Opposite: **Future star Rod Cameron played hero Rex Bennett in two of Republic's fastest action serials,** *G-Men vs. the Black Dragon* **and** *Secret Service in Darkest Africa,* **both released in 1943.**

But in 1943 serials were still great. And the two Rod Cameron serials were prime examples. With World War II going full swing, there could be no doubt who the villains were. In *G-Men* it was a Japanese foreign agent named Haruchi, played to the hilt by Nino Pipitone. As head of the American branch of the secret terrorist organization known as the Black Dragon Society, Haruchi manipulated all sorts of sabotage and espionage plots from his headquarters through two of the coldest, most vicious henchmen in serialdom, played by Noel Cravat and George J. Lewis. The heroes were Cameron, as American G-Man Rex Bennett, Roland Got as Chang, a representative of the friendly Chinese government, and Constance Worth as Vivian Marsh, the British member of the team. Some of the fight scenes between the heroes and the two Black Dragon agents were, at the time the serial was released, almost unbelievable. Stuntmen Tom Steele (doubling Cameron), Dale Van Sickel, Kenneth Terrell, Bud Wolfe, Bert LeBaron, Duke Green, Fred Graham and Eddie Parker (just to name a few) staged some of the most incredible rough-and-tumble brawls ever seen on the serial screen. The fight choreography in *Spy Smasher, Daredevils of the West, The Masked Marvel* and these two serials set the standard for the remainder of the serial era. The surprising thing to see, in retrospect, was how much of the fight action Rod Cameron himself took part in. Because of some of the other later serials, where stuntmen are seen to be obviously doing most of the work, it is easy to forget that in some of these "Golden-Age" serials, the leading player was almost as active a participant in some of the action scenes as were the stuntmen. It can certainly be said of Rod Cameron that he did his share.

In *Secret Service in Darkest Africa,* the scene shifted to North Africa — specifically Casablanca — and the villains were German Nazis led by a high-ranking Gestapo officer named Von Rommler, played by Lionel Royce, who disguised himself as a trusted Arab leader and directed his spy activities from that leader's own office. This time, Rex Bennett's allies were a French diplomatic officer, played by Duncan Renaldo, and an international female journalist, portrayed by Joan Marsh. Frederick Brun was "Wolf," the vicious Nazi hatchetman assigned to carry out Von Rommler's orders, and the action was just as fast as *G-Men*.

It has been said — and I have said it often — that in any listing of serials, the four Dick Tracy serials and *Perils of Nyoka* would have to be included as examples of the very best produced by Republic studios. In that vein, it is fair to say that *G-Men vs. the Black Dragon* would rank right in with the Tracys for action and sheer thrills; and *Secret Service in Darkest Africa* combined the elements of the Tracy serials with the exotic trappings of *Nyoka* to result in one of the most exciting chapterplays ever filmed. It is obvious to anyone that these are the serials most hearkened to by the producers of recent thrill features such as *Raiders of the Lost Ark, Indiana Jones*

Following leading roles in two Yvonne De Carlo pictures at Universal—*Salome, Where She Danced* and *Frontier Gal*—Cameron's career was off and running to stardom in major films.

and the Temple of Doom, Romancing the Stone and The Jewel of the Nile. The knock-down-drag-out, thrill-a-second action of the Nyokas, the Tracys, and these two Rod Camerons is precisely what they were seeking to re-create. And, in a number of priceless scenes—praise be!—they came awfully close.

Rod Cameron passed on a while back, but it was my personal privilege—and innermost thrill—to screen *Secret Service in Darkest Africa* several years ago at the Charlotte Western Film Fair, with "Rex Bennett" himself in attendance. His presence in the room gave new life and perspective to what had always been one of my favorite serials. And, between reels, when fans would congratulate him on a job well done, or ask a question about how something had been done, he was very generous and gracious with his answers.

A star of major importance in the film business, Rod Cameron was truly one who learned his craft the best way: by doing it. And every serial fan who idolized Rex Bennett in the midst of World War II was sincerely gratified that he did become a star. To us, he was—even then.

It may be presumptuous to say that stars like Gene Autry, Johnny Mack Brown, Bill Elliott, Allan Lane, and Rod Cameron would not have become stars without the continuous weeks of exposure provided by serials. And, it may be argumentative to claim that others like Frances Gifford, Ann Rutherford, Jennifer Jones, and Ruth Roman were helped by their one appearance in a serial. It would certainly be ridiculous to maintain that Donald Barry, Ray Benard, and Gordon Elliott couldn't have gone on to better things without picking up their nicknames from serial characters—they were good actors and would have done well anyway. But, there is also one thing for sure:

It didn't hurt.

Chapter 6

"Look, All You Gotta Do Is Shave the Moustache!"

"Things are not always what they seem to be." Even before Alfred Hitchcock made the moviegoing public so keenly aware of that fact, the serials had made it their stock in trade. The villains of serials were a devious lot and showed many faces. So, it was in that category that real acting ability was absolutely required. The basic premise of serials — as well as of series westerns — was that the forces of good must continually battle the forces of evil and that good must always win. The lines were clearly drawn, and there was little deviation from that fundamental concept. So, in a serial, little room was left for any conjecture concerning which was which. It was plain who the good guys were, and just as plain who the bad guys were. That was the starting point.

The actors who played the bad guys had to be convincing in their portrayals because the audience had to believe there was a threat in what they were doing, or else the whole thing would have been academic.

Good at Being Bad
May 1985

The real secret to a good cliffhanger was a bad villain. No matter how handsome and dashing the hero might appear; nor how bright and resourceful he might promise to be; it just wasn't as exciting and enjoyable to watch unless the villain was mean and heartless and cruel. The meaner the heavy, the greater the challenge; and that made for good fireworks.

There were a handful of men who portrayed serial villains many times, and helped give them the colorful image they had. Three very gifted character actors played the cliffhanger heavy only once, but did so with such flair that they remain memorable for that one role. And, three others became the unquestionable leaders — the maestros of menace. Unsurpassed.

As early as 1932, Noah Beery, Sr., and Leroy Mason were menacing serial heroes—Beery plotting against Harry Carey in Mascot's *The Devil Horse*, and Mason trying to corral Lon Chaney, Jr., in R.K.O.'s *The Last Frontier*. Beery was a big, gruff, swaggering bully of a man, who could lower an eyebrow and growl out a line that made you know he meant the hero no good at all. Mason conveyed the same feeling with a tight-lipped sneer and oily leer.

Beery repeated his approach to outright villainy in four more serials: *Fighting with Kit Carson* (1933), *Zorro Rides Again* (1937) and *Adventures of Red Ryder* (1940) at Republic, and *Overland Mail* (1942) at Universal. Mason connected with nine more: *Phantom of the Air* (Universal, 1933), *The Painted Stallion* (Republic, 1937), *Overland with Kit Carson* (Columbia, 1939), *The Tiger Woman* (Republic, 1944), *Federal Operator 99* (Republic, 1945), *The Phantom Rider* (Republic, 1945), *King of the Forest Rangers* (Republic, 1946), *Daughter of Don Q* (Republic, 1946) and *Jesse James Rides Again* (Republic, 1947).

Suave, sophisticated and crafty, actor James Craven worked both sides of the street in cliffhangers. As a distinguished-looking man—supposedly a gentleman—he gained the confidence of the good guys while working against them at every turn. Starting with *The Green Archer* (Columbia, 1940), Craven schemed his way through a total of seven serials, including *White Eagle* (1941), *Captain Midnight* (1942) at Columbia, and *The Purple Monster Strikes* (1945), *Federal Agents vs. Underworld, Inc.* (1948), *King of the Rocketmen* (1949) and *Flying Disc Man from Mars* (1950) at Republic.

Henry Brandon and Eduardo Ciannelli each created a classic serial villain in the same year. Brandon became the unique Dr. Fu Manchu, and Ciannelli chilled serial audiences as the dreaded Doctor Satan—both at Republic in 1940. Prior to *Drums of Fu Manchu*, Henry Brandon had played villains at Universal in *Jungle Jim* (1936), *Secret Agent X-9* (1937) and *Buck Rogers* (1939), but it was as Sax Rohmer's famous archcriminal Fu Manchu that he made his greatest mark on serials. His interpretation of the character was different than Karloff's, but stands in many people's memories as the "real" Fu. Ciannelli's Doctor Satan could easily rank as one of the top three or four villain portrayals in all serial history; and it was done without any costumes, gimmicks, special make-up or effects—just straight acting ability and performance. He went on to make *Sky Raiders* in 1941 and *Adventures of the Flying Cadets* in 1943 at Universal; and, while great in both, his characterization in

Opposite: The Painted Stallion—**Republic, 1937—featured as the head villain Leroy Mason, who was "good at being bad" in serials for over 15 years. From left: Ray "Crash" Corrigan** *(with hands up),* **Maston Williams, Leroy Mason, and (as a bad guy for a change) Duncan Renaldo.**

In *The Purple Monster Strikes*—Republic, 1945—James Craven *(left)* was one of the bad guys who switched sides easily, from villain to solid citizen, and then back again. He is shown here with Dennis Moore and Linda Stirling.

Republic's *Mysterious Doctor Satan* in 1940 still remains one of the best ever.

In 1939, Irving Pichel played the villain Zarnoff in Republic's *Dick Tracy's G-Men*. He went on to become one of the industry's outstanding directors, including such feature films as *She, The Happy Land, And Now Tomorrow, A Medal for Benny, Miracle of the Bells, Destination Moon* and *Santa Fe* in his credits.

As the mean and nasty Wolf Reade in *Riders of Death Valley* (Universal, 1941), Charles Bickford played his only cliffhanger role with such vigor that it became one of the most memorable things about one of Universal's most memorable serials. Bickford was one of the screen's most respected character actors, with outstanding performances given in films such as *Song of Bernadette, A Wing and a Prayer, Mr. Lucky, The Farmer's Daughter* and *Johnny Belinda*.

George MacReady was a first-rank heavy in many feature films, especially as an arrogant despot in costume dramas; but played Professor

Flash Gordon's Trip to Mars—Universal, 1938: Just about everyone's favorite serial villain was Charles Middleton *(left)* when he played Ming, the Merciless. Flash was played by Buster Crabbe *(right)*.

Ernst, the mad scientist bent on ruling the world, in Columbia's *The Monster and the Ape* in 1945, as if he were vying for an award.

Pichel, Bickford and MacReady all were representative of the professional talent that serials often employed in their search for actors who could bring the thrills of the cliffhangers to the audiences by playing convincing and appropriately menacing villains.

Without much argument, it is generally agreed that the three absolute top villains of sound serials were Bela Lugosi, Charles Middleton and Roy Barcroft. Together they spanned the entire era, and separately they accounted for some of the most mean, sneaky and unforgettable villains ever hissed at by America's youth. They are the ones we think of when we think of actors being "good at being bad." They were the best at being the worst.

Lugosi, one of the true screen legends because of his early portrayals in *Dracula* and other horror features, starred in five serials, starting with *The Whispering Shadow* for Mascot in 1933. His next was *The Return of Chandu* (his only serial role as a non-villain) for Principal Pictures in 1934, followed by Victory Pictures' *Shadow of Chinatown* in 1936, *S.O.S. Coast Guard* for Republic in 1937 and *The Phantom Creeps* for Universal in 1939.

Middleton's first was as Zaroff in Mascot's *The Miracle Rider* in 1935; but it was as Ming, the Merciless in *Flash Gordon* the following year at Universal that he became the epitome of the cliffhanger villain—evil personified. He repeated the role in *Flash Gordon's Trip to Mars* in 1938, and that year also played the cruel, heartless Pa Stark, who led his five sons in crime, in Republic's *Dick Tracy Returns*, and a ruthless frontier badman in Universal's *Flaming Frontiers*. In 1939 he was the scheming mastermind known only as 39-O-13 in Republic's *Daredevils of the Red Circle;* and, after doing Ming one more time in Universal's *Flash Gordon Conquers the Universe* in 1940, came back in 1942 as Cassib, the right-hand man of the villainess Vultura in *Perils of Nyoka* at Republic. He finished out his career in serials with roles in *The Desert Hawk* and *Black Arrow* (1944), *Who's Guilty?* (1945) and *Jack Armstrong* (1947), all at Columbia. Barcroft played many minor parts in serials until 1944. That year he took the lead villain's role in *Haunted Harbor* at Republic, and launched an amazing career.

For the next ten years, he played a succession of bad guys probably unequalled by any other actor in the field—pirate, outlaw, gangster, crooked cop, spaceman, renegade, crooked sheriff, saloon keeper, politician—you name it. He was Republic's top villain for those ten years, and the man the fans "loved to hate." His characterizations in 1945 of the re-incarnated pirate, Captain Mephisto, in Republic's *Manhunt of Mystery Island*, and the Martian space invader in their *The Purple Monster Strikes*, stand next to Charles Middleton's Ming as truly memorable screen villains. He appeared in more than a dozen Republic serials from 1944 to 1954 as the top or second heavy, in addition to playing in more of their western features during that time than one could accurately account for. Variety is the spice of life, they say; and who will disagree? That being true, then, Roy Barcroft was the "spice" of Republic serials.

And all the "good" villains—who were "good at being bad"—gave serials that something extra that provided audiences with what they came for: the opportunity to cheer and hiss; to praise and to boo—and to be royally entertained in the process.

The way that villains were portrayed by these outstanding players never left any doubt as to the evil menace involved or the dreadful threat to society that the good guys were trying so hard to overcome. These actors were the ones who were so skillful in spelling out the danger in the plot that kept things interesting and mysterious.

To make things even more interesting, however, the villains sometimes posed as honest, upright citizens—causing things to seem to be other than what they were—or portrayed to the world a deliberately contrived false image of some weird or outlandish fetish creature for the villain, to create revulsion, superstition, or just plain fear.

Fear of the unknown has always been the greatest fear. Not knowing what we have to deal with—so that we have no idea of how to arm or prepare ourselves—is our most enormous dread. From a child's first day at school—with all the unfamiliar sights and sounds—to a person's final encounter with death—with all its unanswered questions and imagined facets—our most frightening apprehensions are about things we don't know, can't identify, or don't comprehend. Something that may turn out to be a small thing when explained can loom large and threatening until we know about it.

Use of the fear that we all have—the idea of an unknown mystery villain, masked and hidden from view—elevated the classic good-bad struggle to epic proportions. And serial fans loved it.

Who's Behind That Mask?
August 1988

A friend of mine just recently borrowed *Adventures of Captain Marvel* to show at a boys' summer camp. For a number of years, he has been showing a serial each summer to the boys attending camp, one chapter a night. But not just any serial—only the ones with a mystery villain, whose identity is not revealed until the last chapter. As the boys watch each chapter, there is a running contest in which they vote on who they think the masked or hooded villain really is. After the final chapter, a prize goes to the lucky boy, or boys, who have guessed correctly. In *Captain Marvel* they get to vote on the unknown hooded villain called the Scorpion.

This is a lucky bunch of kids. Not only do they get to enjoy the slam-bang action of a great serial, but they get to participate in what kids in the 1930s and 1940s enjoyed regularly—the mystery villain guessing game, or "Who's behind the mask?"

Since way before the Rattler in *Mystery Mountain*, Ken Maynard's 1934 Mascot serial, and way on past Captain Mephisto in *Manhunt of Mystery Island*, Roy Barcroft's swashbuckling pirate villain reincarnated by "metamorphosis" in the 1945 Republic classic, kids have argued vehemently about which suspect in the cast was the mystery villain, and why. Many times they would even come to blows over the issue. And it was all great fun. They had great mystery villains to work with, and many of them were very colorful. There were the Wrecker in *Hurricane Express* and the Rattler in *Mystery Mountain*, who wore face masks to look

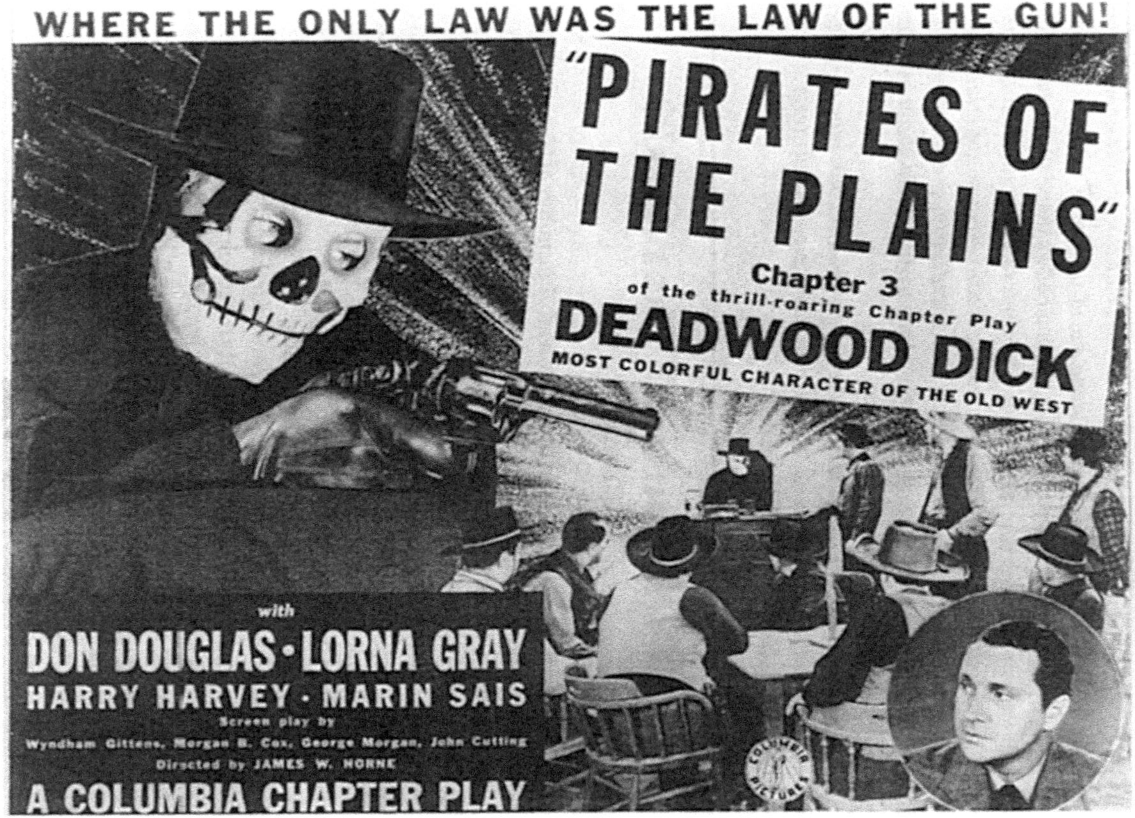

WHERE THE ONLY LAW WAS THE LAW OF THE GUN!

"PIRATES OF THE PLAINS"

Chapter 3 of the thrill-roaring Chapter Play

DEADWOOD DICK

MOST COLORFUL CHARACTER OF THE OLD WEST

with

DON DOUGLAS • LORNA GRAY
HARRY HARVEY • MARIN SAIS

Screen play by
Wyndham Gittens, Morgan B. Cox, George Morgan, John Collins
Directed by JAMES W. HORNE

A COLUMBIA CHAPTER PLAY

like anybody in the serial they wanted to—even, at times, the hero. There were the Black Ace in *Mystery Squadron,* Bob Steele's only serial; El Shaitan in *The Three Musketeers,* which starred John Wayne; the Tiger Shark in *The Fighting Marines,* Mascot's last serial; and the Dragon in *Ace Drummond,* Universal's 1936 air adventure that featured John King as the hero.

All of these were very mysterious and very deceptive, but the next decade would bring a new trend in villains. They began to develop certain personality aspects of their own that resulted in categories, or types, of mystery villains. Some were very picturesque or bizarre; some "faked" a physical disability of some kind; and some based their names and visages directly on morbidity or death. Several even became the "star" of the serial, so to speak, by having their name used as the title. Two of the most bizarre and picturesque were the Lightning in *The Fighting Devil Dogs,* the 1938 Republic serial, and Don Del Oro in *Zorro's Fighting Legion* from Republic the next year. The Lightning was almost certainly the inspiration for Darth Vader, the villain in the *Star Wars* trilogy forty years later; and Don Del Oro hid under the guise of a large, life-size figure of a golden statue, which he purportedly brought to "life" to impress and inspire a tribe of Mexican Indians known as Yaquis. These two villains are remembered as much for their unique appearances as for who they really turned out to be.

The Spider in *Dick Tracy*—also known as "The Lame One" and "The Unknown One"—assumed a clubfoot, which he dragged along as he walked, and a ragged-looking head disguise to conceal his identity; the Octopus in *The Spider's Web* also "faked" a clubfoot and used a cane as he entered his secret headquarters to issue orders, but added a lame arm to protrude from his white robe, so he could use his second "good arm" to shoot down any of his followers who got out of line; and, in one of the best portrayals of a mystery villain of that time, Trevor Bardette played Peg-leg in Wild Bill Elliott's *Overland with Kit Carson,* assuming a scarred facial disguise to cover his true identity, and effecting the "loss" of one leg and use of a peg leg to further throw off suspicion.

In *Deadwood Dick,* the master villain dressed in a black hat and cloak and wore a skull-face mask to hide behind. He was appropriately called the Skull. Six years later, a similar but large skull-face mask was used to cover the face of *The Crimson Ghost* in the serial that bore that name as its title. During that time, a couple of other serials were released with the title the same as the villain's name: *The Master Key* and *Mysterious Mr. M.*

Opposite: **The mystery villain known as "the skull" in *Deadwood Dick* was one of a long line of such colorful bad guys who kept everyone asking— right up to the last chapter—"Who's behind that mask?"**

Some years earlier, the same thing had occurred with *The Whispering Shadow*, *The Clutching Hand* and *The Iron Claw*.

There were numerous other mystery villains—the Tiger Shark, the Wasp, the Dragon, the Gargoyle, the Ghost and the Wizard, to name a few—but they were cast, more or less, in the old, traditional mold of mystery villains. The one thing that they all shared in common was "The Mask"—or hood, or disguise—which concealed their true identity so no one would know who they really were.

Movies in general—and serials in particular—seemed to have a preoccupation with this ploy, and it has caused students of the cinema to wonder why. Aside from being a handy tool in a mystery story, what was the reason for movie makers' fixations on masks and hoods for its bad guys? It's a logical question, and one answer seems very logical to me.

Several weeks ago, I saw a "Hollywood" documentary on public TV which featured the two productions that brought about major changes in early Hollywood movies—*The Great Train Robbery*, which was the first film to tell a story, and *Birth of a Nation*, the first major feature of epic proportions. Prior to *The Great Train Robbery*, all movies were just moving pictures, with no story or plot. It was enough to see the novelty of movement. This film changed that forever. It gave audiences something to get interested in, caught up in, and excited about. And that's what movies became forever. Then, when D. W. Griffith produced his epic feature based on the book, *The Clansman*, and released it as *The Birth of a Nation*, it was seen for the first time what impact a motion picture could have on the general public, and it was stupendous. The reaction was staggering.

Griffith portrayed the actions of the Ku Klux Klan in post–Civil War America during the Reconstruction. As he portrayed them, the Klan was a group of hooded and robed avengers who meted out revenge for injustices done to the South by evil "carpetbaggers" and "unfair" Reconstruction laws. The people of the South saw this as the way it was; but other people elsewhere saw the Klan as a ravaging pack of raiders who violated the law and took justice into their own hands. As a result, there was general controversy about just what was being shown in *The Birth of a Nation*. That controversy still continues today—over three quarters of a century later.

The one thing that was clear to both sides, however, was that no one could be brought to answer for those actions—good or bad—because no one knew who the men were. They all wore hoods and concealed their identities. This was a chilling fact—about the Klan in the movie, and

Opposite: **Reminiscent of the mystery villains of the silent movies, *The Iron Claw* created the proper sense of fear and suspense until he was exposed in the final episode.**

about the Klan in real life. The mystery was thus established. And the movies recognized it.

During the 1920s, 1930s, and into the 1940s, there were many different movies dealing with that dread—that chilling factor: unknown men concealing their identity, threatening others with the fear of violence and death and not being accountable for it because no one knew who they were—and it could not be surpassed as the primary ominous menace of the visual theatre. And in serials the factor took firm root because it was being addressed primarily to young and unsophisticated viewers. It was the thing that sold best. So, one after another, serials were released with the mysterious, unknown, masked or hooded villain preying upon society. And the serial heroes had their work cut out for them. One after another, they had to cut through the fear and superstition and mystery, and unmask the villain for what he was—one of us, using our own worst fears against us—and by unmasking him, let us see who he was, and breathe a sigh of relief.

That may not be the exact way it happened, but it seems logical to me. The whole idea of masked villains may not be traceable to *The Birth of a Nation*, but we all know that the movies take lessons from other movies; and they firmly believe in the adage that "nothing succeeds like success." So, I think it probably did. And, anyway, we sure did enjoy a lot of action and suspense watching the villains tracked down and exposed—whether that was the way it started or not.

The serial villains, then, were usually the primary element in determining whether each production would be a success or not. Portrayed in the open, using the considerable talents of excellent actors, or portrayed as unknown, outlandish characters, whose real identities became part of the mystery, the villains held the key to the whole thing. And it is impossible to remember any good serial without remembering who the villain was.

Most of the actors who played villains almost always played villains. You didn't really expect them to play anything else. It's what they were good at. A veteran serial watcher could recognize the bad guys the moment they came on the screen—not because of what they were saying or doing necessarily, but simply because of who they were. They were typecast. And seldom did they ever appear in any other kind of roles.

But, once in a while they did, and when they did, it was usually a memorable situation.

Opposite: One of the most memorable of all the masked villains of serials was the Ghost, who had the technology to make himself invisible, as well as unknown, in the final Dick Tracy sequel.

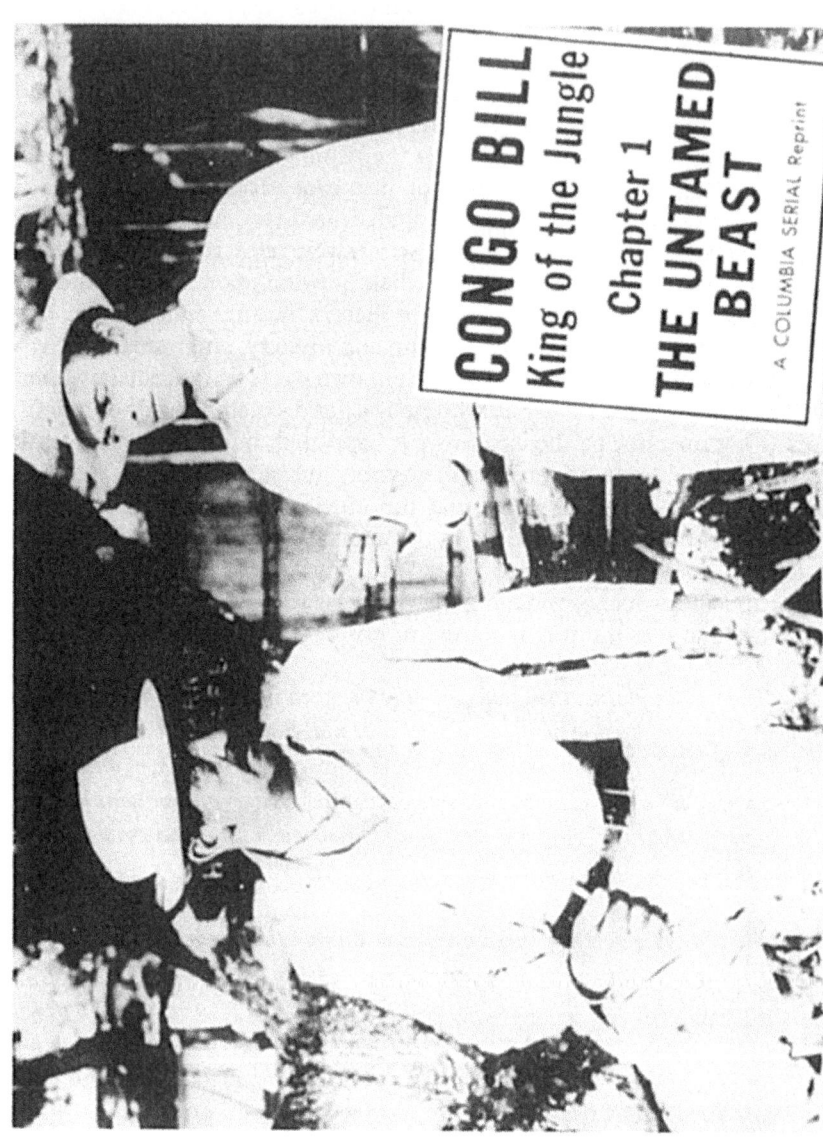

When the Leopard Changed Its Spots
February 1988

It always seemed safe to assume when you saw Charlie King in a serial that he would be a bad guy—or an ornery galoot, at least. The same thing was true of a host of other weather-beaten veterans of cliffhangers such as Jack Ingram, George Chesebro, Stan Jolley and Bob Kortman. The reason is that they always played bad guys, and were good at it. They were a special breed of rough and tumble, no-nonsense, outdoors men of action. Most came to the movies from cattle ranches or rodeos—or both—and were hired because they could ride, shoot, and handle themselves in fight scenes without a lot of direction or coaching. They were naturals: men with practical experience doing what they were experienced in doing. (The same thing could not be truthfully said about many of the leading men who came along. Some of them, unfortunately, had to be coached on the very basics before they would even look right *sitting* on a horse.) So, when one of the bad-guy veterans turned up in a good-guy role—or even a sympathetic one—it was sometimes a little disconcerting, or uncomfortable. You couldn't help wondering,

"Okay, where's the catch? When does he double-cross the good guys and show his real colors?" You couldn't help but be suspicious.

Charlie King is the prime example. After some 20 years in serials playing mostly bad guys, he showed up in Columbia's *Adventures of Sir Galahad* in 1949 playing Sir Bors, the staunchest ally of hero Sir Galahad, fighting side by side with the young knight throughout the serial, even saving the hero's life several times. After all those years of his playing all those scurrilous villains, it wasn't easy to watch.

Several leading men had very successfully played both sides of the issue—switching from good guys to bad guys—and one actress was particularly adept at it. But they were thought of as actors, and you sort of expected it from actors. From the veterans, you expected to see what you had always seen: bad guys playing bad guys. Clayton Moore made ten serials during his career, and in two of them—*The Crimson Ghost* in 1946 and *Radar Men from the Moon* in 1952—he had played heavies. Charles Quigley was a memorable hero in *Daredevils of the Red Circle* in 1939, *The Iron Claw*

Opposite: **Charlie King (left) was a better actor than many people gave him credit for. When he "changed his spots," it was a shock, but entirely credible. Leonard Penn, another "leopard," is on the right.**

in 1941, and *The Crimson Ghost* in 1946, but turned bad guy for *Brick Bradford* and *Superman* in 1948. John Crawford, who had played heavies in several Republic serials, showed up as a hero in *Blackhawk* in 1952, and played in the title role of *The Great Adventures of Captain Kidd* in 1953. The hero of Republic's last really good serial, *King of the Rocketmen* in 1949, was Tristram Coffin, who had always played sophisticated bad guys. And the lady who did it so well was Lorna Gray, when she played good girls in *Flying G-Men* in 1939, *Deadwood Dick* in 1940; bad girls in *Perils of Nyoka* in 1942 and *Federal Operator 99* in 1945; then a good girl again—after a career name-change—as the female hero in *Daughter of Don Q* in 1946, using her new name of Adrian Booth.

There were even some of the veteran bad guys who had achieved the status of character actor, playing all kinds of roles, good and bad. There was Edmund Cobb, who could be seen at various times as the sheriff, the banker, the rancher, the mine-owner, the trail boss, or just one of the bad guys. Likewise, there was Jack Rockwell, who could turn up anywhere at any time as anybody, and you would believe it. In *Riders of Death Valley* (as in many others), he was just one of the outlaws. There were Ed Cassidy, Budd Buster and Jack Kirk who could do the same. Perhaps the best known of all these was Tom London, who played everything in serials from a "dog heavy" to the "brain heavy," and from an "old coot" to the territorial governor. And, in dozens of them, he was just one of the bad guys.

Occasionally there was a shock when a player you had always associated as a good guy turned up in a serial as a crook. One such was Raymond Hatton, who usually played sympathetic parts, barking orders to Unga Khan's henchmen, as Gasspon their captain, in *Undersea Kingdom* in 1936. You just couldn't believe that lovable old rascal was really one of the baddies. The very next Republic release after that, *The Vigilantes Are Coming*, exonerated him, though. In it he portrayed Whipsaw, rugged frontiersman and loyal ally of the hero, the Eagle.

In *The Painted Stallion* in 1937, it was easy to despise most of the bad guys: Charlie King, Maston Williams, Duke Taylor, Leroy Mason, etc.— except for Mason's right-hand man, the sly and sneaky Zamorro, played by handsome, clean-cut Duncan Renaldo. It was just hard to accept him as an outlaw.

But, the real test of credibility came when Ernie Adams, who portrayed not only bad guys, but sneaky, yellow, cowardly bad guys, was cast in the role of Rusty Fenton in *The Phantom* in 1943, and you had to believe that the hero would have in him a good, trusted ally. It was like believing that Jan of the Jungle, a hero played by Noah Beery, Jr., in *Call of the Savage* in 1935, could really trust the big native sidekick they gave him. He was played by Harry Woods, one of the most ornery, no-good

Zorro's Black Whip—Republic, 1944—costarred one of the "leopards" who changed his "spots." George J. Lewis *(right)* usually played a bad guy, but in that one was the staunch ally of the Black Whip, played by Linda Stirling.

villains ever to sneer and swagger his way through dozens of bad-guy roles.

George J. Lewis was a slick, smooth-talking bad-guy who appeared to have no heart in most of his roles in serials. It was easy to dislike him as soon as he appeared on screen, because usually crimes were going to be committed and people were going to be killed as matter-of-factly as one goes to his office every day. Two memorable standouts are his roles as Matson in *Captain America* and Morgan in *The Tiger Woman,* both in 1944. In both, cold-blooded murder to get what he wanted was just simple operating procedure for him. He then surprised everybody by turning up as a hero named Vic Gordon, the Black Whip's ardent champion, in *Zorro's Black Whip* later the same year. Throughout the 12 chapters of that classic serial, he was just as zealous a co-hero as he ever had been as a bad guy. Then, lest we get too attached to him, he was back at his old tricks as villain Jim Belmont the following year in *Federal Operator 99*.

After hating Monte Blue as the villain Unga Khan in *Undersea Kingdom*, the treacherous Yellow Weasel in *Hawk of the Wilderness* in 1938, and the scheming Davis in *Riders of Death Valley*, it was strange to see him playing not only a captain of Texas Rangers, but the father of the hero in *King of the Texas Rangers*.

It was not quite so unusual to see veteran star Hal Taliaferro (formerly known as Wally Wales) play good guys in *The Lone Ranger, Overland with Kit Carson,* and *Adventures of Red Ryder*, after playing so many ruthless outlaws; but it is still unnerving to see good-guy performances from such well-known and long-despised baddies as Richard Alexander (Prince Barin in *Flash Gordon*), Kenne Duncan (Ram Singh in *The Spider's Web*), and Bud Osborne (Tulsa, the hero's sidekick, in *Son of Geronimo*).

The dread of every actor is to become type-cast. That is what happened to Buster Crabbe, Ralph Byrd, George Reeves and many others. It becomes very difficult to get other acting jobs when you are known only as Flash Gordon or Dick Tracy or Superman. But, being type-cast as a western-action bad-guy kept many of the men who played them working for a long time, when regular actors couldn't get work. So, as one of them said to me once,

"You shouldn't mind, if you can stand the grind."

Tom London appeared in the very first movie to tell a story—*The Great Train Robbery* in 1903—and played in the final co-starring film of Joel McCrea and Randolph Scott—*Ride the High Country*—in 1962. During that time, he made countless serials as well; and played a bad guy in most of them. His remark summing it all up was,

"It kept groceries on the table for a long time. I worked steady for fifty-nine years."

Nice work if you can get it.

Some of the major serial villains were adept at playing any kind of role, and did, because of their professional acting ability. When they appeared in major features, it could be as any character, and their credibility was sound. A good example is Stanley Andrews, who played many different parts in big pictures, as well as the kindly and trusted old ranger in the television series Death Valley Days, *after creating one of the serials' most hated villains, the outlaw Jeffries, in Republic's* The Lone Ranger. *Charles Bickford seemed to be absolutely without any feelings as the swaggering bandit leader Wolf Reade in* Riders of Death Valley, *but then played those many sympathetic parts in features, including the wise and gentle priest in* Song of Bernadette *and the lovable, irascible butler in* The Farmer's Daughter, *with Loretta Young. And, in addition to being much-despised villains in a half dozen or so of the best serials—including the colorful Ming in the three Flash Gordons—Charles Middleton played kindly*

Buck Peters in a couple of Hoppy westerns, a wise family doctor in 20th Century-Fox's Jesse James, *Gene Autry's father in one of his films, and a number of other assorted characters in many other features.*
But in serials, they were always the villains.

Once the area of good-bad switch playing was entered, there was an interesting response from readers about other actors who had successfully—or unsuccessfully—switched from good- to bad-guy parts, or vice versa, and which way the readers liked them best. Some time later, I decided to pursue the idea and added some more thoughts to it, going a bit more into detail about several of the people already mentioned that the readers had asked about.

The Double Take
March 1990

Until recently, when I watched the 1943 Charles Starrett action western, *The Fighting Buckaroo*, that I had acquired from my good friend Graham Talbott, it had not occurred to me that there was one other good-bad guy who played in serials. Robert Kellard, billed as Robert Stevens, showed up in the Starrett picture as the mean, rough-talking, unshaven, generally despicable sidekick of boss-villain Wheeler Oakman. Together they were either going to take over young Stanley Brown's ranch and use it to route stolen cattle across the border, or else they were going to expose him as a former member of their gang (despite the fact he had seen the light and gone straight), which would ruin him in the community. Kellard/Stevens just wanted to go on and shoot Brown, and take the ranch anyway (If there had been a dog around, I'm sure he would have kicked it), but Oakman held him back, wanting to use the young rancher as a front for the rustling plan.

As a good guy in serials, Robert Kellard had distinguished himself as co-hero Allen Parker in *Drums of Fu Manchu;* as Corporal Tom Merritt, Jr., valiant partner of Allan Lane's Sergeant King, in *King of the Royal Mounted;* and, billed as Robert Stevens, was the full hero, Sergeant MacLane, in *Perils of the Royal Mounted*. Five years later, again billed as Kellard, he was the hero in the title role of *Tex Granger*. So, it was somewhat of a shock to see the handsome young good guy playing such a no-good, despicable felon. He wasn't the first serial actor to switch-hit, however, nor would he be the last. There were a number of others who managed to swing back and forth from one side of the law to the other. And, just as when heavies like Charlie King showed up now and then on

the side of the good guys, it always came as a surprise to see our hero "out of character" as a bad guy. When it happened, our minds always did a "double take."

There were some actors who were good enough to convince you either way. Reed Hadley, with his deep, resonant voice and dark good looks, could be either the dashing and romantic Don Diego Vegas in *Zorro's Fighting Legion*, or the melodramatic, swashbuckling bandit leader, Rahman Bar, in *Adventures of Captain Marvel*. In either role, you felt he meant business and he was thoroughly believable. In two serials, Victor Jory played absolute hero roles: as Lamont Cranston in *The Shadow*, and as Spike Holland in *The Green Archer*. In both, he was all you would expect from a serial hero—brave, courageous, daring, honest, upright and pure. However, in most of his roles in westerns—such as the Hopalong Cassidys—and in major features with major stars—such as *Dodge City* with Errol Flynn, and *South of St. Louis* with Joel McCrea—he was mean, despicable and cowardly. And you accepted him both ways without question.

Another actor who followed this course was Robert Kent, who played a government agent on the trail of Bela Lugosi, the villain, in *The Phantom Creeps;* was a masked rider seeking justice for the Indians in 1945's *The Phantom Rider;* and a detective investigating murders in a mysterious old mansion in *Who's Guilty?* that same year. The hero in all three serials, he most usually played a crooked gambler or greedy politician in westerns— or a rude, arrogant playboy from "back East," if it happened to be an Autry.

Sometimes it seemingly reflected whether an actor's star was rising or falling by which side of the law he was on in a serial: going up—bad guy to good guy; going down—hero to heavy. The latter seemed true in the case of Charles Quigley, sure enough. In 1939, he played one of a trio of acrobats known as "The Daredevils of the Red Circle" in a serial with that title. Along with Olympic champion Herman Brix and ace stuntman-actor David Sharpe, he was a co-hero of one of the finest action serials ever released. Two years later, he was the lead hero, a newspaper reporter named Bob Lane, in Columbia's mystery serial *The Iron Claw*. Again, in 1946, he played hero Duncan Richards, a crimefighting physicist in *The Crimson Ghost*, the last serial directed by William Witney. His next serial role came in Columbia's *Brick Bradford* nearly two years later, only this time it was a featured role and he was playing a heavy known as

Opposite: Robert Kellard *(center)* was one of the good guys who occasionally switched to playing a bad guy in westerns, thus causing viewers to do a double take. John Davidson *(left)* almost always played a bad guy, and Allan Lane was always a hero.

Laydron, and leading a gang of bullies comprised of the likes of Jack Ingram, Fred Graham and Charlie King. His final role was that of a Dr. Hackett, one of the henchmen of the Spider Lady, the lead villainess in Columbia's *Superman*.

Moving in the other direction, Harry Lauter started in serials playing a henchman named Drake, who carried out the dirty work planned by chief heavies James Craven and Gregory Gay (as an aircraft inventor and an alien visitor from Mars who enlists their aid in a plan to invade the earth) in *Flying Disc Man from Mars*. As his stock rose at Republic, he was cast subsequently as a mounted policeman named Clark in *Canadian Mounties vs. Atomic Invaders;* as hero Tom Rogers in *Trader Tom of the China Seas;* and finally as highwire acrobat Bert King in the last serial released by Republic, *King of the Carnival*.

Some guys specialized as one kind of character and changed over to the other side only a couple of times, thus adding a little variety to their careers. And there was one who played crooks in serials every time except one, which made that time all the more memorable.

John Crawford almost always played bad guys. In serials like *Adventures of Frank and Jesse James, Dangers of the Canadian Mounted, Ghost of Zorro, Radar Patrol vs. Spy King, Invisible Monster, Zombies of the Stratosphere, Son of Geronimo* and *Trader Tom of the China Seas*, he played the classic serial henchman, engaging in fist fights, gun fights, races, chases and splashes and crashes, all trying to do in various heroes. He then played the hero in one—*The Great Adventures of Captain Kidd*—and a co-hero (along with five other guys) in another one—*Blackhawk*. But he will be remembered by serial fans as the guy who managed—somehow—to figure out a way to knock the gun out of the hero's hand when he "had the drop on 'em," and thus start the inevitable brawl.

On the other hand, Clayton Moore mostly played good guys: Nyoka's fighting protector in *Perils of Nyoka;* a reformed (and misunderstood), fighting Jesse James in *Jesse James Rides Again* and *Adventures of Frank and Jesse James;* a fighting F.B.I. agent in *G-Men Never Forget;* a fighting masked avenger in *Ghost of Zorro;* fighting frontiersmen in *Son of Geronimo* and *Gunfighters of the Northwest;* and a fighting mining engineer in *Jungle Drums of Africa*. In two of his ten serials—*The Crimson Ghost* and *Radar Men from the Moon*—Moore played the perennial menacing, glowering, threatening, arrogant, just-plain-mean henchman of the "brain-heavy." The character was exactly the same in both serials, but his name in the first was Ashe, and in the second was Graber.

As early as 1939 (one of the "Three Powers" representatives in *Dick Tracy's G-Men*) and 1940 (the governor's secretary, Wells, in *Mysterious Doctor Satan*), Tristram Coffin was playing small role sin serials. But, it was with the release of *Holt of the Secret Service* in 1941 that he came into

***Trader Tom of the China Seas*—Republic, 1954—featured Harry Lauter as hero Tom Rogers. As his career advanced, Lauter switched from playing a bad guy to doing good-guy parts.**

his own, playing Valden, the number two heavy and field commander of a gang of counterfeiters being investigated by Treasury agent Jack Holt. Shortly thereafter followed the role of Drake, a traitor in the employ of the Mask, in *Spy Smasher*, and the sneaky Count Benito Torrini in *Perils of Nyoka*, and serials had yet another great villain. Subsequently, Coffin played heavies in serials such as *Jesse James Rides Again*, *Federal Agents vs. Underworld, Inc.*, *Bruce Gentry*, *Radar Patrol vs. Spy King* and *Pirates of the High Seas*. Then, all at once, without warning, along came *King of the Rocketmen* in 1949, and the hero was—wha-a-at?—Tristram Coffin! That just didn't make any sense, yet there it was: Tris Coffin was the hero, not the villain. There must be a trick, we thought. So, we watched the first few chapters to see if they were going to pull a Murkland-Cameron trick on us, like in *G-Men Never Forget*. But, no, they were serious. And it wasn't a bad serial, either, once we got used to it. It has become what most serial fans remember about Tristram Coffin. That, plus the fact that his best role in television was also a good guy—Captain Tom Rynning of the Arizona Rangers, in the classic series, *26 Men*.

As for the Murkland-Cameron trick, here's what happened: As

Republic's *G-Men Never Forget* opens, there is this police commissioner named Angus Cameron, played by Roy Barcroft, one of serialdom's most prolific villains. Barcroft? Playing a police commissioner? What's going on here? But, wait! There's also this gangster named Vic Murkland who is escaping from prison. He is also played by usual-villain Roy Barcroft. So, that's okay—Barcroft as a villain. But, that's one too many Barcrofts. So the Murkland/Barcroft goes to "Doc" Stanley Price's sanitarium and gets his features altered to look *exactly* like the other one—Cameron/Barcroft. Now, there's a good-guy/Barcroft and a bad-guy/Barcroft, and they look just alike. So, bad-guy/Barcroft has good-guy/Barcroft kidnapped and taken to "Doc" Stanley's place, where he has him strapped to a chair and then takes his place. Now, there's good-guy/Barcroft out of circulation, strapped to a chair, and bad-guy/Barcroft sitting at good-guy/Barcroft's desk acting like thePolice commissioner.

So, in a way, Barcroft is now playing a good guy; but, he's really a *bad* guy playing the *good* guy. Confused? Well, don't worry. It works out anyway; because hero Clayton Moore eventually tracks down (through a nervous habit he's known to have) the phoney Vic Murkland, and is about to rescue the captive police commissioner, Angus Cameron, when a big fight starts. During the melee, Murkland is shot and killed by—guess who!—that's right: Commissioner Angus Cameron!

Now, let's see: usual-bad-guy/Barcroft, playing good-guy/Barcroft, shoots usual-bad-guy/Barcroft playing bad-guy/Barcroft disguised as good-guy/Barcroft, and then there's only one Barcroft left. But, wait! The one left is good-guy/Barcroft, and we know Barcroft always plays a bad guy!

Oh, well, let's just forget it and go watch *Dr. Jekyll and Mr. Hyde.*

The switching from one side to the other by some of the actors with whom we had grown so familiar just added to the perception that things are not always what they seem to be in serials. The year that Charles Middleton and Miles Mander, the fine British actor, collaborated to create the ultimate personification of that perception—the escaped convict number 39-0-13 (Middleton) disguised and posing as a wealthy industrialist named Granville (Mander), whom he had kidnapped and held captive, in Republic's Daredevils of the Red Circle—*was the same year that the same perception was illustrated to the general moviegoing public in a classic children's movie.*

In 1939, Metro-Goldwyn-Mayer released The Wizard of Oz, *in which the mighty wizard, played by Frank Morgan, was shown to be a trickster and a charlatan, rather than a magician or sorceror, as he purported to be. Things are not always what they seem to be.*

An interesting thing about The Wizard of Oz *is that Frank Morgan, who* was the brother of actor Ralph Morgan, became a "star" character actor at M.G.M., while his brother, Ralph, who was every bit as good an actor, never made it above the level of serials and "B" pictures. In the movies, there is some indefinable quality that taps some actors for success, while leaving others—just as much, or maybe more, talented—to work in the daily grind and hope for the big break.

And, while these actors were moving up or down, occasionally the call came to step out of the ordinary and do something different. After all, they would tell you, "All you gotta do is shave the moustache!"

Chapter 7
"Who Knows What All This May Lead To?"

Since the beginning of mass-market commercial television in 1949, it has often been stated that Republic Pictures was the university for TV, meaning that a great many people who helped design, set up, and produce the shows for early television were taught and trained at Republic. And it is specifically pointed out that early TV was able to survive and flourish by following the practices of the budget-minded creators of series westerns and serials. In those days, when a lot of television shows were presented live, it was obvious to anyone what the advantages were of being able to "do it as well as you can, but do it only once." Even producers who had never seen Republic studios had to learn the value of that old adage, and it became the hallmark of 1950s television.

Who would have thought that the penny-pinching, tight-fisted ways of Nat Levine of Mascot serials in the early 1930s; of Herbert J. Yates of Republic in the late 1930s and the 1940s; and of Sam Katzman of Columbia Pictures in the late 1940s and 1950s would be the forerunner of an entire industry—and that television would be the movies' biggest competition since motion pictures were invented. Probably no one during the entire 26-year life of sound serials ever paused to observe about them, "You never can tell what this may lead to."

The same thing is true about actors who went along doing their parts, collecting their pay, and hoping for better things. Rather than pausing to observe that "you never can tell what this may lead to," many of them probably were thinking, "How the hell do I get out of this rut and on to the real thing?"

It definitely happened with some of the production people because they held entirely different attitudes about their credits and accomplishments during the serial years than they came to hold later. This change in attitudes makes it awkward when one comes to do effective research on a given period. The official credits just don't tell the accurate story.

Take writers, for instance....

The Futile Wish
August 1986

"Oh, if I could only do it over again, knowing what I know now...."

How many times have we all uttered that most futile of all wishes? All my life I have heard it implored, but never have I known anyone who was granted that wish. The judgments we make as we go along are the ones we inevitably are stuck with, it seems. So we just have to keep doing the best we can. And going with what we know when the deadlines fall. But, at least, I have this space to try and clarify something I have just learned that caused me to utter the "futile wish."

Most readers of this column know that its predecessor was a series titled *In the Nick of Time*, which was the publication in installments of the manuscript of the book with the same title published in 1984 by McFarland & Company. Your acceptance of the series prior to publication, and the reception of the book since then, have been very gratifying. Most of the critical response has been quite candid and, thankfully, complimentary; and I am glad that the book has become what I hoped it would be: a good resource for those who love serials, and a dream realized for me.

In doing the research for such a project, however, it is necessary to look in many places, speak to many people, examine many pieces of evidence, evaluate a great deal of documentation, and ultimately use whatever you can get; and still risk coming up short—or even being wrong—when you commit it to paper. Several well-known authors I have talked to agree that this is the main challenge in writing—to assure as much as possible the integrity of your research. Sometimes it is never possible to know for certain sure whether you were right or not—or whether you came up short. Because no one who could know better ever comes forward to say.

But, sometimes it can happen otherwise, and you find out what "might have been." Just such a time came for me recently. And, although my research information was not wrong, I have found that it may not have been comprehensive enough to have covered the whole story in one area of the sound serials—that of the writers, those people referred to in the book as "The Plotters of Peril."

In recent years I have come to know Oliver Drake, and from him have received a new perspective on the serial writers. If I had known him before, and could have had his vast experience to draw from, the chapter on writers would have come out differently.

"Oh, if I could only do it over again, knowing what I know now...."

In official studio credits, Oliver Drake has only one for a serial at

The Lone Ranger—Republic, 1938—had a major impact on the Lone Ranger "legend," the origin of which was conceived for the serial by a writer who received no screen credit for it.

Republic—the screenplay for *Undersea Kingdom*—and one at Universal—the original story for *Riders of Death Valley*. That's all. The lack of any other listed credits leads a researcher to believe he had no other serial involvement. Consequently, his name was not included in the book as one of the major serial writers of that era. And, knowing him to be a prolific songwriter and story writer of western features during that time, it was natural to conclude that his activity lay mainly in those areas, and not in serials.

That's what the records show, but "that ain't the way it was." Oliver Drake was deeply involved in serials during the 1930s, and he should be included with the other writers as one of the primary "Plotters of Peril." While researching *In the Nick of Time*, I wish I had known him then as I know him now, so that the chapter on writers could have included him and had the benefit of his recall.

One of the early sound serials produced by Mascot was *Phantom of the West* in 1931, and starred Tom Tyler and Dorothy Gulliver. Drake worked on it as well as many other projects for producer Nat Levine during the early 1930s. In 1936, when Mascot and several other small companies

Dick Tracy Returns—Republic, 1938—was another Republic serial partly written by Oliver Drake, but without any screen credit.

merged and became Republic, he worked for the new company and continued writing—serials as well as westerns and songs. After *Undersea Kingdom,* however, Drake relates that he continued to write serials for several years, but without official writing credit. As he related it to me, since he was writing stories and screenplays for the Gene Autry features, stories for the new Three Mesquiteer western series starring Robert Livingston, Crash Corrigan and Max Terhune, and stories and screenplays for many of the current serials' chapters, plus new songs for Autry and his comic sidekick, Smiley Burnette, one of the people in the Republic head office complained one day,

"Say, doesn't anybody around here but Oliver Drake write anything any more?"

At the request of studio production chief, Sol Siegel, Drake continued to write serials, but did so without official screen credit, which he did continue to receive on the features and songs.

Some of the fascinating stories he has told me concern working on such classic cliffhangers during that period as *Dick Tracy, The Painted Stallion, Zorro Rides Again, The Lone Ranger, Dick Tracy Returns,* and many

Renegade Ranger—RKO, 1939, with *(from left)* **Lucio Villegas, Tim Holt, Ray Whitley, and George O'Brien**—was written for the screen by Oliver Drake, who also wrote stories for Ray Whitley's short subjects and a later feature starring Tim Holt.

others—all without official writing credit. His work during those years on the western series starring Gene Autry, The Three Mesquiteers and Don Barry at Republic; George O'Brien at RKO Radio; Bob Steele, George Houston and Buster Crabbe at P.R.C.; The Range Busters and The Rough Riders at Monogram (even a Joe E. Brown comedy at Columbia) all did receive official credit, and led up to his becoming a producer at Universal in 1942.

At Universal, he produced westerns starring Johnny Mack Brown, Tex Ritter, Russell Hayden and Rod Cameron, and wrote many of them as well. At the same time, he wrote several more for P.R.C. which co-starred Dave O'Brien and Jim Newill as "The Texas Rangers"; and then produced the series starring Jimmy Wakely at Monogram, followed by a number of independent productions after that.

With so much in the western field to his credit, it is easy to see why those early Republic serial accomplishments could be left unnoticed for all this time. But, it so happens that those were key, pivotal years for the cliffhangers, and vital to any accurate record of their existence. So, Oliver Drake's role in them during that time needs to be recognized, and that is what we are attempting to do now.

"Oh, if I could only do it over again, knowing what I know now...."

Well, it can't be done *over*. But, it is being done: right now there is in the works the official autobiography of Oliver Drake. He has told me that the manuscript should be completed later this year, or early in 1987. The working title, based on a popular song he wrote for Jimmy Wakely, is *Saturday's Heroes*.

"...If I could only do it over again..." is not possible. But, the man who was there can do it for me, and that is even better. Coming from Oliver Drake, who was right in the middle of production of some of the best-loved classics in both the western and serial fields, *Saturday's Heroes* should be a book we will all want to have. As a matter of fact, I am placing my order right now. And Ollie, old friend, thanks for agreeing to share your memories with us. We can hardly wait.

Since this article appeared, Oliver Drake's book has become a reality. Written, Produced and Directed—By Oliver Drake was published by Outlaw Press in 1990. The autobiography of a unique filmmaker, it is a fascinating account of the life and career of a man who, although largely not recognized for it, played a great part in the early development of Republic serials and westerns before going on to bigger things. It is the story of a remarkable man in a remarkable business.

One of the most remarkable things to learn about Oliver Drake and his accomplishments with serials was his involvement with The Lone Ranger *at Republic. This is one of the serials that does not bear his name, but has become—because of facts revealed in diligent research—one of his most lasting contributions to the history of serials.*

Just as weeks of exposure led to public recognition and stardom for some actors; as years of experience at Republic, working on tightly planned productions, provided some technical people with training for their later success in television; and as the economically motivated groundwork laid by Nat Levine, Herb Yates, and Sam Katzman led to television's eventual supremacy in making low-budget series, the character of the Lone Ranger—as conceived by Oliver Drake and the other, credited, writers of the 1938 Republic serial—was altered permanently, and the legend was born that became part and parcel of one of America's most beloved literary action heroes for decades to come.

Kemo Sabe and the Cliffhangers
February 1989

Try to imagine the Lone Ranger without the influence that movie serials had on him, and the result would be pretty bland. The character we came to know, the radio program, the television series, and both of the 1950s big-budget features, would all fade into something altogether different than the great show business legend we all remember and love so well.

Chances are, all we would have left would be something similar to the insipid attempt at "warm-over" that we got in 1981, when the producers ignored all that "the Ranger" had become and tried to replace it with a more modern, "contemporary" concept. (This was the only time the Lone Ranger has been presented without the serials' influence, and it was a total "bomb.")

In whatever form—books, comics, television or movies—when presented as originally conceived for radio and then embellished by the serial influence, the Lone Ranger has always been the essence of high adventure, principled enforcement of law and order, and the championing of the good and virtuous. And America has loved it!

Between David Rothel's great book titled *Who Was That Masked Man?* and David Holland's new one titled *From Out of the Past*, there is very little still unknown about one of America's all-time best known fictional heroes, the Lone Ranger. A reading of these two books will give anyone interested "everything you ever wanted to know" about the famous masked rider of the Plains and his faithful Indian companion, Tonto. I have just had the pleasure of looking over the copy of *From Out of the Past* belonging to my good friend, Jim Scancarelli (who writes and draws *Gasoline Alley* for the newspaper comic strips), and will very soon have a copy of my own. It is a terrific piece of work!

Covering every conceivable facet of the Lone Ranger phenomenon since it was first created in the early 1930s as a live adventure show for radio in Detroit, *From Out of the Past* traces the development of that creation through the years in all the forms to which it could possibly be translated. And it was a major success in each medium.

The thing that impressed me as a serial-devotee, however, was the strong, deep and lasting effect its transposition to a movie serial had on the character and the legend. Radio was its birthplace and its continuing stronghold until the advent of television, but it was the movie serial that gave it body, color, depth and dimension. After *The Lone Ranger* in 1938 and *The Lone Ranger Rides Again* in 1939—both produced by Republic

Oliver Drake is the uncredited author of "Heigh-yo, Silver," Chapter 1 of *The Lone Ranger*—Republic, 1938. In it he created the "origin" of the Lone Ranger, which was then adopted by the writers of the radio series and became the basis of the Lone Ranger legend.

Pictures—the legend would never again be the same as before, when it had been primarily a radio kid's show. And the effect of serials—the two Lone Rangers plus others—continued to bear upon the radio program (and the legend) for more than 20 years thereafter, throughout its life and the life of the succeeding television show.

First of all, Dave Holland states in his book that no attempt had been made during the first five years of the radio program to establish an origin for "The Lone Ranger," and that Republic's serial writers—specifically our old friend Oliver Drake—came up with the idea and the first draft of a script describing an ambush of a party of Texas Rangers who were all killed except one. Then, after being found and nursed back to health by an Indian who had witnessed the ambush, the lone survivor vowed to bring the ambushers to justice and masked his face to conceal his identity. This idea was later adapted to radio (and subsequently television) and became the basis of the Lone Ranger's legend.

In the serial, the Ranger was represented as being one of five young ranchers who had banded together to try and ward off the reign of terror perpetrated by a villain who had murdered and assumed the identity of a government official named Jeffries. Which of the five ranchers was the Lone Ranger was not known until the last chapter; but, in placing the hero in jeopardy, he was shown in a more human light than by portraying him merely as a wandering nomad without any roots. To continue showing the Ranger as a man with a real and human background, the radio shows later began to include a new character: a young man named Dan

The Lone Ranger—Republic, 1938—featured *(from left)* **Hal Taliaferro, Herman Brix, Chief Thundercloud, George Letz, Lynn Roberts, Lane Chandler, and Lee Powell. As did the "origin" of the Lone Ranger, this serial's musical score also became a permanent part of the radio program.**

Reid, who was the son of the Ranger's brother Jim, the captain of the ranger party killed in the ambush. (As time went on, it was further developed by implication that Dan Reid was to be the father of a young fellow named Britt Reid, who would become a modern, Lone Ranger–type crimefighter called the Green Hornet.)

In addition to a genesis for the masked hero, perhaps the greatest contribution made by Republic Pictures to the Lone Ranger radio program was music. The incidental themes and passages (called "cues") written by Alberto Columbo, William Lava, and other members of the Republic music department to go along with the central theme of Rossini's Overture to *William Tell,* were acquired by George W. Trendle, producer of the radio series, and thereafter became permanently identified with the Lone Ranger. Thus, the broadcast subsequently aired from coast to coast by the Mutual Radio Network, contained the finest and most exciting musical scores of any action show on radio. Also, as a result of their contact with the serial influence, the radio show's writers always managed to time the story so as to arrive at a suspenseful or anxious moment midway in the episode, just as the break came for the sponsor's commercial: no accident or coincidence. And this "cliffhanger" break was usually announced by a grand outburst from Franz Liszt's *Les Preludes,* or by an appropriate passage of the "Republic" music.

Two actors best known for playing the Lone Ranger on radio, although there were several in all who did it, were Earl Graser, who was killed in a tragic auto accident, and Brace Beemer, who was the one most remembered because he played him the longest. Others only did it briefly or—like Fred Foy, the announcer—filled in during a crisis. During the Lone Ranger's heyday in movies and television, there were four actors who played the part—and all four were veteran serial actors.

In *The Lone Ranger,* the young rancher named Allan King turned out to be the Lone Ranger, and was played by Lee Powell, who became a real-life hero several years later. During World War II, he was killed in action while serving as a U.S. Marine on the island of Tinian in the South Pacific. In addition to *The Lone Ranger,* Powell co-starred in the serial *The Fighting Devil Dogs* for Republic and was featured in Universal's *Flash Gordon Conquers the Universe,* a 1940 serial.

Robert Livingston was the masked rider in *The Lone Ranger Rides Again,* the sequel made by Republic a year later. A star of Three Mesquiteer westerns (playing Stony Brooke), Livingston had starred previously as a masked hero in the Republic serial *The Vigilantes Are Coming* in 1936, playing the daring Zorro-type hero known as the Eagle.

When the Lone Ranger television series was being planned, a widespread search for an actor to personify the legendary hero produced Clayton Moore, who will now always be associated with the role and thought of by millions as being the "real" Lone Ranger. For anyone who has seen an episode of the TV series, or either of the movie features, it is just not necessary to explain why. Seldom has an actor become so immersed in a role that he actually seemed to "become" the character. But, that is just what happened with Clayton Moore. Before and during the run of the television series, Moore was featured in no less than ten serials—more than any other lead actor in Hollywood. Playing the hero in eight of them, he is only surpassed in that department by Buster Crabbe, who played the hero in nine serials. In two of his featured roles, Moore played bad guys, but even then he played them "to the hilt."

The fourth actor to play the Lone Ranger (and the only other one to play him on television) was John Hart, who took over the role when the show's producers and Clayton Moore's agent failed to come to terms on renewal of his contract after the first year. Hart did a great job as the masked rider, and it looked as though his playing the role would be permanent; but, after one year, and a great deal of clamor from loyal fans of

Until the television show, the only other actor to openly portray the Lone Ranger on the screen was Robert Livingston, who starred in the 1939 sequel from Republic. Former western star Rex Lease stands beside Silver.

Moore, the producer and Moore came to an agreement and he returned to the series. John Hart had played in a number of serials, starring earlier in *Jack Armstrong, the All-American Boy* for Columbia, and several years after in *Adventures of Captain Africa* for them.

All four of these men had learned from making serials that the important thing in an action picture is ACTION! People who watched shows like *The Lone Ranger* wanted to see their hero act like a hero, and—as the kids say today—DO STUFF!

And that's what these men had been trained to put across on the screen: men of action, who were doing stuff! Other so-called action series on radio and television—while good in their own ways—never seemed to catch that spirit of urgency and excitement that came through the set—radio or television—when the Lone Ranger was on: The same excitement the kids had felt every Saturday at the theatre when the serial came on.

As a radio show, *The Lone Ranger* had that from the start. But, I think it is safe to say that the show's experience with Republic's serial makers helped make it grow, expand, bloom and burst forth, forever thereafter,

The most lasting images of Tonto and the Lone Ranger are those portrayed on television by Jay Silverheels and Clayton Moore.

as a genuine entertainment legend, unsurpassed for what it was in any form to which it was adapted: A true phenomenon of our time.

Hi-yo....

In his book, From Out of the Past, *Dave Holland bases his statements about the origin of the Lone Ranger on an original manuscript for Chapter 1 of* the Republic serial, The Lone Ranger, *which his research turned up. Plainly stated was the author's byline. It read: By Oliver Drake.*

"You never can tell what this may lead to!"

Writing the beginning of The Lone Ranger *the way he did was, at the time, all in a day's work for Oliver Drake. To start a 15-chapter serial, they needed to explain how this masked guy who rode the big white horse and fought outlaws came to be. Until that time, the radio program had not tried to do that. There had been no need. He* was *the Lone Ranger. He was just there. That's all the radio program needed to say. So much of radio was in the listeners' minds, anyway, that each listener could decide where the guy came from and what he looked like. But, that wouldn't do for the movies. The origin had to be conceived. It had to be shown. So, Drake conceived it and wrote it: all in a day's work.*

But, as it turned out, it was much more than that. It was actually the start of something pretty big. And serials did that every once in a while—started something big. As a matter of fact, three of them, released in 1932 and 1933, started the career of one of the biggest motion picture stars of all time.

The Start of Something Big
November 1989

Recently I acquired in a trade a print of *The Hurricane Express*, a Mascot serial released in 1932. As I watched a few chapters, I began to realize why I liked it so much.

It certainly isn't because it's one of the "great" serials—it's not. And it is surely not because of any outstanding stunt work—the action scenes are all rather hectic and confusing. There are no impressive special effects to speak of—the few miniature shots attempted were somewhat obvious. And it couldn't be any fascination with the plot development—there is a heck of a lot of "just talk" throughout the whole thing. So, what is it?

When I saw *Hurricane* the very first time was in 1947, and it was 15 years old at that time. As a teenager, I thought it was pretty primitive stuff, and even laughed at parts of it. Had you asked me, I probably would have said I didn't like it. Yet, there was something, even then, that intrigued me about it—that made me want to see it again. Years later, when I did get to see it again, I was amazed at how much it had improved with the passage of time. By then, I had seen a good many classic films of the silent era, and some good movies from the early sound era; and *Hurricane Express*—when measured against those other films of its own time—somehow looked a lot better than it had when I had only the current late–1940s crop of releases to compare it with. Since then, I have seen it several times and have grown to like it more with each viewing.

There is a certain enthusiasm and excitement contained in this serial that makes up for any shortcomings in its production values and professional virtue. The players performed as if their very lives depended on it, and sometimes even overdid it a little. That came largely from experience in recent silent movies for many of them. And, when they needed to shoot scenes on, around, or otherwise involving locomotives and railroad yards, producer Nat Levine and his crew just packed it all up and went out to the railroad yard and did it with real trains. (That was the cheap way to do it then; but that kind of location work now would ruin a budget by running the cost into literally millions of extra dollars.) In scenes calling for fist fights between the good guys and the bad guys, they went head to head against each other and arms flailed in all directions. The result of all this was what we used to call "knock-down-and-drag-out" head bangers. All in all, *The Hurricane Express* is as much fun to watch as any serial of that era I can think of. And that is one reason I like it so much.

The other big reason is John Wayne. He was still in the learning phase of what was to become one of the most brilliant and long-lasting careers of any motion picture star. *Hurricane* was the second of three serials produced by Nat Levine and released by Mascot in 1932 and 1933 that starred young Wayne—the first was *Shadow of the Eagle* and the third was *The Three Musketeers*—and no one could yet accuse the handsome young athlete of being an actor. That would be a long time coming in a career that would eventually span half a century. He had been making movies for nearly five years, and would not become a major star until seven years later—with the release of John Ford's *Stagecoach*—so was still "chewing the scenery" and "leaping the hedges" as a bright-eyed young hero.

The three Mascot serials gave young Wayne a total of 36 consecutive weeks of exposure to the action-loving public; and this, along with a series of westerns being released by Warner Bros. during that time, made his a familiar face to American moviegoers, who seemed to like him more and more with each appearance. Another series of westerns produced by Paul Malvern for Monogram release as "Lone Star Productions," and a series of features with Malvern released by Universal, plus a stint as Stony Brooke in the Three Mesquiteers series for Republic, continued to build on the exposure gained by his three serials and led Wayne up to his *Stagecoach* role, which was the turning point in his career.

In effect, his roles in *The Hurricane Express* and the other two serials were for John Wayne, "The Starting of Something Big." And now, watching that great old fun serial, one can't help but think of that, as well as the other serials that were, for other future stars, also "The Start of Something Big."

The very next Mascot release following *The Three Musketeers* in 1933 was a 12-chapter western titled *Fighting with Kit Carson*, which was released in July. Its star was a young All-American football player named Johnny Mack Brown, who had been recruited for movies a couple of years before and played leading man to several leading female film stars including Joan Crawford. Until *Kit Carson*, he was regarded as just another soft-spoken, good-looking Southern boy who was easy to look at, but no actor. Twelve continuous weeks of exposure as a western hero led him into a career that included four more serials (for Universal release)—*Rustlers of Red Dog*, *Wild West Days*, *Flaming Frontiers* and *The Oregon Trail*—and a career as a top western star at Universal and Monogram for the next 20 years, most of which he occupied a spot in the Top Ten Money Making Western Stars in the Motion Picture Herald Exhibitors Poll.

On the heels of *Rustlers of Red Dog*'s January, 1935, release, came another Mascot serial on February 23rd. The title was *The Phantom Empire*, and its star was a young singer of western songs brought to Hollywood from Chicago's National Barn Dance by Nat Levine to play in a Ken Maynard western, *In Old Santa Fe*. Seeing him go over so well in that appearance, Levine cast him as the hero of *Phantom Empire*, which gave Gene Autry 12 consecutive weeks in which to make his mark with the moviegoing public. By Chapter 12, it was a foregone conclusion that Autry would star in his own pictures, and he went on to become as much an American institution in his field of endeavor as did John Wayne. For Gene Autry also, a serial had been "The Start of Something Big."

In 1936, Republic released two 12-chapter serials: *Undersea Kingdom* in May and *The Vigilantes Are Coming* in October. The hero of the first was Ray "Crash" Corrigan, and the second was Robert Livingston. These two young actors, teamed with comic-ventriloquist Max Terhune, another transplant from the National Barn Dance, became the trio known as The Three Mesquiteers in 18 of Republic's finest action westerns, and then went on to individual stardom in western films.

In July, 1938, "the Start of Something Big" for actor Gordon Elliott came with the release by Columbia of the 15-chapter serial *The Great Adventures of Wild Bill Hickok*. So impressive each week as the legendary lawman was Elliott, that Columbia immediately cast him as the star in his own series of action westerns, and changed his name from Gordon Elliott to Bill Elliott, and proudly advertised him as "Wild Bill Elliott." He also rose to major stardom following two more serials and five years as a western star.

It is well documented that serials were "the Start of Something Big" for many other actors also. Donald Barry, known throughout his career as

In *Three Texas Steers*—Republic, 1939—John Wayne replaced Robert Livingston as one of the Three Mesquiteers just before his "big break" came in John Ford's *Stagecoach*. Three earlier serials at Mascot were the start of something big for Wayne.

Don "Red" Barry because of his role in *Adventures of Red Ryder*, became a very fine actor by any standard, receiving a nomination for an Academy Award in the middle 1940s for his performance in the 20th Century–Fox picture, *The Purple Heart*. Famous motion picture stars Rod Cameron, Lloyd Bridges and Ruth Roman; and beloved television star Milburn Stone (Doc Adams in *Gunsmoke*) played in serials when they were starting their careers.

At the Western Film Fair, as well as at other film festivals and gatherings, we celebrate the early careers of some of our favorite actors and actresses when we were kids. At times it has mystified some of them, who cannot seem to understand why we want to remember them for roles they had in "cheapie" westerns, when they went on to much more substantial and meaningful things—things that were so much bigger and better.

And we haven't always been able to tell them why. We just say that we liked them then, and also liked them later. One way we might be able to express it is like the TV commercial of a few years ago, when the announcer said,

"Honey, you're not getting older; you're just getting better."

That's the way we like to remember those we "discovered" when they—and we—were young. As we enjoyed them later, when they were truly "Something Big," we like to recall that we liked them just as much when it was only the "Start of Something Big."

Although John Wayne became one of the biggest superstars in the motion picture business—some would say the biggest—those who knew him would say that he never lost sight of his beginnings—that he never forgot what the three serials he made for Mascot in the early days of his career did for him. That's one of the reasons he continued to be the top favorite of series western and serial fans for his entire career. It was always a relationship of "you're one of ours, and we helped to make you a star because we love you," from the fans and "I know it and appreciate it, and I won't let you down" from Wayne in response.

Now, maybe it wasn't really just like that. But it sure seemed to be.

Not being able to tell what this may lead to applied not only to actors and production people, but to a complete form of entertainment that was new and unique in the 1930s. Sound serials were little more than four years old when Universal tried something else new and produced its first chapter film based on a comic strip. Tailspin Tommy *was released in October 1934, and, within the next 18 years, about four dozen serials were released by Universal, Republic, and Columbia combined, based on comic strips appearing in daily newspapers or in comic books. They almost became the staple of the serial business.*

Since that time, there have been numerous new productions—Broadway stage presentations and television series, as well as motion pictures—and it is still going on today. Talk about what something may lead to!

Remakes and Side Effects
July 1990

Each time Hollywood has attempted to produce a brand new, ultimate, definitive motion picture adaptation of a popular comic strip, it has somehow turned out as a very expensive remake of something they had already done years ago. The main difference has been the lending of current-generation views to characters that began in another time. The reason for that is that the people making movies now do not have the concept of what these characters were really about, and have only their own views and values to assign them. Sometimes—as in the case of *The Legend of the Lone Ranger*—the result has been rather confusing. What these younger filmmakers think they saw in the earlier films is not what was put there at all, mainly because the younger guys fail to "get the point" of what earlier filmmakers were doing. Today it seems real hard—for some reason—for young filmmakers to produce a picture just to entertain, and for no other reason. They seem compelled to "build in" some kind of "message," and they don't comprehend that a picture can be made "just for the fun of it." And that is too bad. The positive side effect, however, has been that the renewed interest in the characters has created outright revivals of some of those earlier efforts, which those of us who are old enough to remember their beginnings can enjoy.

Such is the case with the latest one—*Dick Tracy*—which came out last month and is now playing in theatres all over the country. While adhering to many of the qualities of the original Tracy comic strip—portraying Tracy as a "straight arrow" honest cop who would qualify as the first of "the untouchables"; showing the romance between him and Tess Trueheart as a man-woman relationship with no phony psychological hang-ups; and giving credence to the theory that a tough young kid from the streets could, when convinced that he was "for real," learn to admire a man like Tracy enough that he would take his name for his own (thus becoming Dick Tracy, *Junior*)—it also included some of today's movie ingredients: notably, having the very sexy Madonna sing some songs that are geared strictly for this generation's appreciation; including as special effects some vintage automobiles doing things those real cars couldn't possibly have been capable of doing; and presenting a "rogues gallery" of villains who, despite being made up as a motley crew of dangerous hoodlums Tracy has faced down over the years, came across as a gang of tough-talking punks like those the police have so much trouble with today, who sneer and snarl a lot, but who are really cowards and sneaks. All in all, *Dick Tracy* is a pretty good picture, when accepted as what it is—that old/new combination type film that *Batman* was last year.

So far, the side effects are pretty good, too. As a result of the renewed interest in Dick Tracy, all four of those great Republic Tracy serials have become available to the public on videotape, and people can now see the first movie concept of Tracy as portrayed by the late Ralph Byrd— the no-nonsense, action hero shown as a crime-fighting F.B.I. agent (with no romantic involvements) whose aim was to rid America of villains such as the Spider (*Dick Tracy*—1937), Pa Stark and his five sons (*Dick Tracy Returns*—1938), master spy Nicholas Zarnoff (*Dick Tracy's G-Men*—1939) and the Ghost (*Dick Tracy vs. Crime, Inc.*—1941). These serials were a definite departure from the comic strip, omitting key characters such as Tess, Pat Patton and Chief Brandon, and emphasized Tracy as the ultimate dedicated lawman, asking no quarter and giving none in his battle against crime. Even as kids we knew that liberties had

been taken in transferring Dick Tracy to the screen, but as action fans we didn't care.

Also available now are the four features produced by R.K.O. in the mid-1940s based on Chester Gould's famous detective—*Dick Tracy, Detective* and *Dick Tracy Versus Cueball* starring Morgan Conway (the only other actor besides Byrd to play Tracy until Warren Beatty); *Dick Tracy's Dilemma* and *Dick Tracy Meets Gruesome*, which returned Ralph Byrd to the role he originated on the screen. In addition to videotape, these features were being played by a number of television stations to coincide with the opening of the new *Dick Tracy* in June; and some stations even aired some of the episodes from the short-lived TV series that had starred Byrd. This was an extra bonus for me, as I had never before seen any of the TV shows. So, if you don't care for the new Beatty movie, you can enjoy any or all of what the movies and TV have previously done with America's favorite comic strip detective.

About 30 years ago, following its successful run as a Broadway musical, Paramount Pictures released Al Capp's *Li'l Abner* as a lavish screen musical starring Peter Palmer in the title role. It was a terrific job, and brought immediate attention to a little black and white comedy done about 20 years earlier that featured Granville Owen as the big bashful hillbilly romeo, with such venerable supporting players as Buster Keaton, Edgar Kennedy, Chester Conklin and Doodles Weaver. Since then, just about every collector I've known has, at one time or another, owned a 16 millimeter print or videotape of the black and white *Li'l Abner* as a result. But I don't see too many who collect the big color musical.

Another comic strip character to go from Hollywood to Broadway and back to Hollywood was that greatest superhero of all—Superman. From comic strips, the Jerome Siegel and Joseph Shuster creation was first presented on the movie screens as a series of animated cartoons released by Paramount in the early 1940s. Next came the two serials featuring Kirk Alyn as the "man of steel," which was produced by Sam Katman and released by Columbia Pictures in 1948 and 1950. Then came the television series starring George Reeves in the 1950s. In the middle 1960s, Broadway presented *It's a Bird, It's a Plane, It's Superman*, a lavish musical based on the exploits of the visitor from Krypton. And, in 1978, Warner Bros. Pictures released the fantastic *Superman: The Movie*, which became the first of four big-budget super grossers for that studio. Some time after that, the two Columbia serials (which had been concealed from the public for over

Opposite: **Dick Tracy has been depicted in serials; a series of low-budget features; a radio series; a television series; and, eventually, a multi-million-dollar blockbuster movie. None of them was better or more exciting than the four serials made by Republic.**

Dick Tracy Returns—Republic, 1938. During fight scenes, such as this one involving Ralph Byrd and a heavy, the thrilling background music kept things at fever pitch. The contribution of music to serials cannot be overlooked.

30 years) became available on videotape, and nearly everybody now has them. All along, the TV series has still continued to play in syndication, and the cartoons have been marketed as kids' videos. There wasn't much that could be done to revive interest in the Broadway musical—it was pretty irrelevant, anyway.

Much the same happened following the release of big-budget productions in recent years of *Flash Gordon* and *Buck Rogers*. Even though their resurgence was brief and more limited, it did result in videotapes of the Flash Gordon serials becoming available. Not so successful were the remakes of *The Lone Ranger* in the early 1980s (a picture titled *The Legend of the Lone Ranger* that didn't click; no serial revival); *Little Orphan Annie* (a big musical titled *Annie* that bombed, did not revive the earlier, better black and white version); and *Sheena, Queen of the Jungle* (a lavish outdoor film that failed to make it, and earlier television series starring Irish McCalla still lay dormant).

Now promised as "coming soon" are *Brenda Starr, Reporter* and *Captain America*. It will be interesting to see how they are handled, and what the result will be. There are quite a few fans who would like to see a revival of the two serials with the same titles (*Captain America*—Republic, 1944, and *Brenda Starr*—Columbia, 1945) and whether the new, big-budget productions bear any resemblance to them, or to the comic strips they're based on, for that matter. Let us only keep a good thought.

My own choice for a big-budget remake some day—but only if it is handled as it was in print, and with the proper respect and attitude toward the mystique of the character—is Maxwell Grant's "The Shadow." Although the 1940 Columbia serial was pretty good, and is remembered very fondly by a lot of us because of the work of Victor Jory, it did not get into the real mystery and fascination of the character depicted so well in the pulp magazines and in the comics (even the highly successful radio show could not accomplish that); and the movie features starring Kane Richmond in the mid-1940s were, to say it kindly, no good at all. If someone would take the character as written by Grant (real name Walter Gibson) and portray him that way—as the ill-fated World War I pilot named Kent Allard, who sends socialite Lamont Cranston on a world cruise and then takes his place in order to operate as the Shadow, and direct his unique group of crimefighting experts in their sophisticated battle against the underworld, employing knowledge and techniques he had learned in Tibet while recovering from a near-fatal war injury—then there are all kinds of possibilities for mystery, intrigue, suspense, special effects, stunt work, and whatever else can help make an exciting movie. Wouldn't that be great?

And if it revived the serial, the radio series, the features, and even the pulps themselves, then so be it.

The year after Dick Tracy: The Movie *made a successful mark at theaters across the country, the Columbia Broadcasting System presented a new television series based on a comic strip character that had never been adapted before. As a mid-season replacement, CBS began a weekly, hour-long, big-budget series called* The Flash, *based on the D.C. Publications superhero with amazing powers of speed caused by a chemical ingestion received in a laboratory explosion (sound familiar?). When last seen, it was still going strong.*

The one area that is probably least perceptible as one in which the serials produced the start of something big was the one in which serials were clearly well blessed—the music. The men who composed the music for serials—and who, earlier, had selected the appropriate themes from the classics to back up the action of the cliffhangers—all went on to bigger and better things at the major studios or in television but, because of the nature of music credits, were not noticed as much by the general public. As a matter of fact—let's face it—musical directors have always been taken for granted.

But, they continued to compose music for movies and television—even for the Broadway stage—and the public continued to benefit from their considerable talents. Unfortunately, though, like the stuntmen, their contributions have remained almost completely anonymous to all but the most discerning credit-roll reader. Only within the past several years has the music of one of them come to light. It was like a giant ray of sunshine.

The Beat Goes On
February 1986

I wish someone would do for Universal serials and westerns what James King has done for Republic. King has produced an album of background themes and chase music written for Republic's western and serial productions and titled it *The Music of Republic*. It has a sub-title: *The Early Years—1937–1941*. I understand if the response is good, there may be a Volume II.

Normally, it is not my thing to write fan letters, but I had to write one in this case. The quality of the performances, the fidelity of the arrangements, and the obvious devotion to the task of re-creating as accurately as possible the "feel" and "drive" of the original composer concepts, came through unmistakably clear. Mr. King's early addiction to and continuing appreciation of the unique compositions of Republic music men such as Alberto Columbo, Paul Sawtell, Mort Glickman, Cy Feuer, and especially William Lava (with whom he later worked and studied at the Warner Bros. and Disney studios) is evident throughout the album. He apparently worshipped the work of these men. When I ordered my second copy, I had to write and tell him so. And I now want to publicly congratulate him. It was well done.

As a serial lover, I wanted to see this kind of album produced for many years. Time after time it has been pointed out—by me, as much as anyone else—how much the music of the classics was used in serials: "Les Preludes," "Flight of the Bumblebee," "Ride of the Valkyrie," "William Tell Overture," "The Flying Dutchman," "Rienzi," "Egmont," etc., etc. But not much has been recorded about all the original music that was written by the studios' music men; and that is a shame, because some of the best and most memorable came from them. Now, by virtue of some original manuscripts he has become heir to, James King has begun to preserve some of this great music.

After a typical Republic-logo fanfare, the album starts with a series of selections from Three Mesquiteers westerns by Lava and Feuer, who went

***Daredevils of the Red Circle*—Republic, 1939—contained one of the finest musical background scores ever written for a serial. William Lava was the composer.**

on to become leaders in the music world—Lava at Warner Bros. and the Walt Disney studios, and Cy Feuer as a highly successful Broadway producer—and ends with a final classic chase composition by Paul Sawtell, who later became a top composer-conductor for Universal and Paramount. In between are selections that thrill the soul of a serial lover: opening theme selections from *King of the Royal Mounted* and *The Painted Stallion,* the driving action music from *The Fighting Devil Dogs,* the classic chase theme from *Daredevils of the Red Circle* (I defy you to keep your toes from tapping), and even Little Beaver's theme from *Adventures of Red Ryder.* Let's hope this album is successful, so that Volume II will become a reality.

And while we're hoping for good things, let's keep a good thought that maybe one day the same thing might happen for the music of Universal. In addition to their use of the classics, Universal's serials and westerns also provided music that was unique and unforgettable for the fans of the 1930s and 1940s. If someone like James King could get hold of those original Universal manuscripts and record them with a full concert orchestra—as he did with Republic's—then we would really have something to listen to and enjoy.

Some of the finest musical talent in Hollywood comprised the music department at Universal Pictures. After working at Republic, and writing some of their most familiar chase passages, Paul Sawtell joined Charles Previn, Frank Skinner and company at Universal, where he continued to turn out exciting background music. Although Charles Previn was the music director, Skinner is generally credited with being the studio's "resident composer," and as such wrote most of what became Universal's "library" of incidental musical cues; but Sawtell added his own considerable contribution to the exciting musical heritage that was Universal's. The thrilling chase sequences that immediately branded a film as "Universal," along with themes composed for appearances by certain characters (Fuzzy Knight, for example, had his own "intro" theme that was used for no other player) all received input from Sawtell before he moved on to Paramount to become a composer-conductor on many of their technicolor action specials. Those Universal musical "calling cards" would also make a terrific album.

My first nomination for a spot in such an album would be the *Destry* title credits theme by Frank Skinner used in almost all the westerns and western serials. To me that *was* Universal. Other passages from the Johnny Mack Brown serials *Wild West Days*, *Flaming Frontiers* and *The Oregon Trail* would also have to be included. And the fight scene music in just about every serial from 1937 to 1943 (used at least twice in each chapter of *Gang Busters*) could be heard no where else in the world outside of a Universal "chapterplay." Can't you just imagine hearing it all the way through?

It would not have to be confined to western and serial music only to include a lot of cues that were used in Universal serials. The music of Universal naturally includes the memorable themes and passages written for such classic features as *Dracula*, *Frankenstein* and *The Invisible Man*, and later used in serials like *Flash Gordon*, *Jungle Jim*, *Red Barry*, *Buck Rogers*, *Junior G-Men* and many others. There is a wealth of original material composed by Skinner, Previn, Sawtell, Hans J. Salter, and the other Universal music men. It would be great to have it come back to life in an album recorded by a full orchestra and a dedicated conductor.

As for the music of Columbia serials, the main thing I remember is the extensive use of the classics—primarily Wagner, Liszt and Beethoven—and the apparent absence of much original music. Mostly, any original music cues used were to augment or blend in with the classical passages selected, and were not in themselves readily recognizable, as the original cues at Universal and Republic were.

The first year of Columbia serials benefitted from the talent of Abe

Meyer, one of the outstanding composers of movie background music, and his score for *Secret of Treasure Island* was terrific: unique and different, and used in features for years thereafter. Then, Morris Stoloff's ingenious musical cues for *The Spider's Web* were sharp and exciting; and Lee Zahler followed up for the next several years with good solid action and mystery cues that served well to blend in with the classical music passages he used so much. But, the overall effect was one of not knowing which passages were the borrowed classics and which the original music used as the bridge between them. In that context, the music of the classics came off much better than the music written by Columbia's music men. So, there may be an album in the music of Columbia, but I don't readily see it as I do with Universal.

To sum up: For *The Music of Republic*—Thanks, Jim. For *The Music of Universal*—let's keep a good thought. And, for *The Music of Columbia*— well, what do you think?

Since the publication of this article, James King produced another album, this one entitled The Music of the Lone Ranger. *The album consists of two parts—first, the Republic serial music that was secured by the producers of the Lone Ranger radio program as part of the negotiations for rights to produce the motion picture serial based on their character and, second, the rewritten versions of that music used on the radio program in the 1940s, during and following an extensive strike by the musicians' union, which forbade the broadcasting of material not especially written for radio. Most of the Republic music was rewritten to meet the criteria set by the union, but much of it retained the quality and feel of the original compositions. This album provided the opportunity to compare the two versions. And it more than qualified as Mr. King's promised Volume II.*

Just suppose that a chance to "do it over again—knowing what I know now" could actually be granted; that actors who seem to have forgotten what serials did for them would recant and tenderly embrace the serials as their "start of something big"; that all moviemakers, as Steven Spielberg and George Lucas have done, would admit the influence that serials had on their own productions; and that someone would take on the job of dealing seriously with The Shadow *as CBS has finally done with* The Flash. *What would be the result?*

Well, we've already seen what happened with "uncredited" Oliver Drake and the Lone Ranger. Because of research by Dave Holland, the truth is now known, and what I could not say in my book, In the Nick of Time, *is now possible to say. If we could get those few people who deny the serials in their past to talk about them, we could learn even more about an era that has had an undeniable effect on motion pictures and television as a whole. If more producers would drop pretension and make more pictures with the action and scope of serials, adventure fans would surely support them as they have the Spielberg-Lucas films.*

And, if one of them were The Shadow, *then this writer would be an extremely "happy camper."*

You never can tell what all this may lead to.

Chapter 8

"Well, Maybe We Could Just Flip a Coin"

During the early 1950s, television took the nation by storm and changed the movie-viewing public's habits forever. In just a few short years, no series westerns were available for movie theaters; few series features (such as Charlie Chan, the Bowery Boys, and Ma and Pa Kettle) were being shown; and, by 1956, the last multichapter action serial was produced. All entertainment of that type had been appropriated by TV and was being dished out to the public in nightly doses, with no admission tickets required. The only price for viewing that continuous flow of movie fare was having to watch the commercials for the products being advertised by the sponsors who paid for the time on the air—the same as today.

By the time the 1960s arrived, one generation of children had begun growing up without the tradition of going to theaters, being a part of an audience watching westerns and serials, and savoring the anticipation and suspense of waiting until the next week to see how a hero would escape his doom. They saw the movies, all right, but they saw them shown on television—at the whim and caprice of TV stations that showed them when it was convenient; at the risk of having the movies preempted by some major sports event, dance recital, egg hunt, or almost anything the station felt like throwing in; and always with the ever-present commercials every few minutes to keep them distracted—which is not the way children had been able to watch them years before.

As the 1960s passed and the 1970s came upon us, several generations had grown up with no knowledge of, or feeling for, the "theater way" to watch westerns and serials. As some of the people who were children when television started entered their 30s and began to experience a need for nostalgia references, they became film collectors and began to acquire 16-millimeter prints of westerns and serials they had seen on TV as children. Unfortunately, having seen the films presented in no particular order, they had no concept of the evolution and development of serials and westerns and began comparing and rating them *against each other without any clear points of reference. The result was confusion.*

With the passage of much time, people tend to forget how things were and what happened as a result of them. In examining anything, if fairness is the goal, one needs to be reminded occasionally that although times change, things produced at a given time, under given circumstances, do not change. Therefore, it is not fair to compare something produced in one period by the standards of a different time. The points of reference are not equal.

The Devil's Due
October 1986

If I believed in omens, then the last Siler City get-together would have to signify one for me. On that same occasion, two friends of mine "pushed" upon me "deals that I couldn't refuse"; and, in so doing, made me conscious of something I had just about lost track of—the importance of the early efforts in producing sound serials.

We almost have a tendency to take for granted that once serials—or any motion picture for that matter—had reached a certain level of quality in production, they could be assumed to have had that same quality all along. Consequently, in comparing films as collectors 40 and 50 years after they were made, it is easy to scoff at one of the early ones as being "second-rate" or inferior because of its having less obvious production features than later ones. And, that comparison is not fair.

In 1930, Universal produced the first all-sound chapterplay, *The Indians Are Coming*, which starred Tim McCoy and Allene Ray. In Siler City, my friend Dave Godwin insisted that I take his print of Chapter Seven and give it a good screening for a possible trade. Now, I had always heard that *Indians* was pretty "primitive" and not too enjoyable—that its main value was as a "historical piece." And, while I respected its place in the history of serials, I never really wanted much to collect any of it. Nevertheless, I agreed to take it and look at it.

Then, from Howard Wheeler, who is a "world-class" veteran of Siler City gatherings, came the most tempting opportunity I have ever had to own a single chapter of *The Last Frontier*, which was the only serial ever released by RKO Radio Pictures. Partly because of that, and partly because it co-starred Dorothy Gulliver, whom we all met in Raleigh two years ago—but mostly because Howard gave me such a good deal on it (one I couldn't refuse)—I took it home, too.

After screening these two chapters, my appreciation for the early

The Last Frontier—RKO, 1932—featured Lon Chaney, Jr. *(left)*, and Leroy Mason *(right)* in a serial that, judged by the technical standards of its day, was a top-notch western. Chaney played in seven serials before making it big in *The Wolf Man* at Universal.

cliffhanger efforts has been fully restored. True, there is no stirring musical score to carry you along as there were in later classics from Republic and Universal. The fight scenes were head-to-head slugfests, without the precision choreography of a Dave Sharpe/Ken Terrell or a Tom Steele/Dale Van Sickel bout. And the photography and editing were not as precisely and surgically processed as they would become later with more sophisticated equipment available. But, the excitement and urgency of telling a good frontier story in a straightforward fashion by use of the best available camera techniques of the time are unmistakenly there. The mixture of silent-film acting methods and the new element of sound make these two serials very enjoyable for anyone except that person who just refuses to accept them and "give the devil his due." And, it is his loss.

Allene Ray had appeared in many silent serials co-starring with Walter Miller, Ed Hearn, Harold Miller, Jack Mower, Johnnie Walker and Bruce Gordon, but *The Indians Are Coming* was a first for Tim McCoy. Miss Ray made no more sound serials after that, but Tim McCoy starred in one other—*Heroes of the Flames*—for Universal in 1931. Director Henry

MacRae proved with *The Indians Are Coming* that sound could be used in an outdoor action picture, and convinced a dubious studio head, Carl Laemmle, that action films had a future with sound.

This serial is credited with re-vitalizing an almost dead interest in serials and restoring their popularity for another 20 years. For that alone—as a historical relic—it has great value. But, to my surprise, it is also a much better picture—judged by any standard—than many, many others that came later and had the benefit of all the subsequent technical innovations. It's just plain "a good old western."

When he was chosen to play the lead in *The Last Frontier*, Lon Chaney's son was still known by his real name, Creighton Chaney. (Three years later, he changed it to Lon Chaney, Jr.) He was just 25 years old and would himself become a screen legend—just as his father had—during the next 35 years. The turning point came in 1941 when he starred in *The Wolf Man* at Universal. After that, he became one of Hollywood's best-known character actors, especially in horror movies or action films. One of his most memorable cameo parts came in *High Noon* in 1952, in which he played the old, disillusioned and embittered ex-lawman who advised star Gary Cooper, as Marshal Will Kane, to get out of town and save his own life, rather than risk it for a town that wouldn't appreciate it. Along the way, Chaney appeared in six more serials after *The Last Frontier*.

Here again, the action and scope of this serial compare more than favorably with western features of that time. Considering how short a time sound had been in use, and the type of equipment that had to be used to get the desired effect on film, it is a shame to withhold the praise it deserves by holding it up for comparison with those made years later after the various sound techniques had been improved and perfected. Judged on its own merit, *The Last Frontier* is also a pretty good western serial.

I'm glad these two chapters came my way, and restored for me what I knew and almost let myself forget—that you judge a film by the standards of what it is, rather than how it compares with something else. When we forget to do this with our beloved films, it's only a short, fatal step away from doing it with the people around us.

And, that is the deadliest mistake we can ever make.

As the 1970s closed and the 1980s got under way, yet another new development appeared that has seemed to increase the compulsion some collectors have to compare and rate all serials. The videocassette recorder has made it possible for individual collectors to acquire more copies of movies (and serials) than was ever dreamed possible. The advent of the VCR has virtually placed the entire output of the motion picture industry within the grasp of anyone with the price of a VCR and the interest to accumulate recorded tapes. This flood of product has turned many an average movie-buff film collector into an instant critic on the comparative qualities and virtues of hundreds of motion pictures. It seems that everybody wants to get into the act....

One of the unexpected and surprising things about this newly acquired access to so much output of Hollywood product is the absolute stance on the quality of certain films that some collectors have been led to take. By virtue of having so many movies in their possession, these collectors seem to think they have become unimpeachable experts on which ones are good and which are not. In dealing with them, others are given to understand that only these collectors can be the judges of what is good and what is not. And, almost always, the contention has been that anything that was not judged to be the best was, consequently, no good at all.

The Comparison Urge: Curse of the Infidel
June 1988

I kept hearing it said so much that I had begun to believe it: The sequel, they said, was so much better than the original in this case because the hero was better cast, the story line made more sense, the action was faster, and the whole thing was just done a lot better than the first one. Therefore, the first one was no good, a big mistake, so forget it. Don't even bother with it. You're wasting your time to watch it. That's the message that came through loud and clear.

We're talking about *The Green Hornet* and *The Green Hornet Strikes Again*, serials released by Universal in 1939 and 1940 respectively. In the first one, the part of newspaper publisher Britt Reid, who was also the Green Hornet, a masked crimefighter, was played by an actor named Gordon Jones. In the latter, Reid was portrayed by actor Warren Hull. Other well known characters such as Kato, the Hornet's faithful sidekick, Miss Case, Britt Reid's glib secretary, and Michael Axford, Reid's well-meaning "bodyguard," were played in both serials by the same actors—Keye Luke, Anne Nagel and Wade Boteler. When released, both were very popular and well-liked serials, and joined other Universal releases such as *Tailspin Tommy*, the *Flash Gordon* trilogy, *Ace Drummond*, *Jungle Jim*, *Tim Tyler's Luck*, *Radio Patrol*, *Red Barry*, *Secret Agent X-9* and *Buck Rogers* as examples of Universal's best efforts to bring comic strip and radio favorites to the screen.

The Green Hornet—Universal, 1939—became a victim of the "comparison urge" when some who liked its sequel better labeled the first one "bad" by comparison. Gordon Jones (as the Green Hornet) holds a gun on John Kelly, while Robert Long *(right)* prepares to slug him with a hammer.

Over the years, however, much discussion has taken place regarding these two serials and their comparative qualities. The result has been a general agreement among serial buffs that *The Green Hornet Strikes Again* was better in many ways than *The Green Hornet,* and no one can argue against a person's right to hold that opinion. But, the strange thing is that, for many, the comparison had gone further than that and concluded that since the sequel was better, then the original was no good. And that's what I've been hearing for many years.

The main objection to *The Green Hornet* seems to be the choice of Gordon Jones to play Britt Reid. Since Jones later became better known as a comedian and comic sidekick in a number of westerns, many people then seeing a 16 millimeter print or videotape of *The Green Hornet* could not accept him as a serious hero—whereas Warren Hull, because of his roles in *The Spider's Web, Mandrake the Magician* and *The Spider Returns,* was readily acceptable as a hero. Also, later viewers of *The Green Hornet* found newspaper publisher Britt Reid's initial indifference to unfolding events, as portrayed by Jones, to be somewhat disturbing—another reason for criticism of his portrayal. (Hull, from the start, was eager and ready to do battle with the underworld, right from the opening scenes of *Strikes Again*.) And the main criticism of the serial itself was of a choppy story line which jumped from one thing to another so quickly, not concentrating on one single issue long enough.

All of these things, it was pointed out, made *The Green Hornet* a bad serial, and I had begun to believe it, because it had been over 40 years since I had seen it. When Robert Smith, a good friend of mine, recently offered to loan me his tape of it to watch, I almost turned it down.

"Why waste my time watching a bad serial," I thought, "with so many good ones now available?"

Instead, I took it home and decided to watch a couple of chapters just to confirm what I had been hearing. I'm glad I did.

Before going any further, let me say that *The Green Hornet Strikes Again* may very well be a better serial than *The Green Hornet*. Since, as far as I know, the sequel is not now available to collectors, I don't know when we will be able to see it again. I would certainly like to. But that's not my point. What I discovered—happily—was that all of those comments about *The Green Hornet* being a *bad* serial, were just not true.

Gordon Jones made a very good Britt Reid, portraying the hero in the same fashion as most other good serial heroes of the 1939 era. The seeming indifference some people had referred to was actually now seen—and only in the first couple of episodes—as Britt Reid's uncertainty about *what* to do about crime in his city, not a hesitancy to do anything at all, as reported. The result of his soul-searching was his decision to create the Green Hornet, who had not existed when Chapter One started. Once he became the Hornet, there was no longer any uncertainty at all in Britt Reid.

As for the so-called "choppy" story line, this was actually basic to the unique format of *The Green Hornet*, and would seem "choppy" only to someone who was not really paying attention. In the serial, the criminal gang—known as the Syndicate—was a group of 12 men, each of whom headed up a different racket preying on the city, all following the instructions of an unknown leader. In each episode, the Hornet dealt with a different one of these rackets, and either caused the arrest or demise of that racket's leader just before or just after the cliffhanger each week. When the 12 rackets were dealt with, he zeroed in on the head man who had been giving the 12 members their instructions. In effect, then, *The Green Hornet* was a *series* as well as a *serial*, which was a very subtle approach back then. The result could, however, cause some to view the whole thing as being a "choppy" story line, if they were looking for only the "usual."

The action portrayed in *The Green Hornet* was above the level of other

Universal serials of that era, and was the result of good direction of Ford Beebe and Ray Taylor. There were several fights throughout, and each was handled as well as you would expect from Taylor, one of the top serial directors of all time. All in all, *The Green Hornet* was a pretty good serial, and Gordon Jones a good Britt Reid. It's a shame that comparison with that thought to be better has given either an undeserved bad name. One could do a lot worse than watch *The Green Hornet*. I plan to—again.

The arbitrary comparison between these two serials is nothing new. The same thing happened with the Flash Gordon serials, the Dick Tracy serials, the two Lone Ranger serials, the Spider serials, and the two made from Zane Grey's character, King of the Royal Mounted. In each case there seemed to be an automatic dismissal as "no good" of the serial that by comparison was judged to be "second best." But, the truth is that many of those "second best" productions were still very fine, action-packed, exciting serials and should be judged as that.

Even now, the compulsion to make comparisons is still with us. How many times have I heard *Star Wars* compared to Flash Gordon serials and heard the serials dismissed as "primitive?" Or *Superman: The Movies* compared to *Superman:* the serials, and heard the serials scoffed at as being "amateurish?" Or *Indiana Jones—The Adventures* compared to the Saturday Matinee Cliffhangers and heard the "cliffhangers" referred to as "yesteryear's kid flicks?"

It's perfectly all right to have an opinion about which film is better than which other film—I have a few myself. But, friends, second time around ain't always better than the first time. And, even when it is, the first might be better than we remembered.

There is a fine line between what is an opinion and what is a rating. An opinion is what any person with any knowledge of a subject may think about that subject and implies the inclusion of personal prejudice. A rating is what a person with expert—or at least extraordinary—knowledge of a subject says is the value of that subject when compared to like subjects with like qualities and implies the exclusion of personal prejudice.

So, if fairness is not the goal, "how about if we just flip a coin?"

On the other hand, if fairness is the goal, why not do whatever possible to make sure there is no misunderstanding. In the late 1980s and early 1990s, a generation of young movie buffs have, in effect, rediscovered the movies, and some of them are trying to learn what they can about what moviegoing was like half a century ago, before television. About the only way they can do so is to learn about the movies that were shown then and listen to people who were part of it tell about those days. The movies, of course, must be obtained on videotape, and *many of these people are looking to experienced movie-buff film collectors to help them select the movies—good or bad—that represent the era. Consequently, it does no good to allow one's opinion to serve as a rating, when advising a novice about which serials to select.*

The 228 Best Serials Ever Made
November 1990

 Not too long ago, I saw a listing by someone of what he said were the "ten worst serials ever made." Over the years I have seen other listings by various people at various times of what they considered to be the ten *best* serials ever made, the top *dozen* serials ever produced, the ten *best* musicals, the ten *worst* musicals, the ten best westerns, the ten worst westerns, the ten best pictures, the ten worst pictures, and so on. It seems that someone, somewhere, is always trying to decide for you and me what the "ten best" and the "ten worst" of things are. And rarely do you ever see—no, never do you see—what criteria these self-appointed critics used to arrive at their conclusions. We are, I suppose, simply to take their word for it because they are somehow more knowledgeable or wise than the rest of us, and the list they have come up with is the result of that superior wisdom or knowledge.

 Well; no, thanks.

 From 1930 to 1956, there were 19 dozen sound serials produced and released; and each one of them has its own merit, its own quality, its own circumstances, and—to the movie-going public—its own unique appeal. From the gloomy depths of the "Great Depression" to the hysterical peak of "McCarthy-ism," they were released during the times of bank failures and economic recovery; gangsterism and an upsurge in law enforcement; World War II dictatorships and the creation of the United Nations; diplomatic "agreement" at political conference tables and national divisions by "curtains" and "walls"; a war that, instead of "war," was called a "police action"; and a peace that, instead of "peace," was called "Cold War." During that quarter-century, Hollywood went from silent movies in black and white to movies with dialogue, music, sound effects of all kind, and ultimately stereophonic "wrap-around" sound; pictures that were photographed in Sepia-tone, Color-tint, Cinecolor, Ansco-, Metro-, Deluxe-, Tru-, Magna-, and Techni- colors; filmed in 3-Dimension, Techniscope, Superscope, VistaVision, Cinemascope and Cinerama; and changed from studio "assembly-line" movies starring well-known, established actors and actresses in stories based on books, plays, current events and classics, to "off-the-wall" independent movies produced by any

"cat" who could afford a movie camera and starring whoever he happened to meet at the beer joint last night, and usually all based on the same premise first presented by H. G. Wells' *War of the Worlds* — an invasion from outer space by some kinky creature. Surrounded by all that was going on, it is a little bit amazing that serials were able to retain as much of their quality and individuality as they did. But, somehow they did manage to retain most of what they were known for, and each one released continued to become its own entity, and a favorite for all time for somebody out there watching it.

At about the time the producers of major features were scrambling to change over to 3-D, Cinemascope or VistaVision, it became fairly obvious to the producers of serials that their remaining duration was going to be for a limited time only. And the reason for both the major studios' scrambling and that sobering conclusion by serial makers was precisely the same — television. When TV hit the market in 1949, it not only changed all the rules of how movies were made, but it changed American life forever. Without trying to outline details, let's just say that unless you lived before the advent of television and saw what changes it brought about, you cannot be told or shown what the differences are. Just believe that things did change. And one of them was that there was no longer a need to go to a theatre every week to follow a serial — there were "cliffhangers" of one sort or another playing every night on the small screen at home, and the exciting "edge" was gone. Six short years after the very first TV sets were turned on in America, serials ceased to be a viable product in the movie business. It is a mystery why some "nerd" can believe he has the wisdom to categorize that much film entertainment.

Many people say that the last really good serial produced by Republic was *King of the Rocketmen*, released in that fateful year of 1949. And I would not argue with that. But, that doesn't mean that all the serials released after that were bad. Just like all the years before, some were pretty good, some not so good, and others were, indeed, pretty bad. The quality had dropped drastically because of lowered budgets (which were already low enough) brought on by TV competition and the reducing number of small town theatres (the serials' mainstay) which were closed by that same competition. Nevertheless, there are some Republic serials released during that time that are considered favorites by many fans. I often hear some of them speak fondly of *Don Daredevil Rides Again, Zombies of the Stratosphere, Man with the Steel Whip* and *Desperadoes of the West*, etc.

Many detractors of Columbia serials have said there were no good ones released after Sam Katzman took over their production in 1945 and

Opposite: *King of the Rocketmen*, released in 1949, was believed by many to be the last really good serial made by Republic.

started turning them out on "shoestring" budgets, like links of sausage. Yet, many of those Katzman serials hold special places in the hearts of many serial fans—favorites like *Hop Harrigan, Jack Armstrong, The Sea Hound, Superman, Cody of the Pony Express, Batman and Robin, Blackhawk* and *Son of Geronimo*, etc.

And, as to the quality of the productions (photography, sound, etc.) during that era, there is no question that it surpassed the quality of those earlier sound serials produced during the 1930s. Many technical advances had been made in the meantime. So, it is only natural for a person who liked those—and did not remember the earlier ones—to say they are better because of that improved production quality; and for a person who grew up remembering the good features of the earlier, less-polished productions, to say they are better, despite the "slickness" of the later ones. That's what makes horse races.

Unfortunately, there has now come along a breed of collector born after World War II who, from his own personal experience, remembers neither of the two eras—much less the middle part—of that quarter-century of serials, but has watched a lot of serials on videotape, and has decided that he can judge what are the best and worst of the entire 19 dozen releases based on his own observations of those he has watched. So, he blithely sets about saying that so-and-so ones are the "ten best" *ever made*, and that so-and-so ones are the "ten worst." He never tells you *why* those ten have been selected as "better" than all the other 218 sound serials, or why the other ten are worse than all those others—just saying smugly that these are the "best" and these are the "worst." If he wanted to be honest, he would say instead that he was listing the "ten he liked the most" of those he has seen, or the "ten he liked the least," but he doesn't do that. Until these guys do, any such "best-worst" list is not worth the paper it's written on.

Now, I have a list of those serials I *like* best, which I will be glad to share with anyone who wishes to share with me the ones they like best. And I have a list of those I like least, but I'd just as soon not "bad-mouth" them, in case someone else has a different opinion. Rather, let's make a list of the "ten worst film collectors in existence"—Okay?

Number One: The guy who insists on making "ten-most" lists....

It seems that most people who ever became involved in movie collecting have invited the opinions of older, more experienced collectors about what to collect. When they ask, "What was your favorite serial?" or "Which serial did you like

Opposite: Branded as "second rate" because it came after *King of the Rocketmen,* **one serial that was well liked by quite a few cliffhanger fans was** *Don Daredevil Rides Again*—**Republic, 1951.**

Blackhawk—Columbia, 1952—is another cliffhanger that is fondly remembered as a good action serial by many, despite the opinions of self-appointed raters that Sam Katzman productions were no good.

the least?" they are prepared to hear a prejudicial report about some serial or other. And, quite often, after they hear the reasons that led to the prejudicial part of the report, they are inclined to agree with the older collector and will either buy or reject the serial in question on the basis of his or her opinion. If the collector, on the other hand, expounds in reply that such and such was one of the best serials ever made or one of the worst, as if that were the final word, then that collector has rendered a disservice because no one can be that expert about all the sound serials ever made.

To be as honest as possible, even those who spent a great deal of their childhood and early teens watching serials during the reputed Golden Age, when those films were evolving before their very eyes into the movie phenomenon they were to become, should be cautious in arbitrarily rating serials by comparison. Just as things are not always what they seem to be, when it comes to serials, it is also true that things are not always what we thought them to be the first time around.

If, indeed, fairness is the game, and older serial lovers want to be a help, rather than a hindrance, to younger movie buffs, it behooves the old-timers occasionally to revisit some of the vintage cliffhangers with an open mind.

A Second Look— And Wrong Again
March 1991

Ever since I first saw it back in 1942, I have thought of Universal's *The Adventures of Smilin' Jack* as not much of a serial. Only recently have I had the opportunity to see it again; and, to my surprise, I came to a much different conclusion about it.

Adapted from Zack Mosely's syndicated comic strip, which was the story of a good-looking, sophisticated, self-confident pilot during the early days of aviation, it was difficult for me to accept young actor Tom Brown in the title role when it first played the State Theatre in Concord. Instead of the classicly handsome, suave Smilin' Jack Martin portrayed in the strip, Brown seemed to come on as the "golly, gee-whiz, let's-charge-in-there-half-cocked" college-hero type, partly because of his round-faced, boyish look, and partly because that's the type roles he had played up to that time. It was sort of like watching Van Johnson doing a part meant for Robert Taylor, or Mickey Rooney playing a role designed for Errol Flynn. It was disconcerting, to say the least. I always felt Universal should have cast Kent Taylor—who had played the hero in *Gang Busters* for them that year—in the part. (Kane Richmond would have been perfect, but he was working at Republic.)

It was during that time also that Universal was experimenting with a new way to introduce each serial chapter, and that added to the confusion. Up to that time, their standard opening each week was to follow the credits with a printed Foreword, headed by the chapter number, which re-capped the events of the previous episode and set up the cliffhanger situation that had led to its conclusion. It then dissolved to the scenes leading up to the cliffhanger, and showed the "take-out" rescue or escape that took place "just in the nick of time." (Columbia's method of doing this was to show quick flashback scenes from the previous episode, with a voice-over by famed announcer Knox Manning narrating the re-cap. Republic used the tried-and-true silent movie technique of showing re-cap "cards," with a picture of one of the characters at the top of each, and a short, printed statement below it saying what he had done in the previous chapter.)

Instead of the printed Foreword, Universal had started opening each episode of its serials with no chapter number or title shown, and no

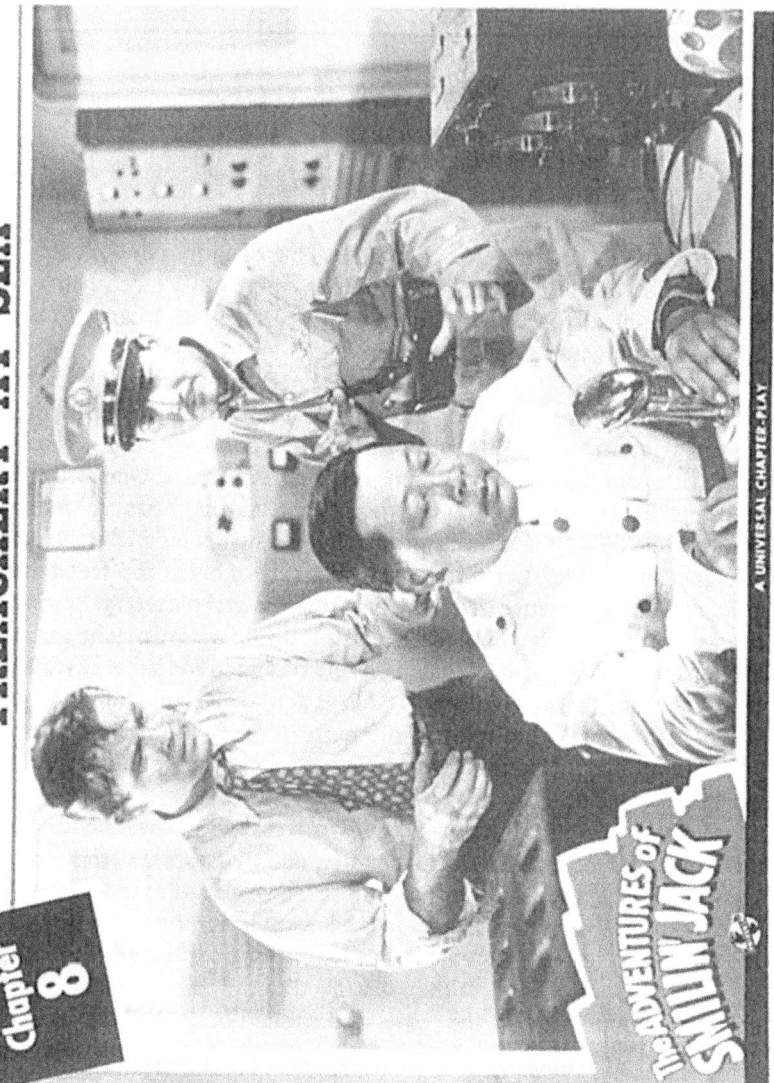

identifiable re-cap. Rather, after the credits, there was a dissolve to a scene that had not been seen in the previous chapter, involving characters who had nothing to do directly with the action last seen the previous week. Those characters would tell each other what had happened in the previous episode and what the hero was doing about it. Then came the scenes leading up to the cliffhanger and the "take-out." The confusing part was trying to figure out sometimes how those folks back at the Embassy—or at military headquarters, or the Consul's office, or whatever—knew what the hero was doing at the moment he was doing it—usually miles away. But, that was just part of it.

To a kid who was used to seeing his serial villains clearly drawn— Ming, the Merciless, the Lightning, Fu Manchu, Doctor Satan, etc.—the main villain in *Smilin' Jack* didn't make much sense. A female Nazi spy named Fraulein Von Teufel, she was portrayed by actress Rose Hobart, who was also playing a member of the hero's group posing as a newspaper correspondent named Trudy Miller. So far, so good; a lot of villains have posed as good guys. But, when she became Fraulein Von Teufel, she did not have a gang, like most villains. Her "soldiers" were members of a Japanese secret society of terrorists known as the Black Samurai, and headed up by a jealous Japanese agent played by Turhan Bey, who hated taking orders from the Nazi woman and seemed to be working against the Fraulein more than for her.

And, to be based on a comic strip about an ace aviator, *The Adventures of Smilin' Jack* had the hero doing very little flying—almost none, as a matter of fact. Most of the action took place on the ground, and the only time Jack flew a plane was to reach a remote mountain village in what looked like an over-sized Piper Cub. All in all, compared to other adaptations to the screen of popular comic strips, I thought *Smilin' Jack* came off second-rate at least, if not outright "bummer."

But, that is where I made my mistake. And that is where I see a lot of mistakes made by other people. Instead of judging the serial objectively, and on its own merits, I had compared it to other things I liked; and, when it fell short of them, I had written it off as "second-rate" or "bad." We do the same thing with other types of movies as well—especially westerns— and I have found that we lose something as a consequence.

When *The Adventures of Smilin' Jack* became available on videotape, I did not run out and buy a copy. Because of my memory of it, I wasn't even sure I wanted to see it again. So I put it off. But, finally I picked up a copy from M. L. Armstrong at the last get-together in Siler City and

Opposite: **Unfortunate comparisons with other serials of its time left** ***Adventures of Smilin' Jack*** **with a reputation as a second-rate serial. It was anything but that.**

carried it home, just out of curiosity. I thought, "Maybe I'll look at a chapter or two and then swap it for something." But it didn't work out just that way.

After I ran Chapter One and Two before going to bed one night, I began thinking, "Hey, that wasn't too bad after all." So, Tom Brown didn't look like Robert Taylor—so what? And, what if he was young and eager? Nothing wrong with that in a serial hero. Besides, America had just entered World War II and was struggling to keep its spirits up in the face of disappointing early battle losses. Who needed "handsome," "suave," and "sophisticated?" Maybe "golly," "gee-whiz" and "get-the-job-done" was better under the circumstances. So I decided to watch a couple more chapters the next night.

As each one began, there was an establishing shot following the credits showing where the re-cap scene was about to take place. As the characters did the re-cap, you could remember from the previous chapter some reference being made to contacting that particular place for advice, instructions, orders or information of some kind, and that explained how they knew what was going on. Ingenious, I thought! Let's go on with a couple more episodes.

By that time, the realization had come that this was a very tight, well-written story about one specific phase of the beginning of World War II. In the ensuing chapters, there were no flashbacks, no crossplots, very few diversionary side-plots (unheard of in a Universal serial), and a cohesion regarding the "weenie" (a secret route through the mountains from China to India) that was almost incredible. Now I had to see the rest of it.

As I watched more, the unrest I had felt over the years concerning the villain, Fraulein Von Teufel, changed to fascination. Rather than feeling disdain for the character that had seemed so senseless, I began to understand that she represented what was, at the beginning of World War II, an unknown enemy—not unknown as to what they were capable of doing, but unknown as to how they related to each other. And, as it turned out that representation was almost prophetic; since, as history unfolded in the next few years, the Axis powers, comprised of Germany, Japan and Italy—because of their jealousy of each other, and their suspicion of the true motives of each other—wound up doing each other almost as much harm as good.

By Chapter 11, I could hardly wait to see how it was going to come out. Along the way, the matter of involving an ace aviator in a battle of wits and intrigue had taken care of itself. Right from the start of the first chapter, Jack had voiced the fervent desire to go back home to the United States and become a flyer for his country; but, being in a certain place at a certain time had "side-tracked" him into a more important job. And that paralleled the situation that all America was in at the time:

Wanting to be what it had always been, it had been diverted into becoming the leader of the free world in order to help keep the world free.

I owe *The Adventures of Smilin' Jack* an apology. It was always a pretty good serial. It was just ahead of its time, and a lot of us failed to see that.

My answer to an inquiry about The Adventures of Smilin' Jack *would have been entirely different before I viewed it again 45 years after it was first released. My opinion would have been negative, to say the least, and if I were into doing arbitrary ratings, my assessment would have been even lower. So, even giving an opinion is risky, but, at least, it's honest.*

Sometimes it is difficult just to state an opinion and let it go at that. Even when every effort has been made to be fair and objective regarding the quality of certain serials, one may still be strongly tempted to try to convince another collector of the superiority of serials released in one era over those released at a different time. Because of factors that you consider important, the desire to convince the other collector may be strong, even though he or she tends to favor those you do not recommend. When that happens, an important truth is realized: In the absence of official judgment, the other person's opinion is just as good as yours; his or her points of reference may just be different.

Your View or Mine
May 1990

Although it bore little resemblance to the movie serials of 40 years ago, last year's feature production of *Batman* was an exciting and enjoyable experience. It was seen by a lot of people—so many, in fact, that it has taken a place among the leading box-office grossers of all time. To an old serial-lover like me, the enjoyment came, not from seeing one more re-make of the Batman story that had been shown in the two serials (as exciting as they were), nor the adaptation to something called "camp" that had been shown in the television series (as silly as it was), nor the condensation to a feature-length "comedy" as shown in the 20th Century–Fox film released to capitalize on the series (as embarrassing as it was), but in seeing the character presented essentially as he had first been conceived back in 1939.

To an 11-year-old boy at the "trailing edge" of the gangster era, the first Batman was some kind of a hard-nosed dude, and much to be admired. Having seen his parents murdered by criminals—and the law seemingly helpless to do anything about it—young Bruce Wayne went to the

Batman and Robin—Columbia, 1949: Your view or mine depends upon when you began watching the Boy Wonder and the Caped Crusader, here played by Johnny Duncan *(left)* and Robert Lowery *(right)*.

trouble to prepare himself to wage his own battle against crime—only wage it to win, no holds barred. And, for a year or two, it was something to see: our hero struck fear into the hearts of criminals and brought a lot of them to justice. He was doing what most of us—in our heart of hearts—would have liked to be doing.

Then, for some reason a lot of us never did really understand, they rang in this young kid called Robin, who was depicted as a pretty good crime fighter himself; but, for practical purposes, only got in the way and slowed down the Big Guy. Maybe that's what was intended—who knows? Anyway, from then on, "Batman" and "Robin" became "Mr. Squeaky-Clean and his sidekick, Chuckles," and were off on the "high road" as respectable law enforcement allies, leaving the "make-my-day" Batman behind. The action was good, so the kids continued to buy it, and the rest is history. But a lot of us missed the "real" Batman.

Through the years, the character underwent many other changes—from becoming nearly a superhuman like Superman at one extreme, to a pathetic, almost sub-human jerk, wallowing in doubt and self-recrimina-

Atom Man vs. Superman—Columbia, 1950: One of the "best," one of the "worst," the "most favorite," the "least favorite," one of the "top 10" or the "bottom 30"—be your own judge. Meanwhile, Noel Neill (as Lois Lane) seems happy to be in the arms of her hero, played by Kirk Alyn.

tion, at the other—but most of his fans stayed loyal. By the 1980s the character still had one of the largest followings of any modern fictional character. The interesting thing is, they weren't all loyal to the same Batman.

It depended on when you "came on board" as to which Batman you liked. Some of us still clung to the original, looking for evidences of him in everything the subsequent ones did. Others remembered the high-adventure of the wartime Batman with his cheery little buddy. Still others placed him right up there with Superman, where he was when they had "joined up." Those now in their late 30s and 40s think of the "twinkle-toed" Adam West Batman of the 1960s, with his "golly, gee-whiz" Robin; and those in their 20s and early 30s see him as the schizophrenic "dark knight," ruled by some compulsion he himself does not understand that drives him to do crazy, impulsive things in the name of "justice."

Now comes along the new *Batman* feature which depicts the hero as a combination of the original and the latest—and no mention of the boy wonder. It stands to reason that those who began their following of

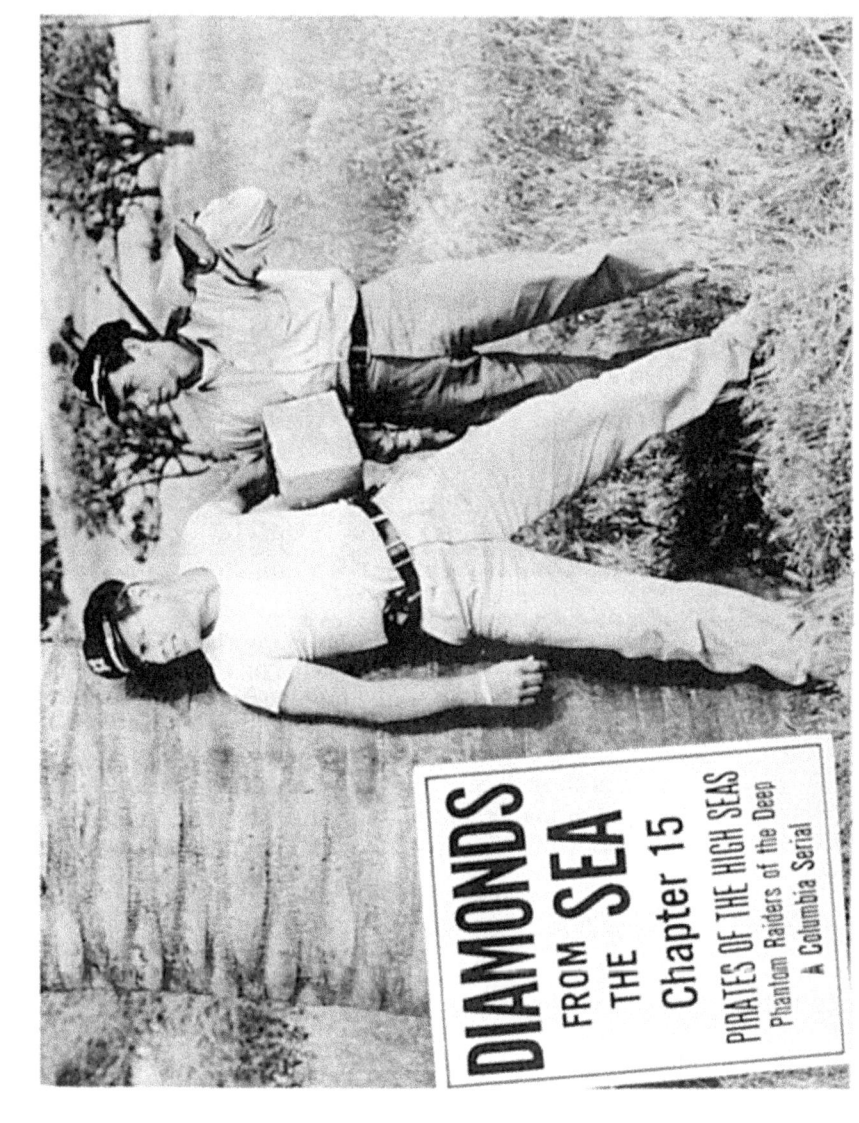

Batman with the strip, the serials and the television shows that included Robin, would like to see him included. He was a part of it for them. And maybe they missed some of the "humor" they had grown up with—that, too, is understandable. But, to me, it was a joy to see things come full-circle and show Batman as he first was. I'll hang on to my tape of it, because I feel certain that any sequels that are made will start "monkeying" with the Batman character again. It's only human nature—to fix "what ain't broke."

Several years ago, I witnessed almost the same parallel situation in film collecting. As a serial and western fan who had gotten in on the good stuff in the middle 1930s, I remembered western stars like Hopalong Cassidy, Tex Ritter, Johnny Mack Brown, Wild Bill Elliott, Gene Autry, George O'Brien, Dick Foran, Tim Holt, Charles Starrett, Roy Rogers, Bob Livingston, Crash Corrigan and Don Barry, who were just reaching their peak in the outdoor adventure films so loaded with action and excitement. Very soon afterward, there came along Rod Cameron, Buster Crabbe, Robert Mitchum, Kirby Grant and Allan Lane to join them. Still going strong were already established stars like Buck Jones, Bob Steele, Ken Maynard, Hoot Gibson and Tim McCoy. And, even though he had already made his last film, the legend of Tom Mix was still alive and well. Other stars were to come along later, and westerns would undergo many changes; but, to me, these were the cream of the crop. I was looking forward to enjoying them again.

The serials of that same era that still stood out for me as great were *The Vigilantes Are Coming, Flash Gordon,* the *Dick Tracy* four, *The Painted Stallion, The Fighting Devil Dogs, The Lone Ranger, The Spider's Web, The Great Adventures of Wild Bill Hickok, Daredevils of the Red Circle, Zorro's Fighting Legion, Drums of Fu Manchu, Adventures of Red Ryder, King of the Royal Mounted, Doctor Satan* and *Captain Marvel.* Later, during World War II, such outstanding entries as *Spy Smasher, Perils of Nyoka, Valley of Vanishing Men, G-Men vs. the Black Dragon, Batman, Daredevils of the West, The Phantom* and *Captain America* joined the list as classic adventures in cliffhanging; but, after 1944, there seemed to be a downward shift to a long string of "same-ness." Universal stopped making serials when they merged with International Pictures, and Columbia turned over serial production to Sam Katzman, who ground out one serial after another with an amazing degree of similarity. They were almost like one long production, with only the leading characters changing from title to title.

From the end of World War II until television wiped them out in the

Opposite: **Buster Crabbe** *(left)* **and Tommy Farrell** *(right)* **in a tense scene from a Sam Katzman serial. "Best," "worst," or "favorite?" Who cares? The word is: Enjoy!**

Although not many serial fans consider *Captain Video* one of the best (or even anywhere near it), others have a great affection for it. Your view or mine?

early 1950s, both series westerns and serials had declined remarkably from what they had once been. At least, that was my thinking, as one who had come on board during what was called the Golden Age. I assumed that everyone shared the same views regarding the relative quality of pre-war and post-war productions. After all, I surmised, it was pretty obvious.

To my surprise, when I began meeting and talking to many western film collectors, I learned that instead of the ones I thought would be obvious choices, their favorite western stars were Lash LaRue, Sunset Carson and Whip Wilson (whom I thought of as "johnny-come-latelys"); Eddie Dean and Monte Hale (whom I thought of still as "supporting" players); Jimmy Wakely (an Autry clone), and—for heaven's sake—Rex Allen (a Rogers clone)! The only one I could relate to the so-called Golden Age was Allan Lane, because of his slam-bang serial roles (especially in *Daredevils of the West*).

Those guys were recalling with a great deal of relish serials like *Jack Armstrong, Jesse James Rides Again, Brick Bradford, Tex Granger, Batman and Robin, Son of Zorro, Adventures of Sir Galahad, Captain Video* (believe it!) and *Zombies of the Stratosphere,* and using words like "super" and "great" to describe them. Now, wa-a-it a minute, I thought!

All of this was quite a shock until I realized that many of these guys were a lot younger than I, having seen their first westerns and serials in the post–World War II era. It was only natural that they would remember what had first grabbed their attention. And, whether I agreed or not, the stars and serials they remembered as "great" were great to them. I still held the strong opinion that the ones I held dear were better (and still do, having lived through the entire 20-year period and seen them all) but, it made me stop and wonder what someone ten years older than I might think—some one who had gotten "hooked" in the mid-1920s on silent serials and stars such as Fred Thomson, Harry Carey, William S. Hart, and the great Tom Mix. I'm sure they would say those were the great stars and serials, and my favorites were not as good.

There is an old riddle about a bus that starts out on its route and, at each stop on its run, lets off so many people and takes on so many. As it progresses from stop to stop, you are told how many get on and get off, and your head begins to boggle trying to keep track of how many are left on the bus at any given time. Then, when the punch line comes, the riddle is not how many people are left on board (the obvious); but, how many stops did the bus make? (the overlooked).

So, in our discussions with fellow film buffs, instead of assuming that others will have the same favorites that we do (the obvious), we could begin to listen and learn from each other the good points of what the other guy likes (the overlooked), and thereby gain a better understanding of the whole riddle, "why do we like serials and westerns so much?"

The people I feel sorry for are those under 35, who only have television to remember.

But, wa-a-it a minute! There was *Sky King*, and *Fury*, and *Time Tunnel*, and *Gunsmoke*, and *Lost in Space*, and *Have Gun—Will Travel*, and *Star Trek*, and *Bonanza* and....

No type of motion picture has enjoyed the fierce loyalty and firm dedication of its hard-core fans as have action serials and series westerns. The appeal of these movies is not universal, as it once was, but, then, neither is the appeal of the big, color musical. The unique, indefinable mystery of these serials has not been recaptured by any other type of motion picture since their demise as viable entertainment products, but, then, neither has the thin-lipped, steely eyed private detective movie so well played by Humphrey Bogart, Robert Mitchum, William Powell, and Alan Ladd. And, their incessant urgency that compelled moviegoers to return to the theater week after week—knowing the hero would surely escape— has not been replaced or duplicated by any better technique—but, then, neither have the bright, sophisticated, fun-oriented comedies of Clark Gable, Spencer Tracy, Katharine Hepburn, Cary Grant, Claudette Colbert, and Fred MacMurray.

Yet, nowhere do we see musical film fairs or private eye film fairs or comedy film fairs, as we do the annual Western Film Fairs, which include the western's brother, the serial. Nobody expects serials or westerns to return to motion picture theaters. Audiences have become much too aware, discerning, and blasé for that to happen. But, serials will continue to be important to serious students of cinema and to the fans who grew up with them.

And we all know which ones were the best, don't we?

No? Well, how about if we just flip a coin?

Chapter 9

"But, Dad, That's Not What You Said a Serial Was!"

Even though modern movies and television have not recaptured the indefinable mystery of serials or replaced their sense of urgency by a better technique, it has not been because no one has tried. On the contrary, a number of efforts have been made to duplicate the excitement and urgency that serials had, but all have fallen short. Having pumped millions of dollars into major adventure epics and produced some excellent, action-packed movies as a result, several current filmmakers have earned the everlasting gratitude of movie fans who had begun to wonder if motion pictures would ever come to life again. And the trend continues as this is written. But, to a serial lover who can remember the sense of urgency that the real series had, there is still something missing.

The basic reason that movies no longer contain the urgency of serials is that the cliffhanger, as such, is gone. There is no waiting for the outcome; no talking with buddies about possible takeouts until the episode next week; no anticipation or dread that perhaps, this time, the hero may not make it—even though you privately know he will. The American public has developed into a strangely blunt, egocentric, impatient "mob" (observe any local traffic scene or any crowd entering or leaving a public event), and they won't tolerate—much less try to enjoy—being made to wait for anything. Filmmakers wouldn't dare challenge that intolerance with real, honest-to-goodness cliffhanger movies.

When television has toyed with the cliffhanger technique, it has usually treated it tongue in cheek or with outright cynicism. The results have not been good. The only exceptions have been those that have clearly been labeled cliffhanger shows, so people could choose to watch them or not and thus have not been suddenly surprised. The few times the technique has worked have been delightful to watch.

Drums of Fu Manchu—Republic, 1940—*From left:* **Robert Kellard, William Royle, and John Bagni. Along with** *Perils of Nyoka* **and** *Secret Service in Darkest Africa,* **this was obviously an inspiration for the Lucas-Spielberg Indiana Jones epics 40 years later.**

Counterfeit Cliffhangers
December 1984

Ever since it came out in 1981, *Raiders of the Lost Ark* has been compared to the serials of the 1930s and 1940s. And now, *Indiana Jones and the Temple of Doom* has joined it as the subject of a rising gleeful chorus of folks who say the "good old days" of serials are back. Before that, those people were saying how much *Star Wars* and its sequels were like the old cliffhangers—so it must be the "new and improved" versions of cliffhangers we were beginning to see. People were saying that because, for a change, the action in these pictures was fast-paced, loose, free-wheeling and unrestrained—"just like the old Saturday matinees of long ago." I've even heard the Indiana Jones pictures compared to *Perils of Nyoka* and *Secret Service in Dark Africa,* and the *Star Wars* trilogy compared to the *Flash Gordon* and *Buck Rogers* serials. It has almost become the "fashionable" thing to say, when talking about current movies, to make

Flash Gordon's Trip to Mars—Universal, 1938—*From left:* **Frank Shannon, Buster Crabbe, Donald Kerr, and Jean Rogers. Reportedly, the three Flash Gordon serials served as models for the *Star Wars* blockbuster epics produced in the 1970s and 1980s by George Lucas and Steven Spielberg.**

the comparison of these features with the old "Saturday serials of long ago."

Well, I won't take a thing away from the quick-moving, wide-swinging action of these movies. It's a long overdue treat to see movies "move" again, and action pictures contain some real bone-crushing action. (It still flips me out to think about "Indy" crawling all over, around, and under that Nazi truck—Yakima Canutt style—in *Raiders of the Lost Ark*, and how he ultimately resolved that situation.) And, if proof were needed of what originally made movies great, they are proof again that most people go to see films to be entertained and thrilled, rather than educated or enlightened. Also, the new era of computerized special effects gives a dimension to fantasy action films that couldn't be reached back in the old days. These films are fun, and they are great.

But, to say that these movies are the "new cliffhangers" just ain't so.

No matter how great the action sequences are, or how compelling the special effects appear, or how bold the hero may be, these films all lack the one basic, central element unique to the cliffhanger serials—the suspense of having to wait to see how a dangerous threat is resolved, and then

knowing the relief of seeing it done. That element just cannot be put into a feature film, and that's what all of these great, current action hits are—features.

As far back as the early 1940s (even earlier in some cases), there was a practice of re-editing successful chapter films into 70 to 80 minute condensed versions, and re-releasing them as features. To do so, all the cliffhangers had to be closed in and resolved in a running sequence, or eliminated altogether. When television came, this was done to nearly half of Republic's total serial output, only these were put together in 100 minute versions to serve a two-hour TV format, allowing 20 minutes for commercials. Again, all the cliffhangers were re-edited into uninterrupted sequences and resolved on the spot, without any need for any waiting until later to see what would happen. Thus they became the exact opposite of what they started out to be. Instead of suspense-building, mind-nagging, teaser attractions, provoking you to come back to see the next chapter (and, oh yes, see the newest action feature or western as well, while you're here), they became the "action feature," just like the rest. They were still crammed with fist-slingin', gun-poppin' action, but they were no longer *cliffhangers.*

So, the current crop of action features are *very much* like the feature versions of the old Saturday serials, but they're not like the serials themselves—and cannot be.

Admittedly, this is a puristic view. Many arguments could be made regarding comparisons and similarities, but in defining the cliffhanger, the basic point of difference is format and purpose. The feature's is to present a complete story in one telling, with no loose ends and no unanswered questions after the end; and the serial's is to give you the story in pieces, and do it in such a way as to keep you interested enough to want to come back and see more. Loose ends and unanswered questions are what it's all about—the more the better.

Currently on TV, there are a number of "dramatic" serials—*Dallas, Dynasty, Falcon Crest, Knots Landing,* etc.—which have found the successful formula for enticing TV viewers to return each week, by leaving several stories unfinished and unresolved and at crisis points at the end of each episode.

Imagine what we would have if someone put an Indiana Jones-quality adventure series into the *Dallas-Dynasty* format. Now, speaking of cliffhangers....

Opposite: *Zorro Rides Again*—Republic, 1937—was one of the early serials edited for theatrical release as a feature. Along with *S.O.S. Coast Guard,* it showed that a profit could be made after a serial had completed its runs, even though the cliffhanger concept was entirely gone.

There is nothing wrong with making a wonderfully exciting motion picture. Every true serial fan loved action features as well as serials. And, it is clear—as he forthrightly stated in interviews—that Steven Spielberg, who directed the Indiana Jones pictures, was influenced by the serials. It is easy to see by their finished work that many producers of the later pseudo-serial adventures were, also. The only thing wrong, from a serial-lover's viewpoint, is to call what they made "cliffhangers." It just ain't so.

To some people, the point may be academic. To them—because of their lack of exposure to the real thing—the designation "cliffhanger" serves as a noun, when it should—if used at all—serve as an adjective. That is, an exciting scene in a movie, where the hero's life is seriously threatened and, in just a matter of moments, is miraculously saved, is, to them, a cliffhanger. In reality, it is a cliffhanger-type scene (adjective), but not a real cliffhanger (noun). It would only be a true cliffhanger if the audience had to stop there and come back much later—not in just a few moments—to see the situation resolved. A fine point, maybe, but, it is the difference.

The cliffhanger as a technique suffered the most damage when it was treated dishonestly, tongue in cheek, or cynically. For it to work, the audience had to believe that there was a real threat to the hero's life and whatever happened to save him from that threat had to be credible. When a solution was not credible or was too farfetched, then the whole thing became suspect. It may sound high blown, but between the serial makers and the serial watchers, there was a substantial element of trust. When a phony or obviously contrived takeout was used, that trust was violated. The feeling it produced was, "We were cheated!"

It would be easy to lay the blame for most of this kind of thing on television; however, in all fairness, the serials themselves were, from time to time, guilty of betraying the audience's trust.

Just Say It Wasn't So...
December 1986

As Gilda Radner's kookie newscaster, "Roseanna," on the TV show, *Saturday Night Live,* used to say—"Ne-e-ver Mind!"

That's the same feeling many had after the opening episode of the CBS television series, *Dallas,* this fall: "Ne-e-ver Mind!"

Opposite: In the 1950s and 1960s, more than a third of all Republic serials (26 of the 66) were adapted to 100-minute feature versions to be shown on television. *Spy Smasher* **was retitled** *Spy Smasher Returns.*

Over the years, some serials have been edited into feature versions, eliminating the cliffhangers and thereby making something different than what was originally conceived. *The Lone Ranger* serial became a feature entitled *Hi-Yo, Silver*.

In the *Saturday Night Live* skit, Radner used to come on with a wild, screwball explanation of some news event that was designed to tell the audience what she thought of some particular issue of the day—only, instead of the real issue, hers would be something different that she had assumed it to be. In its own peculiar way, and to anyone who might share a somewhat similar outlook on life, it even made a modicum of sense, until colleague Jane Curtin would correct the character's mistaken basic assumption; whereupon the whole thing would collapse as the totally ridiculous and implausible idea that all but "Roseanna" already knew it to be. She then would look into the camera, grin impishly and—as if to erase all she had said—dismiss it with, "Ne-e-ver Mind!"

Well, *Dallas* did the same thing this fall with an entire season's episodes. They looked straight at the American television audience and dismissed them all with a casual, "Ne-e-ver Mind!" And, in so doing, television put to rest any competition there might have been in the credibility department between the movie serials of yesterday and the television series of today.

It took television to bring to perfection what movie serials danced

'MYSTERIOUS DOCTOR SATAN'
A REPUBLIC SERIAL IN 15 CHAPTERS

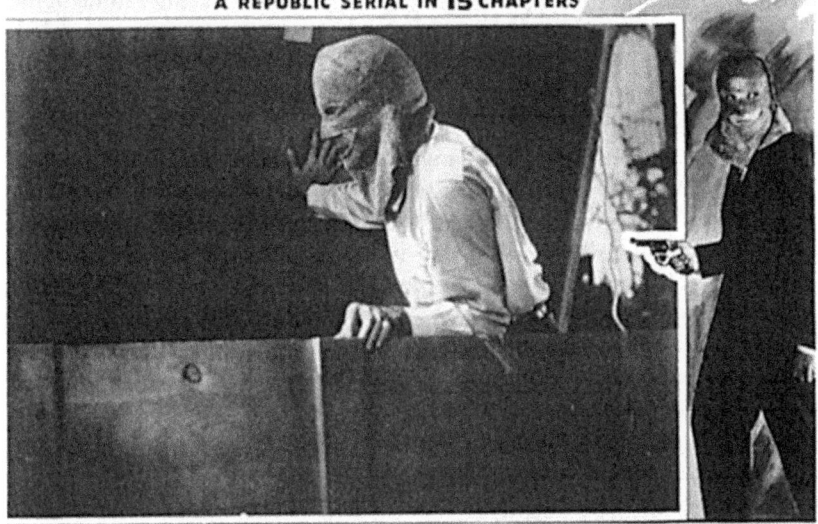

Episode 15 'DOCTOR SATAN STRIKES'

Sometimes serials were guilty of actually "cheating" the moviegoers in resolving their cliffhangers. Otherwise one of the best ever, *Mysterious Doctor Satan* contained such a resolution.

around and flirted with for their entire existence — and have received much criticism for — but were actually never really very good at: the "cheat" resolution of the cliffhanger ending.

First, let it be said that all cliffhanger resolutions involved a certain degree of cheating. It's the only way they would have worked; and everybody — producers and audiences alike — knew it. When a hero was left in danger at the end of an episode, everyone knew that certain little things not shown in that sequence would suddenly turn up in the next chapter to enable the last-second rescue just in the nick of time. But, there was rationale to support this voluntary suspension of credibility. Usually, everything was happening so fast you could say, "Well, why not? It could have gone that way. He could have leaped from the car in that last instant. He could have dived under the cleft in that rock that quickly. The sidekick could have somehow gotten there quicker than it seemed he would. Yep, it *could* have happened that way." So, we joined in the deception and made it mutual so it would work. And, in the doing, we accepted that minor bit of cheating because it supported our desire to try and figure out which of the possible solutions would be brought into play. It was all a game, and the "rules" were being applied.

But, when the "rules" were dropped, and a totally implausible solution was offered, it then became a "cheat" resolution, because none of the "rules of expectation" could be applied, and the game became one-sided, therefore unfair. Those are the ones movie serials have had to answer for all these years—and rightly so.

It was one thing to see a vault door blown off its hinges and crash down on the unconscious hero lying on the floor at the end of one chapter of *Adventures of Red Ryder*. You figured next week he would swiftly roll out of harm's way in the instant before the door hit and be all right. You didn't expect to see him come to, get up, survey the situation, and hop up a stairway to safety *before the explosion occurred*. But, that was the resolution used, and aficionados are still arguing whether it qualified as a genuine "cheat" resolution, or just a near-"cheat." Later, in the final episode of the same serial, the hero and villain together took a header off a high mountain bridge and plunged apparently to both their dooms. Fade-out. In the next scene, the hero is being eulogized for being such a gallant fighter, when up he rides *with only his arm in a sling*.

"We thought you were dead, Red Ryder," exclaims his sidekick, Little Beaver. And, the hero's answer:

"Well, this time we fooled 'em, sprout." Fade-out. Now, that's a real "cheat."

Other examples of genuine "cheat" resolutions occurred in similar gambits in *Mysterious Doctor Satan* (1940) and *Batman* (1943). In the former, a large box containing the hero, the Copperhead, is delivered to the hide-out of Doctor Satan in Chapter 14. Suspecting the box contains deadly gas, the villain places it unopened in a huge furnace and raises the flames to the maximum. As the box begins to burn, the chapter ends. In the beginning of Chapter 15, the box is once again placed in the furnace and begins to burn. As it burns, Doctor Satan closes the furnace door and the box is consumed. The hero did not escape from it! Zowie! The scene switches to the heroine's house where the phone is ringing. She answers it and is astounded to hear the voice of the Copperhead, who tells her in flashback how he really got out of the box and filled it with sandbags before it was carried into the hide-out. In *Batman,* the box was dumped into a crocodile pit instead of a furnace, but the "cheat" resolution was the same. In neither case could the viewers in the audience expect that the peril would have been resolved before the cliffhanger occurred, but that they wouldn't be told until afterwards—and then in flashback. In the spirit and essence of the serial, that is blatant cheating.

These ploys, and others like them, have been subjects for discussion among serial followers for years. Most agree that they were breaches of the game and should be recognized as such. There is really no excuse to offer for them other than they were expedient. So be it.

Dick Tracy's G-Men—Republic, 1939: Some serials had "flashback" chapters consisting primarily of scenes from earlier episodes, which many fans considered "cheat" chapters. After a flashback session, Ralph Byrd, Kenneth Harlan, and Ted Pearson *(from left)* are "trapped" in a gas-filled taxicab.

We now come to the *Dallas* ploy, which is the most blatant cheat of all, and done for the most expedient of motives. All of the "cheat" resolutions in serials were devices of production continuity used for their expediency and didn't change the story or plot in any way. They could just as easily have been rigged another way and the result would have been the same. They were, if you will, tactical decisions. What the *Dallas* writers did was create an entire 1985–86 season of plot and character developments leading up to a final episode with not one, but three cliffhangers to hold the audience over the summer. Then, in order to restore a key character that had been killed at the end of the 1984–85 season, wiped out those cliffhangers plus the entire current year's season, by making it only a "dream" by that character's wife. They said, in effect, that nothing that happened all that season really happened at all; that any characters introduced did not really exist; that any development of known characters that was shown did not really take place; and that any conversations held and words spoken were not really said. What they said to us was: "Ne-e-ver Mind!"

And their motive was to put back in the show a popular actor they had written out a year before by killing off his character. I suppose you would have to admit it was the only way to do it. But, there is now a question as to whether it was worth it. Most of the people I have talked to say they don't feel they will ever be able to trust that show's integrity anymore. That's a high price to pay. It's one thing to suspend credibility to make a technique like cliffhangers work. It's another thing to blithely shove it aside for an obvious commercial gain.

Can you ever watch *Dallas* again without wondering whether they will suddenly look out at you again, grin impishly, and casually say, "Ne-e-ver Mind?"

Boy! Doesn't television have a way of making old movies look better and better?

For the most part, serial lovers were a patient bunch, realizing that there had to be that suspension of credibility to some degree to make the whole thing work. It was only when their patience was abused or ignored that they reacted in a critical way. Serials and their cliffhangers were much like professional wrestling and their overtheatrical antics: As long as the "game" is played in the proper spirit, the fans—serial or wrestling—will go along and enjoy it.

But, it was and is a mistake to insult the fans' intelligence.

Outside movies and television, in what many call "real life," the greatest proponent of the cliffhanger technique in the early part of the 20th century was the legendary Harry Houdini, world-renowned escape artist and illusionist. Taking his magic to the actual locations of the dangers from which he planned to escape—rivers, caverns, oceans, skyscraper roofs, jungles, mountains, whatever—he would set the stage elaborately, build up the suspense through media coverage, and then perform the feat—usually with large crowds of witnesses to spread the word about his incredible "escape" from an impossible situation. It was the essence of showmanship, and the epitome of the cliffhanger technique.

Today, there is a successor to the famed Harry Houdini. His stage, like Houdini's, is an actual location where the danger exists or will be made to exist. His vehicle for reaching millions of people at once—rather than Houdini's hundreds, or thousands—is television.

In 1988, he came to Charlotte:

 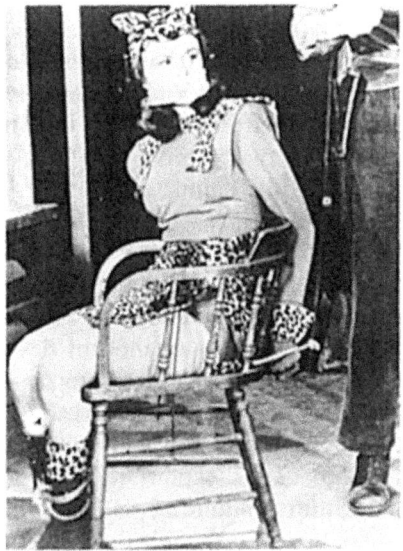

Kay Aldridge *(left)* in *Perils of Nyoka*—Republic, 1941—and Linda Stirling *(right)* in *The Tiger Woman*—Republic, 1944—were not Houdinis, but were continually being captured by the bad guys, bound up and gagged. Their situations, though not as elaborate as Houdini's, were no less urgent to serial viewers.

Countdown to Destruction
December 1988

The Queen Charlotte Hotel stood for 64 years as an integral part of downtown Charlotte. It would be impossible to record all that took place there during that time—there was so much. Its imposing outline was a central part of that city's skyline for all those years; and its presence was taken for granted.

Several Sunday afternoons ago, the Queen Charlotte disappeared in a matter of eight seconds—the subject of a demolition process known as implosion. Strategically-placed explosive charges were fired in sequence, blasting the building's lower foundations out of place just enough to cause the massive structure to crumble under its own weight into a huge pile of rubble right on its own base. The only effect on nearby buildings was a thick layer of dust that resulted from the collapse.

It was there, and then it was gone.

I never get over the feeling of awe when I see that happen; and the first time was in a newsreel stock-shot used as a cliffhanger ending in a serial in 1942. The serial was Universal's *Gang Busters,* and the implosion was the cliffhanger of Chapter Six, *Under Crumbling Walls.* Searching for a story, girl reporter Vicki Logan, played by Irene Hervey, had gone into a new building that had been threatened with destruction by villain Professor Mortis, played by Ralph Morgan. Hero Kent Taylor, as police detective Bill Bannister, went in looking for Vicki as the deadline for destruction approached. Apparently before they could clear the building, Professor Mortis began setting off the charges by remote control and the building started to collapse. To this 14-year-old, the resulting scene was spectacular, even though I suspected that it was a newsreel shot. I had never seen such a method of destruction before. In serials, there were plenty of explosions, fires, storms and other forms of natural and manmade disasters, but there was something insidious about turning a structure's own size and weight toward its own devastation.

Most serial explosions were carefully planned and staged to show a maximum amount of damage—much like a choreographed fist-fight, where broad, telegraphed punches were employed to display the utmost in physical movement and individual athletic prowess. At Republic, the Lydecker brothers, Howard and Theodore, and their special effects crew, built miniatures and blew them apart for some of the most memorable scenes in action filmmaking. Who can forget the famous "Republic barn" being blown to smithereens in so many serials and westerns? Or the Republic carpenter shop (doubling as a warehouse, a factory or a hangar) blowing apart, with pieces flying all over the screen? Or the various shacks, cabins, houses, oil rigs and other assorted structures being blown literally all over the landscape? There was something re-assuring about seeing a movie explosion blowing something all to pieces. It seemed to be logical. So, an implosion came as somewhat of a shock.

Needless to say, the opening of Chapter Seven of *Gang Busters* showed Bannister and Vicki getting out of the doomed building before the implosion just "in the nick of time." But, every time I have seen a similar demolition in movies or on the TV news since then, I have always thought of *Gang Busters.* I guess I always will.

Traditionally, the escapes from explosion cliffhangers in serials have been many and varied. Some have been very logical, while others have made no sense at all. But, of course, the same thing could be said of most "take-outs." In most of them—like Chapter Six of *Gang Busters*—it is made to appear that the blow-up takes place before the hero can get clear of the area; but the next episode shows him getting clear just in time. Some of them show a gimmick "take-out"—such as a tight sequence in Republic's *Spy Smasher*—when the hero seems hopelessly trapped, but suddenly makes a spectacular dive through a window to the outside and safety just before the blast. And, all too many—especially in Universal and Columbia

Zorro's Black Whip—Republic, 1944: The overseers of heroine Linda Stirling's predicament in this scene are two of serialdom's all-time outstanding bad guys—John Merton *(center)* and Tom Steele *(right)*.

serials—show the hero struggling to get clear of the blast area before the explosion, but the blow-up coming before he can make it; then, in the next episode, the blast does take place, and the hero crawls out from under the debris, brushes off his clothes, and remarks something like,

"Boy, that sure was a close one!"

The most illogical ones were those like the blasting of the safe in *Adventures of Red Ryder,* in which the hero—tied up in a basement, unconscious and unaware of impending danger as the explosion came to end the chapter—has time to come to, free himself, run up the stairs and out the door to safety before the blast goes off, in the beginning of the next episode. That was really asking the kids to suspend credibility.

But, of course, we did just that, because it was all in fun and we were willing to go along with it to enjoy the action. All in the name of the cliffhanger.

Interestingly, there was a "cliffhanger" also involved in the destruction of the Queen Charlotte:

As the demolition crew were preparing the building for the final blast, world-famous magician and illusionist, David Copperfield, was also there and was hard at work with a camera crew and sophisticated location equipment, rigging a spectacular sequence for use in a planned television special. Two and a half minutes before the building came down, Copperfield was locked in a chained vault inside the doomed building. As the countdown to implosion progressed, Copperfield had to somehow extricate himself from the chained vault on the third floor and get out of the building before it came crashing down.

As his anxious crew focussed on the grand old structure, the seconds ran out and the explosive charges began to sever the building's foundations. The north wing was the first to begin falling. In just eight seconds there would be a large pile of debris where a proud Queen had stood. And Copperfield should have accomplished his much-publicized "take-out."

Did he make it?

The TV special is scheduled for March 3rd.

What makes this feat of David Copperfield's a true cliffhanger is that television audiences had to wait for over three months to see if he would actually get out of the implosion. The expectation that he would, indeed, escape was always there—the viewers were never told anything else but that he would—but, the thing was, they couldn't be absolutely sure and they couldn't figure out how, and they had to wait and see. And wonder. And speculate. Just like the old days.

Without actually planning it that way, for the first time since it began, the Serials-ly Speaking *column had become a part of a cliffhanger. After the column,* Countdown to Destruction, *appeared, a number of letters were received from readers wanting to know how the escape would be effected, assuming that I had some advance access to that knowledge. Since that was not the case, and the Copperfield people probably had never heard of* Serials-ly Speaking, *I was wondering, too. Waiting for the date of Copperfield's next television special was the closest thing to sweating out a cliffhanger in the old days.*

Illusions and Delusions
April 1989

From this column—December, 1988:

"Two and a half minutes before the building came down, Copperfield was locked in a chained vault inside the doomed building. As the countdown to implosion progressed, Copperfield had to somehow extricate himself from the chained vault on the third floor and get out of the building before it came crashing down.

"As his anxious crew focussed on the grand old structure, the seconds ran out and explosive charges began to sever the building's foundations. The north wing was the first to begin falling. In just eight seconds, there would be a large pile of debris where a proud Queen had stood. And Copperfield should have accomplished his much-publicized 'take-out.'

"Did he make it?"

CBS Television—March 3, 1989:

The Magic of David Copperfield, the 11th network special presentation by the master illusionist, had come to its climax: after appearing out of thin air before a group in Costa Mesa, California; performing an astonishing mind-reading routine; changing a 100 dollar bill into a dollar; thrusting swords into a box containing a grown woman; and accomplishing an unbelievable levitation sequence with lovely guest star, Emma Samms; the world-renowned David Copperfield appeared and set the stage for his most spectacular feat—escape from a crumbling hotel building in Charlotte.

After locking him in and chaining the safe—with a stationary TV camera covering it all—the crew and two security officers serving as witnesses immediately vacated the area, and got out of the building as quickly as they could. While the coverage of the safe by the remaining stationary camera was broadcast as an inset, the people leaving the building were covered by a portable, hand-held camera that recorded their departure from beside the safe on the third floor, down the stairs, and then to a point outside and a safe distance away from the building. The camera continued to move away from the building, and came to a stop in a nearby parking lot, where a large, square, steel sheet had been laid upon saw horses to form a thin platform three feet off the ground. On top of the steel sheet lay a folded red cloth with a big black "X" painted on it. The camera continued to focus on that steel-sheet platform, with the hotel beyond (the stationary camera covering the locked safe still being shown as an inset) while the building was blasted loose from its foundations and crumpled into a massive heap. As it began to fall, the inset went blank, as the stationary camera inside was presumably destroyed. It had not shown Copperfield leaving the chained and locked safe.

As the outside camera continued to show the steel-sheet platform with the folded X-marked cloth lying on it, and the billowing cloud of dust and smoke rising from the pile of debris beyond it, there was a moment of hesitation and uncertainty. Then, without apparent reason, the folded cloth began to move and enlarge, unfolding by itself and ballooning up from within until it reached a height of about six feet. At that point, it was thrown back and out stepped the disheveled figure of David Copperfield—alive and well!

So, to answer the question posed in December's column: yes, he did make it! But, if you were to ask how, only Mr. Copperfield and his associates could tell you. And, this is unlike the serials of yesteryear. They always showed you how, even though the "how" didn't always make sense.

The difference, of course, is that an illusion is based on a trick, and the trick must always make sense; because the life and safety of the illusionist is at stake, and the trick must always work. However, the trick must always remain a secret; because, unless it does, the illusion is gone. Only the sense would remain. Then, anybody could do it.

In serials, there was no need for secrecy in extricating the hero from his danger—only the suspense of guessing how it would be; or which of the possible solutions would be employed to save him or her "in the nick of time." We always were quite sure the escape would come; we only had to guess the "how."

In an illusion such as Mr. Copperfield's, we also felt quite sure he would somehow escape. But, none of us expect to ever know "how" he did. I'm not sure we would even want to. It would destroy the fun of being tricked. So, we watch fascinated as so-called "magicians" ply the tricks of their trade—everything from pulling a quarter from behind a child's ear to rising mysteriously in an X-marked cloth from a steel-sheet platform outside a demolished building—and we stare incredulously at the illusion created, and applaud the "magician," knowing there was a trick in there somewhere. But, not really caring, because it was fun to watch.

For quite a long time, I have tried to find something to explain the fascination of serials. Any student of movies—or even those who just "like" them—would agree that serials are a separate breed from most motion pictures that are accepted as part of cinematic "art." They are admittedly—for the most part—"junk," when compared to movies such as *Gone with the Wind*, *Ben-Hur*, *How Green Was My Valley*, *The Lost Weekend*, *Mrs. Miniver* and *Singing in the Rain*, to name only half a dozen. With just a few exceptions, most serials were made quickly, directly, systematically and—most important of all—cheaply. They had no pretense, no claims of artistic integrity, no attempts to achieve realism, no ambitions to "reflect life." They were made to amuse, excite and entertain. They were illusion. Serials were, to motion picture "art," what a magician's illusions are to real life. We viewed them incredulously and applauded their excitement and suspense, knowing there was a trick in there somewhere. But, not really caring, because they were fun to watch.

Even though there were moments when real quality performances were given, most of the actors spoke lines and went through motions that were designed only to further the story along from one action sequence to another. And it was in those action sequences, usually staged by expert stuntmen, where the real quality of the serials came through. They were just plain-by-damn exciting!

***Mystery of the Riverboat*—Universal, 1944—contained the basic element of serial suspense: anxiety about an ominous threat to one of the good guys—the belief that his life was really in danger.**

The locations—especially in the earlier serials—were sometimes excellent stages for the action that was to take place there. But, quite often, those locations—the houses, lakes, dams and forests—were products of the craftsmanship of gifted special effects people. If a moviegoer could accept these for what they were: backdrops for the great action sequences that were to come, then he or she could thoroughly enjoy what the serials had to offer.

The problems always come when someone tries to compare serials with motion pictures that were produced as "art"—features that tried to and did achieve an entirely different goal: either artistic integrity or what is called cinematic realism. When such a comparison is made, serials will always come up looking like "junk"; and that's just the truth of it.

(Unfortunately, the same thing can happen to those movies with artistic integrity or realism when they are compared to the dramatic stage or the written word. Many of them—because of their cinematic "tricks"—also come up looking like "junk" by that comparison.)

Of course, it goes without saying that to know the "how" of a David Copperfield illusion would automatically destroy that illusion. It would become then merely a delusion. To continue enjoying them, we must help the illusionist protect his own secrets from us. So, we don't even ask—most of us—and those who do can no longer enjoy.

Likewise, those of us who enjoy old serials the most are the ones who don't look for the flaws and faults, and debunk the plots. We help the producers protect their own secrets from us—and we just enjoy.

A certain snobbery that still exists among students of the cinema has resulted in the serial getting a "bum rap." Because of the seeming transparency of its thrust, the obvious aim of its main technique, the evident purpose of its creating thrills for the sake of thrills, and the lack of artistic values in its plots and characterizations, the serial has been scoffed at and dismissed as worthless by many of those who purport to understand what motion pictures were and are all about.

If the cinema as a medium of storytelling was charged with some noble mandate to produce and present to an appreciating public only those projects that are aesthetically inspired, intellectually conceived, artistically created, and literarily presented, then the snobs would have a case. But, that case would also apply to most of the products that have come out of Hollywood since its inception and would condemn many of the movies that have come to be known as classics. Only a handful of films that were released in the entire history of the medium would meet the standards of that mandate. And, unfortunately, they would be the handful that most Americans have never seen or, having seen, would dismiss as boring.

For those who study motion pictures, it should be fundamental knowledge that there is no such mandate. The theatergoing public do not want to spend their time watching aesthetic, intellectual, artistic, and literary movies. Simply stated, they want to be entertained. And, if some of the noble educational qualities can be transfused through the entertainment, then all the better. If not, then they still want to be entertained. That is the mandate of the cinema. Nothing more. To try to make it more becomes snobbery.

The people who make movies learned a long time ago that the best way to entertain people is to provide them with two basic kinds of stories: those to which they can relate and those that cause them to dream. The people who go to see movies walk into theaters from lives that are lived on a day-to-day basis, with no promise of what tomorrow will bring. Their lives are filled with joys, sorrows, frustrations, failures, successes, happy times, sad times, love, hate, kindness, cruelty, pleasure, pain, victory, and defeat, in all manners and degrees. When people see these events and emotions portrayed on the screen, they respond from personal feelings and experiences. And their responses are produced by many kinds of movies. Also, all moviegoers have hopes, dreams, ambitions, aspirations, and even fantasies about rising above what is and having everything better and more wonderful. When they see movies that touch that chord in them, they are touched by magic. And, it doesn't take a cinematic "work of art" to do that, either.

Let them say what they will about cliffhangers. The beholder is the judge. But, the existence of these movies cannot be negated or dismissed. They are a fact of life. In one sense, they are life: Humanity, without exception, moves forward in episodes. No life comes and goes without experiencing the changes that come to all. Every human being must wonder what the next day or the next turn or the next development in anything will bring. And we all must wait, to find out.

Chapter 10

"It's Been a Long Tunnel, Guys, But There Is the Light!"

It may be a little high sounding to compare the serial form to life itself, but the parallel simply cannot be denied. No matter what goes on at any given time, it is an episode, a chapter, in the ongoing story of life. For each human being, there is the veritable beginning and the ultimate end, and all else between the two is a continuing, changing saga. Ups and downs, ins and outs, lights and darks, goods and bads—all are variances of that continuing saga.

As time has passed, people who have felt that truth about the lowly serial and who were captivated by its fascinating urgency have conscientiously tried to keep the memory of those old cliffhangers alive. At times they felt alone and at other times, they felt filled with companionship as they learned about others who felt the same way they did. They took heart when somebody else was heard to say what had been going on in their own thoughts for years. And they joined with each other in spirit to keep alive the memories they had tried to nurture alone, sharing with each other their joy each time someone new—or younger—was brought to understand what serials were—and are—because of the dedication of stubborn old cliffhanger fans like themselves.

What television has done to promote the cliffhanger technique has been helpful in keeping alive the concept of the movie serials, but what has really done the most to keep it alive are the little groups of dedicated aficionados around the country who simply will not let it go; who know they are living a serial; who see their daily problems as just little cliffhangers; and who believe—by faith—that everything will come out all right, if you just don't let go. Several years ago, I was involved in a situation that had nothing to do with movie serials, but brought clearly into focus for me the concept that life is a serial and serials are life.

Saga of the First Baptist Church
November 1986

The First Baptist Church in Concord, NC, is celebrating its 100th anniversary this month, and asked me to help them do it. As a Lutheran, my first reaction was,

"Why me? What can I—a non–Baptist—do to help in a project like that?"

The answer was very simple: As a Lutheran, nothing; but, as a film collector and student of movie history, I could serve a very useful purpose. And, as a serial buff, even more so. I could lend perspective to a pageant being planned that would depict the church's growth and response to America's changing social and economic life during that time.

Since I have always viewed life and history as the ultimate serial—the epitome of the continuing story—I accepted their challenge to see what we could come up with that would prove me right, or show me to be wrong. The result was uncanny.

The pageant was to be presented in five parts—each to depict a 20-year period in the life of the First Baptist Church. To introduce each segment, I was to show a short film clip depicting something about life in America during that time; then the live skit would come on showing a development or attitude of the church that either coincided or contradicted the social trend of the time.

Film clip number one—for the time period from 1886 to 1906—opened with a shot of a kerosene lamp, which dissolved to a shot of the first electric light bulb; then a picture of Thomas A. Edison; followed by scenes showing a "horseless carriage" emerging from a horse-barn garage, traffic scenes in New York showing horses and wagons and early autos traveling side-by-side, and finally a shot of the Wright brothers' first flight at Kitty Hawk—all of which changed communication and transportation forever in America. The live skit—done tongue-in-cheek—depicted the first attempted baptism of a reluctant youth in the new Baptist church's indoor baptistry, after years of performing that sacrament in the nearby Coldwater Creek.

To illustrate the popularity of silent movies in the period from 1906 to 1926, we then showed a clip from a movie starring the great Buster Keaton, who was one of America's most famous screen comedians of the time—along with Charlie Chaplin, Harold Lloyd, Fatty Arbuckle and others. The live segment was a very humorous bit about the church's rigid view toward dancing, and how it was beginning to see a subtle change—a new tolerance, almost—of some of the social changes in America that had at first been harshly rejected, but later reconsidered.

The period 1926 to 1946 brought the depression and World War II, which resulted in changing forever the face of rural America and its small towns.

A clip from *So This Is Washington*, showing Lum and Abner, owners of the "Jot-em-down" General Store in Pine Ridge, Arkansas, performing every conceivable home front wartime job, such as draft board, rationing board, tire inspector, air raid warden, etc., set the scene for that era. The live pageant segment followed up by showing some of the post-war problems and concerns of the war veterans and their families, and how First Baptist Church had helped deal with them.

Between 1946 and 1966 came the revolution in music, brought about by rock and roll, and the revolution in social standards which began as the "beat" or "hippie" generation, and is still going on today. The opening film clip was simply the preview trailer of the movie, *A Hard Day's Night*, starring the Beatles, the musical group that became strongly involved as leader in both aspects of the period's two revolutions. The live segment depicted an innocent young Baptist youth going away to college, and returning home filled with the ideas of the "hippie" philosophy, much to the bewilderment of his confused, old-fashioned parents.

The final 20-year period, 1966 to 1986, was the most difficult to typify, as it is still going on and is so contemporary. But, to try, we selected for the film clip an opening shot of astronaut Neil Armstrong explaining the purpose of the Apollo XI moon landing, brief scenes of the blast-off, Armstrong's stepping on to the moon, then a fade back and quick cut to a 60-second promo of a 1970s CBS television season line-up. Thus showing the moon landing and television to be—historically and socially—the most significant events of these past two decades. For the live part in the pageant, a humorous skit showing an *It Pays to Be Ignorant*-type committee, making plans for a move to a new location and construction of a complete new church, which is in reality the most significant event currently in the life of the First Baptist Church.

So, in film clips from the kerosene lamp and the first electric light bulb to television and man's landing on the moon, and in live segments from baptisms in a nearby creek to a multi-million dollar structure housing every conceivable facility for worship, the story of the first 100 years in the life of one church was told—and was told as a five-chapter serial. That's what was so uncanny.

As each film clip ended, and as each live segment concluded, you could almost feel the sense of anxiety in the audience assembled.

"What's coming next?" you could feel them thinking.

"How're they gonna do the next twenty?" you knew they were wondering. And it became very exciting.

Even though I knew what was coming next, I couldn't wait to show it; to see the audience reaction. It was almost like becoming a part of that church's history, and re-living those earlier times in America, to see all of that pass in review. And feel the crowd's response to it.

The essence of the serial.

And the beauty of this episode is—as is true of all the serial of life—it ain't even near over yet.

Granted, the parallel between an old-time action serial and the first 100 years of the First Baptist Church is a distant one. And the similarity has to be clearly established as conceptual for it to make any sense. But, that's the nagging, intriguing, magnetic, almost hypnotic, thing about the cliffhangers—they simply wouldn't let you alone. They fixed it so you simply had to come back to see what would happen next. And, when new serials no longer came along to replace the existing ones, a real void developed in the entertainment world of those who cared about them. It did not seem possible that the serial had come to an end, so many of the serial fans searched vainly on television and in movies for something to replace it. During those dark days of the 1950s, the movie serial as an entity had been floundering at its lowest ebb, virtually undergoing its own supreme cliffhanger. But some faithful fans and collectors just wouldn't let go.

Never again would the movie serial return to its former glory. The new habits of American movie watchers being forever changed and redirected by television, there was no more place for the serial and its purpose. Instead of luring audiences back to the movie theaters with cliffhangers designed for people who relished the excitement of wondering, all movies were being made to be seen, wrapped up, and discarded quickly. The legacy of television was that most viewers could not remember by Thursday what they had seen on Monday because Friday and Saturday were coming with shows that would be forgotten by the next Monday. To suggest that someone wait a week, or even several days, to see how a cliffhanger was resolved was almost a joke. For several years, it appeared that the serial, as a form of storytelling in films, had completely disappeared.

If life were like a feature film, that would be the end of the story. But, life is not a feature; it's a serial. And, although the 1950s were a dark chapter for cliffhangers; for them—as in most worthwhile crusades—there was a slim ray of light: An "underground" force was quietly at work (each person assuming he or she was alone) doing whatever it could to keep the cliffhanger alive.

Through the years, television stations showed serials from time to time, providing hope for the keepers of the flame. Universal's 1936 classic *Flash Gordon* was one that showed up as often as any.

Keepers of the Flame
May 1986

When motion picture sound serials folded in 1956, there was every good reason to believe that they were dead—gone forever. The movie business was undergoing drastic change as it responded to the new threat of television. Almost imperceptibly the moviegoing habits of the American public were altering to reflect a new generation that was going to co-patronize movies and television in a different perspective than before. And television itself was off and running with variety shows, dramatic shows and comedy shows competing with movie features; and action and western series that had in effect replaced serials and "B" westerns.

To survive, motion picture features began to move in a more graphic, explicit, sensationalistic direction, depicting subjects, ideas and concepts that could not be shown on the home screen. By their very nature, serials and "B" westerns could not do that, and thus did not survive. The television westerns and action shows were already more mature and sophisticated than the movie westerns and serials could dare become, so they became the closest thing to what the westerns and serials had been—but were a far cry from actually being it. Westerns and serials—especially serials—appeared to be dead and gone.

Occasionally a serial would show up on TV—as had been true since its advent—but not too many stations kept faith with serial fans by sticking to them once they had started, so you couldn't count on it lasting for its full run. For several years, nothing much happened except in the minds and hearts of those who remembered them and loved them; who diligently searched out whatever information they could find on them; who sat up until after midnight—or got up before dawn—to catch a distant station's running of a chapter; who taped the soundtracks (and sometimes got only hissing) and wrote down credit information as it rolled across a snowy screen; and who thought they were all alone while doing it: the faithful—the *Keepers of the Flame*.

Then, one day it became known that some lucky young man up in New York had fallen heir to a veritable mountain of serial material—press books, still photos, poster advertising, etc.—and was going to publish a lot of it in book form. To serial lovers all over the land—*The Keepers of the Flame*—Alan Barbour became a celebrity. Each time he published some of his material, we all immediately sent for our copies and devoured them the day they came. I daresay most of us still have those first dog-eared copies.

In the late 1960s, one of the most devout of the *Keepers of the Flame* started a chronicle on sound serials that became the standard in quality for the rest of us to follow. Bob Malcomson, who lived in Mt. Clemens, Michigan, began publishing a periodical called *Those Enduring Matinee Idols*. Likening the conception, creation and development of sound serials to the conception, birth and development of a baby into a mature person, Bob traced the history and progress of serials from the introduction of sound to motion pictures in the early 1930s, through the evolution of serials into adventure-strip added attractions in the mid–1930s, up to their role during America's entry into World War II in the 1940s. Due to circumstances known to him, Bob was not able to continue and finish the chronicle, but he had done the important part. By interesting, intelligent and perceptive narrative, augmented by superb selections of photographic illustrations, presented in a highly polished, professional publication, he had not only started telling the story of the serials, but raised the level of their importance and esteem. What had been sloughed off by many as an unimportant by-product of the movie industry had been shown by Bob Malcomson to be an exciting, vital, but unappreciated, part of it. Bob himself may not realize it, but that's the real impact of TEMI—*Those*

Enduring Matinee Idols. Helping him make TEMI the successful journal it became were such knowledgeable *Keepers of the Flame* as Jim Stringham (Bob's Michigan partner), Parky Parkhurst and Harry Sanford, just to name a few. Bob introduced through TEMI several excellent writers on serials.

When TEMI stopped, the torch moved over to the capable hands of Jeff Walton, another *Keeper of the Flame*. A California son, Jeff created *Serial World* and continued to report to all who would read or listen, anything he could find out about the beloved cliffhangers that, by then, many of us knew had not died forever, but were just suspended in time, waiting for a re-birth of interest. We wondered when and how it would come. *Serial World* became Jeff Walton's ode to the cliffhanger, and its herald—taking its place beside TEMI as the continuing book of writ on the American movie serial—while under his steady guidance.

From then to now, there have been several books published on serials. Most of them are good, and all are good to have. There is something in each one (pictures, information, viewpoints, etc.) that adds to the total knowledge a serial lover wants to keep. Our thanks to fellows like Barbour, Harmon, Glut, Tuska, Weiss & Goodgold and the others. They gave us books on other movie subjects as well as serials, and we appreciate them all. And, during that time, *Serial World* was the golden thread that kept it all together.

Jeff has continued to be an outstanding exponent of cliffhangers, and has helped many of us to learn even more about serials as time goes by. He is now an ally of Norman Lynch, the *Keeper of the Flame* in Houston, Texas, who is one of the most devoted serial-lovers in the entire country. Norm has written and distributed a personal newsletter about serials to a group of serial fans known as Norm's Nostalgia Club since 1974. His newsletter features news and views from all over serial world and is distributed quarterly to members who await each issue eagerly.

One of the most knowledgeable, best-liked and highly respected of all the *Keepers*, Norm is one of those who paid his dues by losing sleep because of weird TV scheduling, enduring aggravation because of rotten TV reception, suffering disappointment in seeing a serial discontinued after Chapter Nine, and spending money he couldn't easily afford for pubs that didn't deliver on their promises, in order to collect some audio soundtracks of serials (he loves the music), while thinking he was the only "nut" doing it.

Then, when he found out he was not alone, Norm started his club, and became the go-between for a bunch of other soundtrack collectors

Opposite: **Republic's 1949 topical thriller** *Radar Patrol vs. Spy King* **was another serial that often showed up on television stations.**

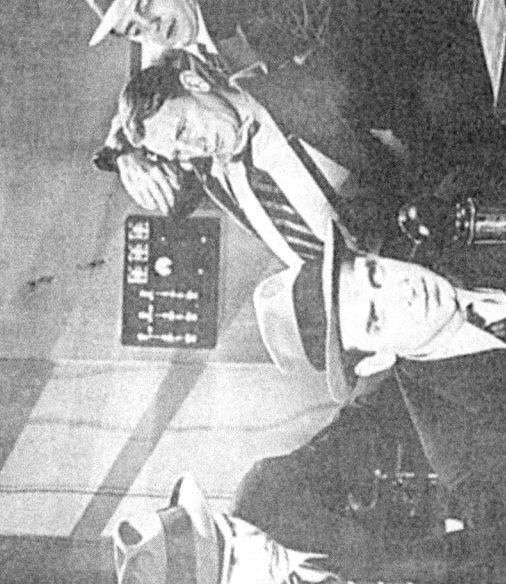

who had also thought they were "nuts alone." Audio graduated to video, and Norm adjusted. But, along the way, his club has cost him more lost sleep, aggravation, disappointment and money—and more than once has tempted him to "chuck it all" and run away. But he hung in there and answered the letters (eventually, in some cases), dubbed the tapes, wrote the newsletters, and swallowed the expense. And, all because he wanted—more than aggravation and disappointments could prevent—to see serial fans sharing what they love most with each other: SERIALS.

Now, that is a Keeper of the Flame.

After the first decade of television, when the newness had worn off and television had become redundant, that medium found itself searching for ways to keep its audience coming back. Every conceivable type of entertainment—from Shakespearean plays and operatic productions to gimmicky game shows and local "talent" contests—had been funneled through the "tube" night after night, until about the only thing that kept people watching was the built-in addiction they had attained from watching so much stuff through the years. Many people didn't know now not to watch.

But, bobbing up here and there out of all the mess were the occasional gems sought out by the keepers of the flame—the serials that were shown once in a while—and those loyal cliffhanger fans did whatever they could to retain and preserve them—first, by making audiotapes of the soundtracks and later, by making videotapes when it became possible to do so.

Some of them began collecting serials and westerns on 16-millimeter film whenever they could find prints. Because early television relied heavily on film for its product, many features, westerns, and serials became available to the market after the stations were through with them. From that source, an amazingly large number of titles began to surface over the years, and collectors were delighted to be able to have them again. To their disappointment, however, there was a list of highly desirable serials that, because of legal or technical restrictions, never made it into the television scene—and, subsequently, to the collectors' market—and still have not today, even after the advent of the VCR. For practical purposes, they are serials that are lost to collectors, as well as to any potential television audience. Included in this group are early favorites, such as Universal's Fingerprints *(1930),* Heroes of the Flames *and* Danger Island *(1931),* Jungle Mystery *and* The Lost Special *(1932), and* Phantom of the Air *(1933). Later ones include* Adventures of Frank Merriwell *(Universal,*

Opposite: From left,** **James Craig, Robert Paige, Bud Geary, and Richard Fiske in a scene from** Flying G-Men**—Columbia, 1939—another of the cliffhangers that were "lost."

Dave O'Brien in *Captain Midnight*—Columbia, 1942—one of the "lost" serials, much sought after by film collectors.

1935; both Lone Ranger serials, *produced by Republic in 1938 and 1939;* both King of the Royal Mounted *serials from Republic in 1940 and 1942;* The Green Hornet Strikes Again *(Universal, 1940);* Captain Midnight *(Columbia, 1942);* Daredevils of the West *(Republic, 1943), and* Brenda Starr, Reporter *(Columbia, 1945). Some collectors have been able to obtain all the sound serials except these and are constantly hoping that these will turn up somewhere, either on film or on videotape.*

As their collections grew, by trading with each other what they had acquired, that little group of dedicated serial lovers managed to keep the cliffhangers alive through the 1960s and 1970s while television was still groping for a way to retain its audiences.

By the time the 1980s rolled around, television producers were beginning to see the light. Even though there appeared to be no way to restore the genuine urgency of the movie cliffhangers, there did seem to be a way to grasp a part of it. Eventually, the guys who make television shows began to realize that and began to inject into their productions—especially the continuing series—the excitement of wondering about what will happen next. As they did so, interest in the shows increased perceptibly, and people were once again talking about what might—or might not—be the resolution of a ticklish or perilous situation.

There were, by the mid-1980s, outright experiments with cliffhangers. Usually, these experiments were confined to the last episode of the season and designed to hold the audience's interest from that show, in April or May, until the first episode of the next season in September. But, at least, that was something.

The Excitement of Wondering
June 1986

You know that a bomb has been planted in his car. As he prepares to leave town, he asks his sister to drive him to the airport in it. As they start out, the phone rings. She goes on, but he answers it and receives a warning about the bomb. Before he can do anything, the car blows up!

The caller on the other end hears the explosion, hangs up his phone and dashes out of his office, leaving a briefcase (which you know also contains a bomb) on the desk. As he gets on one elevator, his wife gets off the other and goes into the office calling his name. An exterior shot of the building shows the office being blown apart—with debris flying everywhere!

The newlywed wakens to find her new bridegroom missing from bed. She gets up and makes her way to the bathroom, where she hears the sound of the shower going. She opens the shower door and sees a young man (presumably her new husband) taking a shower. As he turns to greet her with a cheery "Good morning," she recoils in shock! The young man's face is that of her dead first husband!

These are not the cliffhangers of three separate episodes of a serial. They are the triple cliffhangers of one current television serial—*Dallas*. All three of these shockers will have to wait until September to be resolved or explained, keeping *Dallas* fans on hold for three months.

The same idea is being used in *Knots Landing* and *Falcon Crest* on CBS; *Dynasty* and *The Colbys* on ABC; and *Hill Street Blues* and *St. Elsewhere* on NBC, with varying degrees of cliffhangers being employed. Whether they are violent, emotional or dramatic (in *Knots Landing*, Val sees her husband embrace her sister-in-law and then walk arm-in-arm to her van together), the idea is to keep the fans wondering what is going to happen, so they will return to the series when it resumes in the fall.

Well, they haven't made it yet, but they're gettin' there. The days of the serial cliffhangers, when you had to wonder from week to week how your hero was going to escape from his current dilemma, are long gone, and have not been successfully replaced by anything yet. And, serial lovers still miss the suspense and the excitement of wondering. There have been attempts made, but nothing that really replaced the thrill of the originals. So, these series that use the cliffhangers once a year to keep you hanging over the summer months are better than nothing; but, it still ain't like getting the "excitement of wondering" every week.

The early television series utilized the technique of mystery to recreate the excitement of wondering, and several classics were born as a result. *Outer Limits* and *Science Fiction Theatre* probed outer space and its built-in mysteries; *Inner Sanctum*, *The Invisible Man* and *Alfred Hitchcock Presents* dramatized the bizarre, unusual and unexpected to achieve excitement. And, perhaps the series to best survive the passage of time was *The Twilight Zone*, which delved into all facets of the imagination and our earthly existence to provide wondering and surprise to viewers.

But, none of them used the cliffhanger technique, because all were locked into a rigid 30-minute time frame and had to open, develop and close their story within that time. The hour-long series that came along a little later began using mild cliffhangers for the commercial breaks. In some of them—like *Man from U.N.C.L.E.*, *Mission Impossible*, *Cannon*, *Wild, Wild West*, etc.—the little cliffhangers just before commercials—designed to bring you back to the same channel after your trip to the refrigerator, or around the dial—were often quite good. A few were even worthy of being called genuine cliffhangers; but most were little things like a light switch being activated, or a doorknob turning, while the hero was conducting a clandestine search. When the commercials were over, the story resumed to show the hand or key belonged to a friendly ally, or the hero had quickly found a safe place to hide. But, unmistakably, the cliffhanger theory was at work: create the excitement of wondering, and they will return. For many years, that was all we could hope for or expect from TV.

The mini-series offered a little more. They compressed into five or six nights a compact series of episodes, each concluding with a number of unanswered questions or unresolved situations, which the viewer had to return to the next night to find out about. By the end of the next night's episode, they had been dealt with and advanced to further points of unanswered questions and unresolved situations. Close to the old serials in concept, but still missing the magic ingredient—the cliffhangers.

The most recent "major" mini-series—*North and South: Book II* on ABC—then took another step in what serial lovers would call the "right" direction. One episode of the six-night series ended with one of the primary heroes—a Union army general—captured and held in an infamous Confederate prison, on the verge of being attacked by the brutal warden. Pretty close to being as genuine a cliffhanger as you might want.

And, another concluded with a sensational explosion, as the other hero—a Confederate army general—closed in on a treacherous underground operation aimed at the assassination of Confederate President Jefferson Davis and the overthrow of his government. Involved in the plot was the general's own sister and a former West Point classmate of his. The explosion was the blowing up of the secret arsenal they had amassed. Even though the hero was not in direct jeopardy, the episode ended with that gigantic explosion, and almost—for a split second or so—even "felt" like a serial.

However, these were exceptions rather than the rule, and still just substitutes for actual cliffhangers. So, even though another step in the right direction was taken, we've still got a long way to go.

As a confessed (and admittedly pretty stubborn) purist on the subject, I will continue to wait for the day someone can screw up the courage to produce an action series of the "Indiana Jones" quality (rather than the silly mess they served up in *Golden Monkey* and *Bring 'em Back*) and put it into the *Dallas-Dynasty* format, with a genuine cliffhanger at the end of each episode (not a dramatic or emotional substitute) that would really give us the excitement of wondering. If that series ever comes, and I am still writing this column each month when it does, I will proclaim it to you proudly in all capital letters.

I get excited just thinking about it. But, will it ever happen? I wonder.

After nearly 30 years, there were cliffhangers again. And, though they were only versions and variations, they were cliffhangers. It was good to see them again. For the keepers of the flame, it finally began to feel almost as if there might be a chance of revival for the kind of excitement they had been trying so hard to keep alive. If not exactly that, it was at least movement in the right direction.

George Wallace, as "Commando Cody" *(left)*, and leading lady Aline Towne, in a publicity photo for *Radar Men from the Moon*—Republic, 1952—which was shown on the American Movie Classics channel as a lead-in to "The Republic Pictures Story."

And, even though Dallas *wiped out all its three cliffhangers by declaring that whole season a "dream," we had what looked like the genuine thing for a whole summer.*

Now that the cliffhanger has been restored to some level of its former appeal, the natural thing to wonder is, "What next?" In the format of an action serial chapter, there was usually a scene following the takeout when the principle good guys gathered to decide what their next move would be. Or, there would be a meeting of the principle bad guys to plot their next act of skullduggery. These scenes served to set up the situation and the resulting action for the remainder of that episode, which inevitably led up to the next cliffhanger.

Linda Stirling as the Tiger Woman. *The Tiger Woman*—Republic, 1944—was shown on cable TV's American Movie Classics channel in 1991 under its reissue title, *Perils of the Darkest Jungle.*

In a relative sense, we are now at the point following the takeout, waiting to see what will transpire next in the ongoing saga of the serial story form. On an encouraging note, one of the cable television channels, American Movie Classics, has produced a two-hour special on Republic Pictures, in which the importance of the serial to that studio was stressed. To coincide with its presentation, they ran—one chapter per week—two of Republic's serials, **Radar Men from** the Moon *and* The Tiger Woman, *under its rerelease title,* Perils of the Darkest Jungle. *It caused quite a stir among western and serial fans.*

There are probably no bad guys in meetings anywhere, plotting deliberately to wreck or destroy the cliffhanger's return to prominence, but there are definitely good guys holding meetings in efforts to save and promote that return.

Alive and Well— And Going Strong
January 1990

When you ask director William Witney which serial he thinks was the best of the 24 he directed, or co-directed, most serial fans know that he is likely to answer *Drums of Fu Manchu.* And, that is placing it above 23 others that are considered by almost everyone to be the "best of the best" during the serial's "Golden Age." It was the tenth serial he co-directed with John English and featured young actor Henry Brandon in the title role, with the versatile William Royle as Sir Nayland Smith, and handsome Robert Kellard as the young action hero, Allan Parker. Released in 1940, it was Witney's 12th serial (he earlier co-directed *The Painted Stallion* and *S.O.S. Coast Guard* with Alan James), and marked the midway point, in numbers, of his serial career. After the 17 with English, he directed four solo—*Spy Smasher, Perils of Nyoka, King of the Mounties* and *G-Men vs. the Black Dragon*—and one more after World War II ended—*The Crimson Ghost,* with Fred Bannon as co-director. In addition to the 17 he co-directed with Witney, John English did one other alone—*Daredevils of the West*—and one with Elmer Clifton co-directing—*Captain America.*

Practically every serial buff I ever knew places *Drums of Fu Manchu* at or close to the top of his list of favorites also. It is one great serial, and deserves to be run more than just once, whenever a top-quality continued picture is desired. Which brings me to the subject at hand:

Every Friday night possible, a group of serial and western fans here in the Charlotte area—guys like Larry Reed, Clay Satcher, Bob Green, Graham Talbott, Tommy Hildreth, Ernie Marion, Leonard Kelly and I—meet at Wayne Short's house to look at a couple of series westerns and a serial chapter. Currently, we are showing *Drums of Fu Manchu* for at least the fourth time since the group first met at Clay's house over 15 years ago. And it still seems new and exciting as we wait each week to see the next episode. As much as the good westerns we have watched over the years, it has been the serials that have kept our Friday night group glued together.

Drums of Fu Manchu—Republic, 1940—*From left:* Robert Kellard, William Royle, and four bad guys. Director William Witney's favorite of two dozen serials he directed or codirected during the Golden Age of serials.

And the same is true of many other similar groups. Out of these groups, some pretty nice things have resulted.

The friendship and fellowship established in the Charlotte group led to the desire to share what we enjoyed with others. That led to the establishment of the Charlotte Western Film Fair in 1980, when it was brought over from St. Louis, where it had been held for several years. To properly undergird that venture, a non-profit organization was formed and named The Western Film Preservation Society, Inc., with Wayne Short elected president.

Shortly thereafter, the enthusiasm began to spread; and, in 1981, a chapter of the Society was established in Raleigh, N.C., with Edgar Wyatt as its president. The great western film star, Charles Starrett, was named as permanent honorary president. The Raleigh chapter meets on the third Thursday evening of each month at North Carolina State University's McKimmon Center, and is always well attended.

In 1984, the Raleigh chapter took on the job of hosting the Western Film Fair, partly to give the Charlotte guys a temporary "break," and partly to welcome to North Carolina their beloved honorary president,

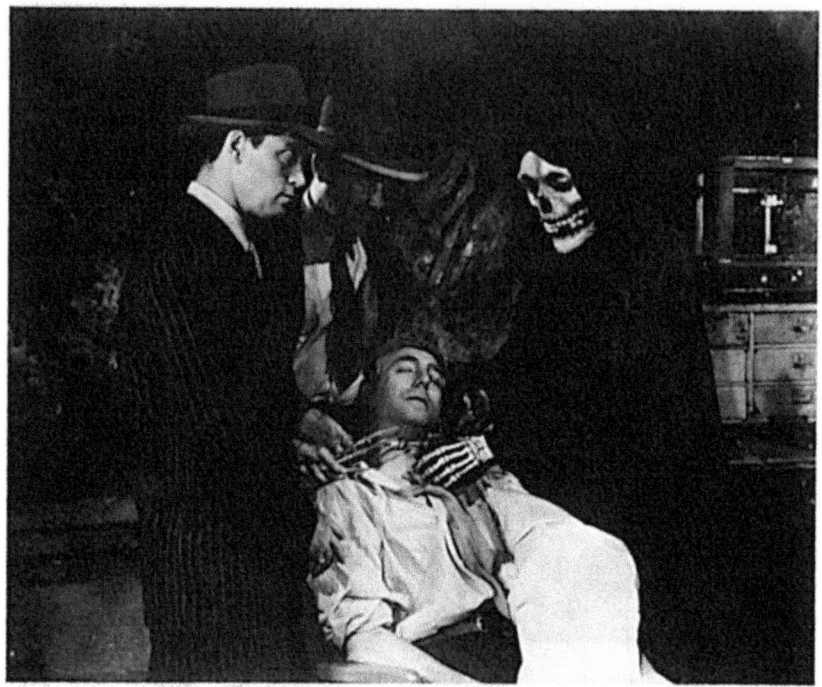

The Crimson Ghost—Republic, 1946: Clayton Moore *(left)*, who usually played heroes—and was soon to become part of the Lone Ranger legend—playing a bad guy; Kenne Duncan *(center)*, one of serialdom's top bad guys, playing a good-guy professor; and a mystery villain in the classic tradition. This serial had it all—and it was the final one directed by William Witney.

the legendary "Durango Kid" himself, Charles Starrett. After four years back in Charlotte, the Film Fair was again hosted by the Raleigh group in 1989.

Helping out ever since the Western Film Fair first came to Charlotte, have been serial and western fans from many other groups like those in the two host cities. For example, one group of men in the Gastonia, N.C., area who meet regularly to show serials and westerns has been strongly supported by friends of mine like the brothers Jerry and Bill Gunter, and veteran film collector Bill Moses. John Rutherford and his friends keep the flame alive in Radford, Virginia; and Mack Houston and a group of his buddies have been gathering to watch "shoot-em-ups" and "cliffhangers" for years in the Old Dominion state.

The print of *Drums of Fu Manchu* now being watched in Charlotte was recently acquired in a trade from a member of yet another great group of action fans in the Hickory, N.C., area who meet on the second Saturday of every month in Sawmills, N.C. That member, Cameron Monroe, is part of a group who call themselves the "Best of the West Film Club," and meet at the home of a member who has dubbed his film projection set-up as "Gwynn's Mini-Theatre," his name being Gwynn Bowman. This group is currently following the adventures of Wild Bill Elliott in the great Columbia serial, *The Valley of Vanishing Men,* using a print borrowed from a member of our Charlotte group. Cameron and fellow-member Bob Mays (who always has a lot of terrific photos, lobby cards and one-sheets for sale) recently visited the Charlotte group on a Friday night, and then extended an invitation for the Charlotte guys to return the visit.

These are just a few of the many groups in the two Carolinas, Virginia and Tennessee, who regularly gather to enjoy the good old "B" westerns and great action serials. There are many others who also keep alive the interest in these great films by meeting and enjoying them with the same enthusiasm as when we were kids and the films were new. And, there is one group to which most of them also belong and lend support—the "granddaddy of them all":

The Old-Time Western Film Club, in Siler City, N.C.

Recently, Siler City, N.C., was the focus of national attention, when one of its most revered citizens passed away. Actress Frances Bavier, who had played Aunt Bee on *The Andy Griffith Show* and *Mayberry, R.F.D.* television shows, had retired and moved to Siler City after production ceased on those shows, and had lived there quietly for about 20 years. When she died in December 1989, the entire nation mourned the passing of Aunt Bee, and the citizens of Siler City bade goodbye to a lady whose presence in the town had become a part of their daily lives. So, for a few days, everybody in the country knew about Siler City. But, western and serial fans have known about Siler City for much longer than that.

Every other month since the late 1960s, western fans from Maryland to Florida have converged on Siler City for an all-day showing of westerns, serials, comedies, cartoons, newsreels, silent classics, or whatever good films Milo Holt could come up with. This gathering is known as "The Old-Time Western Film Club," and was started by Milo as a way to share his interest in westerns with other people who expressed the same interest. Over the years, this gathering has attracted as few as ten or twelve (when the weather was extremely bad) to as many as 150 (when a guest celebrity like Sunset Carson or Lash LaRue was expected to be there). Several years ago, Milo's get-together was held at the Sunset Theatre in Asheboro, N.C.; and, for a while was held at the Curtis Theatre in Liberty, N.C.. But, Siler City is the home of the Old-Time Western Film Club; and it keeps going back there.

Many people who remembered the serials and westerns of their youth have come to Siler City out of curiosity, and left as full-fledged film collectors. (There has always been a lot of "parking-lot trading" going on as well as films being shown.) Some of them have gone back home and started up the local groups that we mentioned earlier. And, it is not possible to say how many lasting friendships have started there between people standing or sitting together and reminiscing about favorite films they love, or sharing movie-related experiences from their childhoods with each other.

There are those who say that the advent of video tape, which makes everything available to everybody at prices we all can afford, has destroyed film collecting as we have known it. And, there is no doubt it has changed things considerably. They say it will eventually destroy interest in old movies, since "familiarity breeds contempt." But, there is one thing we all have observed about video tape that is almost a phenomenon—and what gives me hope that film collecting as such will survive and continue to thrive:

Almost all viewing of video tape is done alone. Or, with one or two others at most. At home. Away from anyone else. By impulse. There is no anticipation; no preparation; no comparison of views; no critique; no sharing. It makes watching a movie a lonely thing to do. And that could, indeed, lead to the disintegration of our hobby.

But, when you get together with eight or ten or twelve—or a hundred and ten or twelve—other serial fans and watch Henry Brandon go through his paces as the evil Dr. Fu Manchu on a movie screen—even for the fourth time—you revive what brought us together in the first place so many years ago: the thrill of enjoying an exciting movie, shared with others who are enjoying the same thrill.

And in that we have hope. For, so long as the small groups of loyal western and serial fans continue to get together to watch films, that thrill is alive and well—and going strong.

When students of the cinema discuss films, they discuss them by specific titles, by the leading actors and/or actresses, by the directors, by the producers, or by the authors of the stories or screenplays. Each film is a separate entity, a complete work, a different subject. There is never any discussion about the form of the film. It is expected that the film will have a definite plot, with an opening, an introduction of characters, a development of story line, a climax, and a close. There is no need to expound on the mechanical structure of the film; it is always the same. It is a motion picture, and all movies are acceptable. But there are two exceptions.

Although films about the West and films presented in chapters have specific titles, actors and actresses, directors, producers, and writers; are separate, complete works on different subjects; and have plots, openings, introduction of

Top: From left: **Louise Currie, William Benedict, and Frank Coghlan, Jr.,** in a tense scene from *Adventures of Captain Marvel*—Republic, 1941. An interview with Coghlan was included as part of "The Republic Pictures Story" on the American Movie Classics cable television channel in March 1991. *Bottom:* **Frank Coghlan, Jr.** *(left),* as Billy Batson, and **Nigel De Brulier** as Shazam, in what is probably the most widely recognized serial photo. *Adventures of Captain Marvel*—Republic, 1941, was, in the opinion of many, the best of the best!

characters, story development, climaxes, and closes, many of the same students of cinema dismiss them with a wave of the hand as "westerns" and "serials," without any serious effort to analyze them as motion pictures. It is almost as if these critics are saying, "Oh, yes. They are films; but they are just types, with no real value."

This is the essence of prejudice, and it is what serials and westerns have had to bear since their creation—from motion picture executives, who created them to save their fortunes; from studios, that depended upon them to stave off bankruptcy; from the critics, who refused to see the value in anything as basic as raw entertainment; and even from some of the actors and actresses who played in them, so they could keep bread on their tables.

The only ones who weren't prejudiced—unless it could be considered "reverse prejudice"—were the people who kept coming back to see them every week.

And, now that these films are again becoming useful, maybe that group will grow. Who knows? Maybe, after all this time, we're getting through at last.

Index

ABC Television Network 82, 234, 235
Academy of Motion Picture Arts and Sciences 63
Ace Drummond 84, 99, 131, 179
Adams, Ernie 45, 138
Adventures of Captain Africa 69, 158
Adventures of Captain Marvel x, xi, xii, 25, 79, 80, 81, 82, 85, 99, 129, 143, 197, 243
Adventures of Frank and Jesse James 99, 144
Adventures of Frank Merriwell 42, 57, 231
Adventures of Red Ryder 8, 26, 75, 79, 85, 99, 106, 125, 140, 163, 171, 197, 210, 215
Adventures of Sir Galahad 69, 137, 198
Adventures of Smilin' Jack 85, 189, 190, 193
"The Adventures of Superman" (TV series) 115, 116, 167
Adventures of the Flying Cadets 41, 117, 125
Aldridge, Kay x, 43, 112, 213
Alexander, Richard 140
"Alfred Hitchcock Presents" (TV series) 234
Allen, Rex 198
Allied Artists Pictures Corp. 99, 109, 111, 115
Alyn, Kirk x, 43, 65, 87, 93, 111, 167, 195
American Humane Association 80
American Movie Classics (TV channel) 236, 237, 243
An American in Paris 6
And Now Tomorrow 126

Anderson, Eve 49, 104, 115
Andrews, Stanley 8, 140
"Andy Griffith Show" (TV series) 241
Annie (stage musical) 168
Apollo Theatre (Hollywood, CA) ix
Arbuckle, Roscoe "Fatty" 223
Arlen, Richard 116
Armstrong, M.L. 191
Armstrong, Neil 224
Armstrong, Robert 8, 76, 117
Ates, Roscoe 109
Atlanta Film and Memorabilia Fair x
Atom Man vs. Superman 195
Atwill, Lionel xi
Autry, Gene 13, 77, 79, 97, 99, 122, 141, 143, 151, 152, 162, 197, 198

Bacon, David 54
Bacon, Rod 54
Bagni, John 202
Bakaleinikoff, Mischa 25
Bakewell, William 117
Ballew, Smith 79
Bandolero 77, 80
Barbour, Alan 227
Barcroft, Roy 45, 46, 47, 54, 127, 128, 146
Bardette, Trevor 10, 131
Barry, Donald "Red" 29, 43, 79, 99, 106, 111, 112, 122, 152, 162, 163, 197
Batman 42, 82, 85, 105, 107, 197, 210
Batman: The Movie 83, 85, 165, 193, 195
Batman: The TV Series 82

245

INDEX

Batman and Robin 42, 69, 83, 85, 187, 194, 198
Batman and Robin (comic strip) 83
Battling with Buffalo Bill 99
Bavier, Frances 241
The Beatles 224
Beatty, Warren 83, 167
Beebe, Ford xi, 70, 77, 125, 182
Beemer, Brace 157
Beery, Noah, Jr. 15, 138
Beery, Noah, Sr. 8
Beethoven, Ludwig Van 172
Belle Starr 12
Below the Border 79
Ben-Hur 6, 60, 61, 63, 71, 75, 218
Benard, Ray 107, 122
Benedict, Billy 93, 117, 243
Bennet, Spencer G. xi, 57, 59, 63, 64, 65, 66, 67, 68, 69, 70, 75
Bennett, Bruce 15
The Best of the West Film Club 241
Best Years of Our Lives 6
Bey, Turhan 191
Biberman, Abner 8
Bickford, Charles 8, 126, 127, 140
The Big Reel xiii
Birth of a Nation 133, 135
Black Arrow 79, 128
The Black Widow 67, 79
Blackhawk 49, 69, 81, 85, 87, 138, 144, 187, 188
Blackhawk Films 3
Blake, Pamela 48
Blazing the Overland Trail 13, 25, 44, 65, 69
Blue, Monte 8, 109, 140
Bogart, Humphrey 199
"Bonanza" (TV series) 47, 199
Bonomo, Joe 1, 52
Booth, Adrian 138
Bosch, Peter 94
Boteler, Wade 179
Bowman, Gwynn 241
Boyd, William x, 146
Brandon, Henry x, 127, 238, 242
Brannon, Fred C. 238
Brenda Starr (movie) 83, 168
Brenda Starr, Reporter 43, 85, 112, 169, 232
Brent, George 6
Brick Bradford 69, 85, 138, 143, 198

Bridges, Lloyd 7, 106, 163
Briggs, Don 57
Brissac, Virginia 48
Brix, Herman 15, 77, 79, 143, 156
Broken Arrow 17, 80
Brown, Joe E. 152
Brown, Johnny Mack 13, 32, 33, 44, 56, 97, 98, 99, 100, 104, 113, 115, 116, 122, 152, 168, 172, 197
Brown, Mary 19
Brown, Max 19
Brown, Stanley 141
Brown, Tom 189, 192
Bruce Gentry 69, 85, 145
Brun, Frederick 120
Buck Rogers 85, 92, 125, 168, 172, 179, 202
Buck Rogers (movie) 81, 82, 85
Buffalo Bill (movie) 12
Burnette, "Smiley" 151
Burroughs, Edgar Rice 83
Buster, Budd 138
Butts, R. Dale 26
Byrd, Ralph 31, 44, 111, 140, 165, 167, 168, 211

CBS Television Network 169, 173, 207, 224, 234
Cagney, James 20
Call of the Savage 138
Cameron, Rod 37, 43, 93, 99, 116, 117, 118, 119, 120, 121, 122, 152, 163, 197
Canadian Mounties vs. Atomic Invaders 144
Cannes Film Festival 48
"Cannon" (TV series) 234
Canutt, Enos Edward 60, 63
Canutt, Joe 61
Canutt, Yakima 38, 41, 43, 48, 53, 54, 60, 61, 62, 63, 75, 92, 100, 203
Capp, Al 167
Captain America 5, 81, 82, 85, 119, 139, 169, 197, 238
Captain America (movie) 168
Captain America (TV movie) 81, 82
Captain Blood 91
Captain Marvel (comic strip) 85

Index   247

Captain Midnight 85, 125, 232
Captain Video 69, 198
Carey, Harry, Sr. xi, 13, 125, 199
Carmen, Jean 41, 43, 48, 49, 104
Carol, Sue 91
Carr, Thomas 65
Carroll, John 15, 54
Carson, Sunset 29, 198, 241
Casablanca 6
Cassidy, Edward 138
Cassidy, Hopalong 56, 83, 116, 143, 197
Chandler, Lane 156
Chaney, Creighton 178
Chaney, Lon, Jr. 2, 15, 125, 176, 178
Chaplin, Charles 223
Chapman, Marguerite 104
Cherwin, Richard 26
Chesebro, George 37, 39, 45, 137
Ciannelli, Eduardo xi, 117, 125
Clancy of the Mounted 20, 99
The Clansman (book) 133
Clapham, Leonard 88, 89
Clarke, Richard 54
Classic Film Collector 3
Clifton, Elmer 238
Cline, Anita 2
Cline, Edna 19
The Clutching Hand 131
Coates, Phyllis 112, 114, 115, 116
Cobb, Edmund 45, 138
Cody of the Pony Express 41
Coffin, Tristram 42, 43, 138, 144
Coghlan, Frank, Jr. xii, 43, 81, 93, 243
Colbert, Claudette 199
"The Colbys" (TV series) 234
Collins, Monte 109
Colombo, Alberto 156, 170
Come to the Bower (school song) 26
Congo Bill 66
Conklin, Chester 20, 167
Consolidated Film Industries 62
Conway, Morgan 167
Cooper, Gary 77, 79, 178
Cooper, Jackie xi
Cooper, Tex 9
Copperfield, David 215, 216, 217, 218, 219
Corrigan, Ray "Crash" 13, 43, 99, 100, 104, 105, 106, 111, 112, 113, 124, 151, 162, 197
Cotton, Carolina 57
The Cousins 91, 92
"The Cowboys" (TV series) 80
Crabbe, Larry "Buster" x, 16, 41, 43, 69, 99, 111, 113, 127, 140, 152, 157, 196, 197, 203
Craig, James 9, 15, 23, 42, 230
Cramer, Richard 109
Cravat, Noel 120
Craven, James 125, 126, 144
Crawford, Joan 162
Crawford, John 41, 43, 100, 138, 144
Crehan, Joseph 8, 117
The Crimson Ghost 67, 99, 131, 137, 138, 143, 144, 238, 240
Croft, Douglas 106, 107
Cunard, Grace 51
Currie, Louise 243
Curtin, Jane 208
Curtis, Dick 45
Curtis, Ken 7
Curtis Theatre (Liberty, NC) 241

DC Publications, Inc. 169
"Dallas" (TV series) x, xi, 205, 207, 208, 211, 212, 234, 235, 236
Danger Island 231
Dangers of the Canadian Mounted 144
Daredevils of the Red Circle 11, 25, 79, 85, 104, 128, 137, 146, 171, 197
Daredevils of the West 13, 14, 31, 99, 119, 120, 197, 198, 232, 238
Daughter of Don Q 79, 125, 138
Davidson, John xi, 142
Davis, Jefferson 235
Deadwood Dick 130, 131, 138
Dean, Eddie 49, 56, 105, 116, 198
"Death Valley Days" (TV series) 8, 140
De Brulier, Nigel xi, 243
De Carlo, Yvonne 117, 121
Delevanti, Cyril 11
De Mille, Cecil B. ix, 44
De Normand, George 43, 91, 92, 93
The Desert Hawk 128
Desmond, William ix, 1
Desperadoes of the West 185

248 INDEX

Destination Moon (movie) 126
Destry Rides Again (movie) 172
Detective Comics (magazine) 83
The Devil Horse 125
Dew, Eddie 116
Dick Tracy 42, 131, 151, 165, 197
Dick Tracy (comic strip) 83, 85
Dick Tracy: The Movie 165, 167, 169
Dick Tracy, Detective 167
Dick Tracy Meets Gruesome 167
Dick Tracy Returns 128, 151, 165, 168
Dick Tracy vs. Crime, Inc. 165
Dick Tracy vs. Cueball 167
Dick Tracy's Dilemma 167
Dick Tracy's G-Men 7, 25, 31, 49, 79, 104, 126, 144, 165, 211
Disneyland 49
Doc Savage, Man of Bronze 83, 85
Dr. Jekyll and Mr. Hyde 146
Dodge City 143
Don Daredevil Rides Again 7, 185, 186
Don Winslow of the Coast Guard 84
Don Winslow of the Navy 84
Downs, Johnny 117
Dracula 127, 172
Drake, Oliver 42, 61, 149, 150, 151, 152, 153, 155, 160, 173
Drums of Fu Manchu 25, 85, 125, 141, 197, 202, 238, 239, 240
Dubin, Joseph 26
Duel in the Sun 17
Dumas, Alexander 83
Dumbrille, Douglas 8
Duncan, Johnny 83, 193
Duncan, Kenneth xi, 45, 140, 240
Durante, Jimmy 20
Duryea, George 91
"Dynasty" (TV series) 205, 234, 235

Eagle Lion Pictures Corp. 116
Eason, B. Reeves 70
Edison, Thomas A. 223
"Egmont" (overture) 170
Elliott, Gordon 97, 107, 109, 122, 162
Elliott, Wild Bill 13, 32, 35, 44, 77, 79, 97, 99, 107, 110, 111, 112, 115, 122, 131, 162, 197, 241

Elliott, William 97
English, John 67, 70, 238
Equus 60

Fairbanks, Douglas, Jr. 80
Fairbanks, Douglas, Sr. xi
"Falcon Crest" (TV series) 205, 234
Falkenburg, Jinx 7, 104, 106
Fargo 115
The Farmer's Daughter 126, 140
Farnum, William 8
Farrell, Tommy 41, 196
Fawcett, Jimmy 91
Fawcett Publications Corp. 80
Faye, Alice 15
Federal Agents vs. Underworld, Inc. 125, 145
Federal Operator 99 125, 138, 139
Ferguson, Al 37
Feuer, Cy 22, 25, 170, 171
The Fighting Buckaroo 141
The Fighting Devil Dogs 131, 157, 171, 197
The Fighting Marines 103, 104, 131
Fighting with Kit Carson 8, 15, 32, 97, 98, 125, 162
Fingerprints 231
Finley, Evelyn 49, 104, 112, 113, 114
First Baptist Church, Concord, NC 223, 224, 225
Fiske, Richard 230
Flaming Frontiers 25, 32, 97, 128, 162, 172
"The Flash" (TV series) 169, 173
Flash Gordon 15, 23, 92, 128, 140, 168, 172, 179, 197, 202, 226
Flash Gordon (comic strip) 84
Flash Gordon (movie) 81
Flash Gordon Conquers the Universe 128, 157, 179
Flash Gordon's Trip to Mars 127, 128, 179, 203
"Flight of the Bumblebee" 170
Flying Disc Man from Mars 112, 125, 144
"The Flying Dutchman" (overture) 170
Flying G-Men 42, 49, 138, 230
Flynn, Errol 91, 143, 189

Foran, Dick 23, 197
Ford, Francis 53
Ford, John 161, 163
Fort Apache 12
Foulger, Byron 48
Foy, Fred 157
Frankenstein 172
From Out of the Past (book) 154, 159
Frontier Gal 121
Frost, Terry 143
Fuller, Mary 51
"Fury" (TV series) 199

G-Men Never Forget 99, 144, 145, 146
G-Men vs. the Black Dragon 99, 117, 118, 119, 120, 197, 238
Gable, Clark 15, 199
Gangbusters 25, 75, 85, 172, 189, 214
Gasoline Alley (comic strip) 154
Gay, Gregory 144
Geary, Bud 230
Ghost of Zorro 99, 144
Gibson, Helen 51, 52, 53
Gibson, Hoot 53, 97, 116, 197
Gibson, Walter 169
Gifford, Frances x, 101, 102, 105, 112, 122
Girard, Joseph 8
The Girl Who Dared 60
Glickman, Mort 26, 170
Godwin, David 176
Going My Way 6
Gone with the Wind 6, 37, 218
Gordon, Bruce 177
Gordon of Ghost City 97
Got, Roland 120
Gould, Chester 83, 167
Government Agents vs. Phantom Legion 112
Grable, Betty 15
Graham, Fred 92, 120, 144
Grant, Cary 199
Grant, Kirby 197
Grant, Maxwell 169
Graser, Earl 157
Gray, Lorna 5, 138

The Great Adventures of Captain Kidd 138, 144
The Great Adventures of Wild Bill Hickok 32, 49, 79, 97, 109, 162, 197
The Great Alaskan Mystery 15
The Great Bar 20 83, 85
The Great Train Robbery 88, 133, 140
The Greatest Story Ever Told 6
Green, Bob 238
Green, Duke 92, 120
The Green Archer (silent) x
The Green Archer (sound) 37, 125, 143
The Green Hornet 85, 92, 179, 180, 181, 182
"The Green Hornet" (TV series) 82
Grey, Zane 182
Griffith, D.W. 133
Gulliver, Dorothy 38, 43, 44, 100, 150, 176
Gunfighters of the Northwest 38, 99, 115, 144
"Gunsmoke" (TV series) 16, 45, 47, 163, 199
Gunter, Bill 240
Gunter, Jerry 240
Gwynn's Mini-Theatre 241

Hadley, Reed 15, 54, 143
Hagman, Larry xi
Hale, Creighton 53
Hale, Monte 198
Hallelujah! I'm a Bum! 20
The Happy Land 126
A Hard Day's Night 224
Harlan, Kenneth 211
Hart, John 69, 157, 158
Hart, William S. 112, 199
Hatton, Raymond 138
Haunted Harbor 128
"Have Gun—Will Travel" (TV series) 199
"Hawaii Five-O" (TV series) 8
Hawk of the Hills x
Hawk of the Wilderness 25, 79, 140
Hawks, Frank 67
Hayden, Russell 116, 152

Hayes, George "Gabby" 32, 34, 93, 109
Hazards of Helen 53
Healey, Myron 115
Healy, Bill 54
Hearn, Edward 177
"Hebrides Overture" ("Fingal's Cave") 25
Hellfire 111
Hello, Henry (radio show) 116
Hepburn, Katharine 199
Heroes of the Flames 97, 177, 231
Hersholt, Jean, Jr. 57
Hervey, Irene 75, 76, 214
Heston, Charlton 61
Hi-Yo, Silver! 208
Hickman, Howard 8
Hicks, Russell 8
High Noon 12, 17, 178
Hildreth, Tommy 109, 238
Hill, Robert F. 70
"Hill Street Blues" (TV series) 234
Hillie, Verna 76
Hinson, Lewis 90
Hitchcock, Alfred 123, 234
Hitler's Children 116
Hobart, Rose 191
Holland, David 154, 155, 159, 173
Holmes, Helen 51, 52, 53
Holt, Jack 116, 145
Holt, Jennifer 40, 41, 43, 112, 114, 116
Holt, Milo 241
Holt, Tim 48, 116, 152, 197
Holt of the Secret Service 116, 144
Home in Wyomin' 79
Hop Harrigan 41, 85, 117, 187
Horne, James W. 67, 75
Houdini, Harry 212, 213
Houston, George 152
Houston, Mack 240
Houstoncon 74 93
How Green Was My Valley 218
Hull, Warren 44, 179, 180
The Hurricane Express 8, 129, 160, 161
Hutchison, Charles 67

In Old Cheyenne 79
In Old Santa Fe 162
In the Nick of Time (book) ix, xiii, 1, 4, 5, 19, 41, 149, 150, 173
Indiana Jones and the Last Crusade 84, 85
Indiana Jones and the Temple of Doom 120, 121, 202
The Indians Are Coming 13, 44, 97, 176, 177, 178
Ingram, Jack 37, 45, 48, 137, 144
"Inner Sanctum" (TV series) 234
International Pictures Co. 197
The Invisible Man 172
"The Invisible Man" (TV series) 234
The Invisible Monster 144
The Iron Claw 132, 133, 137, 143
The Iron Mask (silent) xi
Isley, Phyllis 104, 106
"It Pays to Be Ignorant" (radio series) 224
It's a Bird, It's a Plane, It's Superman 82

Jack Armstrong 85, 128, 158, 187, 198
Jackson, Selmer 8
James, Alan xi, 238
Jesse James (movie) 12, 140
Jesse James Rides Again 67, 99, 125, 144, 145, 198
Jewel of the Nile 121
Johnny Belinda 126
Johnson, Van 189
Jolley, I. Stanford 37, 45, 137
Jolson, Al 20
Jones, Buck ix, 13, 44, 96, 97, 197
Jones, Dickie 109
Jones, Gordon 179, 180, 181, 182
Jones, Jennifer 7, 104, 122
Jordan, Bobby 117
Jory, Victor 37, 39, 43, 143, 169
Jungle Drums of Africa 99, 115, 144
Jungle Girl 25, 101, 102, 112
Jungle Jim 25, 84, 85, 125, 172, 179
Jungle Mystery 99, 231
Jungle Queen 7, 104
Junior G-Men 92, 172
Junior G-Men of the Air 7

Kalem Productions 53
Kane, Bob 83
Karloff, Boris 125
Katzman, Sam xi, 49, 57, 65, 67, 69, 75, 148, 153, 167, 185, 188, 196, 197
Keaton, Buster 20, 167, 223
Keaton, Michael 83
Keene, Tom 91, 113
Kellard, Robert 141, 142, 202, 238, 239
Kelly, John 180
Kelly, Leonard 238
Kemp, Hal 29
Kemp, T.D. 29
Kennedy, Edgar 167
Kent, Robert 143
Kerr, Donald 203
Key, Donald xiii
King, Charles xi, 37, 39, 45, 47, 136, 137, 138, 141, 144
King, James 170, 171, 173
King, John 99, 113, 131
King, Pee Wee 29
King Kong 8, 20
King of the Carnival 144
King of the Congo 69
King of the Forest Rangers 125
King of the Kongo 85
King of the Mounties 8, 31, 99, 119, 232, 238
King of the Rocketmen 42, 125, 138, 145, 184, 185, 186
King of the Royal Mounted 25, 31, 79, 85, 99, 141, 171, 197, 232
King of the Texas Rangers 24, 26, 140
Kirk, Jack 138
Knight, Fuzzy 172
"Knots Landing" (TV series) 205, 234
Kohler, Fred, Sr. xi
Kortman, Robert xi, 137
Kruger, Harold "Stubby" 88
Ku Klux Klan 133

Lackteen, Frank x, xi
Ladd, Alan 199
Laemmle, Carl 178
Landis, Carole 104

Lane, Allan 13, 28, 29, 30, 99, 111, 115, 117, 122, 142, 197, 198
Lang, Harry 31
Langdon, Harry 20
La Rue, Alfred 41, 47, 49, 56, 112
La Rue, Lash 29, 36, 41, 47, 49, 53, 56, 112, 116, 198, 241
The Last Frontier (silent) x
The Last Frontier (sound) 15, 20, 65, 125, 176, 177, 178
The Last of the Mohicans xi
Lauter, Harry 92, 144, 145
Lava, William 18, 25, 156, 170, 171
Lease, Rex 158
Le Baron, Bert 120
The Legend of the Lone Ranger 12, 81, 82, 85, 164, 168
Letz, George 15, 43, 156
Levine, Nat xi, 53, 60, 67, 75, 76, 97, 98, 148, 150, 153, 161, 162
Lewis, George J. 43, 75, 76, 89, 120, 139
The Library of Congress 3
The Lightning Warrior 7
Li'l Abner (black and white movie) 167
Li'l Abner (color movie) 167
Li'l Abner (comic strip) 167
The Lions Club 19
Liszt, Franz 157, 172
Livingston, Robert 13, 43, 99, 100, 151, 157, 158, 162, 163, 197
Lloyd, Harold 223
Loftin, Carey 91
London, Tom 86, 87, 88, 89, 90, 91, 92, 94, 138, 140
The Lone Ranger 13, 15, 41, 49, 79, 81, 140, 150, 151, 153, 154, 155, 156, 157, 160, 197, 208, 232
"The Lone Ranger" (radio series) 156, 173
"The Lone Ranger" (TV series) 99, 158
The Lone Ranger Rides Again 7, 18, 79, 99, 104, 154, 157, 232
Lone Star Productions, Inc. 161
The Lone Star Ranger 91
Long, Robert 180
The Longhorn 115
Lorraine, Louise x
"Lost in Space" (TV series) 199

The Lost Special 231
The Lost Weekend 218
"Lou Grant" (TV series) 7
Lowery, Robert 78, 83, 194
Lucas, George 173, 174, 202, 203
Lugosi, Bela xi, 127, 143
Luke, Keye 179
Lum 'n' Abner 224
Lydecker, Howard, Jr. xi, 214
Lydecker, Theodore xi, 214
Lyden, Pierce 43, 48, 49, 57, 58, 59
Lynch, Norman 229, 231

McCalla, Irish 168
McCoy, Tim 7, 13, 97, 176, 177, 197
McCrea, Joel 88, 140, 143
MacDonald, Edmund 48
McGowan, J.P. xi, 53
McGuire, Don 66
McKim, Dorothy 49
McKim, Sammy 49, 109
McKimmon Center 239
MacMurray, Fred 199
McNear, Howard 16
MacRae, Henry xi, 57, 177, 178
MacReady, George 77, 126, 127
Madonna 165
The Magic of David Copperfield 217
The Magnificent Ambersons 116
Mahoney, Jock 13, 37, 38, 43, 69, 93, 115
Malcomson, Bob 4, 227
Malvern, Paul 161
"The Man from U.N.C.L.E." (TV series) 234
The Man with the Steel Whip 185
Mander, Miles 10, 146
Mandrake, the Magician 85, 180
Manhunt of Mystery Island 67, 128, 129
Manning, Knox 189
Mapes, Ted 77, 78, 80, 92
Marion, Ernie 238
Marsh, Joan 120
Marshall, Tully 8
Martin, Richard 48
The Masked Marvel 54, 88, 93, 119, 120

Mason, Leroy 124, 125, 138, 177
The Master Key 41, 49, 56, 112, 131
Mathews, Carole 78
The Maverick 115
"Mayberry R.F.D." (TV series) 241
Maynard, Ken 13, 76, 97, 129, 162, 197
Mays, Bob 241
A Medal for Benny 126
Melford, Clarence xi
Mendelssohn, Felix 23
Merchants Movie News 19, 20
Meredith, Iris 44
Merton, John 215
Metro-Goldwyn-Mayer Pictures Corp. 15, 20, 42, 71, 104, 146, 147
Meyer, Abe 172, 173
Middleton, Charles xi, 92, 127, 128, 140, 146
Miller, Harold 177
Miller, Walter x, 1, 67, 177
Millhauser, Bertram 67
The Miracle of the Bells 126
The Miracle Rider 13, 77, 97, 128
"Mission Impossible" (TV series) 234
Mr. Lucky 126
Mitchum, John 58
Mitchum, Robert 197, 199
Mix, Tom ix, 13, 77, 97, 197, 199
Monogram Pictures Corp. 32, 42, 99, 100, 115, 116, 152, 161, 162
Monroe, Cameron 241
The Monster and the Ape 79, 127
Montgomery (Letz), George 15, 41
Moore, Clayton 13, 43, 99, 115, 137, 144, 146, 157, 158, 159, 240
Moore, Dennis 48, 56, 115, 126
Moore, Frank 20, 146
Morgan, Ralph 8, 78, 147, 214
Morton, Danny 48
Moses, Bill 240
Mosley, Zack 189
Motion Picture Herald 162
Mower, Jack 177
Mrs. Miniver 218
Mulhall, Jack xi
Murphy, Edna 67
Murray, Forbes 88
The Music of Republic: The Early Years 1937–1941 170, 173

The Music of the Lone Ranger 173
Mutual Radio Network 156
My Darling Clementine 116
The Myrtle Beach, S.C., Sun Times 65
Mysterious Dr. Satan 22, 61, 85, 126, 144, 197, 209, 210
Mysterious Island 68, 69
Mysterious Mr. M 48, 131
The Mysterious Pilot 67
Mystery Mountain 76, 97, 129
Mystery of the Riverboat 219
The Mystery Squadron 97, 131

NBC Television Network 234
Nagel, Anne 9, 179
Naish, J. Carroll xi, 106
The National Barn Dance 162
Neill, Noel x, 115, 195
Newill, Jim 152
Nicholson, Jack 83
Nimoy, Leonard 7
Norm's Nostalgia Club 229
Norris, Edward 104
North and South: Book II 235
North Carolina State University 239

Oakman, Wheeler 141
O'Brien, David 152, 232
O'Brien, George 91, 152, 197
O'Day, Nell 28, 43, 104
Oh, Susanna (folk melody) 26
The Oklahoma Kid 12
The Ol' Time Western Film Club 241
The Oregon Trail 32, 97, 162, 172
Osborne, Bud 37, 39, 44, 140
Osteen, Tom 4
The Outer Limits 234
The Outlaw Press, Inc. 153
Outlaws of Texas 115
Overland Mail 15, 25, 125
Overland with Kit Carson 10, 13, 15, 32, 42, 97, 109, 125, 131, 140
Owens, Granville 167

PRC (Producers Releasing Corp.) 53, 56, 99, 116, 152
The Pacific Electric Railroad ix
Paige, Robert 230
The Painted Stallion 41, 48, 49, 97, 99, 104, 124, 125, 138, 151, 171, 197, 238
The Pale Rider 12
Palmer, Peter 167
Panther Girl of the Kongo 115
Paramount Pictures Corp. 167, 171, 172
Paramount Theatre, Concord, NC 19, 29, 89, 93
Parker, Eddie 55, 92, 120
Parkhurst, "Parky" 229
Pathé Pictures Corp. 53, 67
Patterson, Shirley 42, 44, 105, 106, 107
The Pawn 48
Pearson, Ted 31, 211
Pedreira, Fernando 1, 4
Penn, Leonard 136
Perils of Nyoka 99, 112, 119, 120, 128, 138, 144, 145, 197, 202, 213, 238
Perils of Pauline x, 112
Perils of the Darkest Jungle 237, 238
Perils of the Royal Mounted 38, 104, 141
Perils of the Wilderness 49, 57, 69, 104, 115
Peters, House, Jr. 42, 57
The Phantom 85, 86, 99, 138, 197
The Phantom Creeps 127, 143
The Phantom Empire 77, 97, 162
Phantom of the Air 99, 125, 231
Phantom of the West 99, 150
The Phantom Rider (Republic) 41, 67, 125, 143
The Phantom Rider (Universal) 97
Pichel, Irving 126, 127
Picture Snatchers 20
Pioneer Frontier Days Rodeo 60
Pirate Treasure 52
Pirates of the High Seas 41, 145
Play Ball 67
Pomeroy, Alan 53
Potel, Victor 20
Powell, Lee 9, 79, 156, 157
Powell, William 199
Prairie Gunsmoke 79

"Les Preludes" 157, 170
Previn, Charles 16, 23, 172
Price, Stanley 37, 146
Principal Pictures Corp. 127
Purcell, Dick 5, 54
The Purple Heart 163
The Purple Monster Strikes 66, 67, 125, 126, 128

The Queen Charlotte Hotel 213, 215, 217
Quigley, Charles 137, 143
Quillan, Eddie 104

RKO Radio Pictures Corp. 15, 20, 48, 65, 116, 125, 152, 167, 176, 177
Radar Men from the Moon 99, 137, 144, 236, 237, 238
Radar Patrol vs. Spy King 144, 145, 228
Radio Patrol 85, 92, 179
The Radisson Plaza Hotel 42, 103
Radner, Gilda 207, 208
Raiders of Ghost City 41
Raines, Ella 117
The Range Busters 99, 152
Rawlinson, Herbert 8
Ray, Allene x, 1, 13, 67, 176, 177
Red Barry 11, 85, 92, 172, 179
The Red Rider 97
Red River 12
Red River Valley 79
Red Ryder (comic strip) 85
Reds 85
Reed, Larry 80, 238
Reed, Marshall 43
Reed, Walter 112, 113
Reeve, Christopher 65
Reeves, George 65, 140, 167
Reid, Wallace, Jr. 57
Renaldo, Duncan 13, 44, 120, 124, 138
Renegade Ranger 152
The Republic Pictures Story 236, 237, 243
The Return of Chandu 127

Reynolds, Gene 7
Richmond, Kane 44, 54, 81, 169, 189
The Riddle Rider ix
"Ride of the Valkyrie" 170
Ride the High Country 88, 140
Riders of Death Valley 13, 15, 23, 25, 42, 97, 126, 138, 140, 150
Riders of the Badlands 79
Riebe, Loren 91
"Rienzi" (overture) 170
Ritter, Tex 36, 79, 101, 109, 113, 116, 152, 197
Roach, Bert 20
The Roaring West 97
Robards, Jason, Sr. xi
Roberts, Lee 156
Rockwell, Jack 138
Rogers, Jean x, 203
Rogers, Roy 197, 198
Rohmer, Sax 125
Roman, Ruth 7, 104, 122, 163
Romancing the Stone 121
Rooney, Mickey 104, 189
Rothal, David 154
The Rough Riders 79, 152
The Royal Mounted Patrol 79
The Royal Mounted Rides Again 15
Royce, Lionel 120
Royle, William 202, 238, 239
Rubin, Sam 3
Rustlers of Red Dog 32, 97, 162
Rutherford, Ann 103, 104, 105, 122
Rutherford, John 240

S.O.S. Coast Guard 127, 204, 238
S.P.E.B.S.Q.S.A. 19
Sahara 15, 85
St. Elsewhere 234
St. John, Al "Fuzzy" 49, 99
Salome—Where She Danced 121
Salter, Hans J. 16, 23, 172
Samms, Emma 217
Sande, Walter 84
Sanford, Harry 229
Santa Fe 126
Santschi, Tom 53
Satcher, Clay 238
Saturday Night Live 207, 208

Index

Saturday's Heroes (book) 153
Sawtell, Paul 170, 171, 172
Sawyer, Joe 41
Scancarelli, Jim 154
Science Fiction Theatre 234
Scott, Fred 48
Scott, Randolph 88, 140
Scouts to the Rescue xi
Screen Guild Productions 116
The Sea Hound 49, 187
Sea Raiders 25
Secret Agent X-9 (comic strip) 85
Secret Agent X-9 (1937) 125, 179
Secret Agent X-9 (1945) 7, 106
The Secret Code 42, 67
The Secret of Treasure Island 25, 85, 173
Secret Service in Darkest Africa 37, 67, 93, 99, 117, 118, 119, 120, 121, 202
Sedgwick, Eileen x
Seitz, George B. xi, 67
Selznick Releasing Corp. 91
Sergeant York 77, 79
Serial World (magazine) 94, 229
The Shadow 37, 39, 85, 143
The Shadow (magazine) 169, 173
Shadow of Chinatown 127
Shadow of the Eagle 38, 53, 161
Shane 12, 17
Shannon, Frank 203
Sharpe, David 43, 54, 80, 81, 91, 93, 113, 143, 177
She 126
Sheena, Queen of the Jungle 168
Shields, Brooke 83
Short, Wayne 36, 238, 239
Shrum, Cal 29
Shuster, Joseph 167
Siegel, Jerome 167
Siegel, Sol 151
Silverado 12
Silverheels, Jay 159
Singing in the Rain 218
Skeoch, Thomas 91, 94
Skinner, Frank 23, 172
Sky King 199
Sky Raiders 25, 125
Smith, Brent 109
Smith, Robert 181
Smith, Smilin' Jack 113

So This Is Washington 224
Son of Geronimo 41, 69, 99, 140, 144, 187
Son of Zorro 41, 198
The Song of Bernadette 104, 126, 140
Sousa, John Philip 21
South of St. Louis 143
Southern Attractions, Inc. 29
The Spider Returns 180
The Spider's Web 85, 131, 140, 173, 180, 197
Spielberg, Steven xi, 173, 174, 202, 203, 207
Spy Smasher 80, 81, 85, 104, 119, 120, 145, 197, 206, 214, 238
Spy Smasher Returns 206
Stagecoach 12, 161, 163
"Star Trek" (TV series) 199
Star Wars 131, 182, 202, 203
Starrett, Charles 45, 79, 100, 141, 197, 239, 240
Stars and Stripes Forever 21
State Theatre, Concord, NC 189
Steele, Bob 97, 116, 131, 152, 197
Steele, Tom 37, 43, 54, 55, 86, 88, 91, 92, 93, 94, 120, 177, 215
Stevens, Robert 141
Stewart, James 77, 79, 80
Stewart, Peggy x, 41, 43
Stick to Your Guns 116
Stirling, Linda x, 67, 89, 112, 126, 139, 213, 215, 237
Stoloff, Morris 173
Stone, Milburn 15, 16, 56, 163
Strange, Glenn 45
Stringham, Jim 229
Stuntman (book) 61
Sunset Theatre, Asheboro, NC 241
Superman 63, 65, 69, 70, 81, 85, 138, 144, 182
Superman (cartoon series) 167
Superman (comic strip) 167
Superman: The Movie 167, 182

Tailspin Tommy 81, 84, 164, 179
Tailspin Tommy in the Great Air Mystery 84

Talbott, Graham 141, 238
Taliaferro, Hal 140, 156
Tall in the Saddle 12
Talmage, Richard 52, 53
"Tarzan" (TV series) 83
Taylor, Kent 189, 214
Taylor, Ray xi, 65, 67, 70, 75, 76, 182
Taylor, Robert 189, 192
TEMI 227, 229
Terhune, Max 36, 93, 99, 100, 151, 162
Terrell, Kenneth 91, 120, 177
Terry, Don 84
Tex Granger 79, 85, 141, 198
The Texas Rangers 152
Thayer, Julia 41, 43, 48, 104
Thompson, Bob 36
Thomson, Fred 199
Thorpe, Richard xi
Those Enduring Matinee Idols 227, 229
The Three Mesquiteers 48, 79, 99, 100, 151, 152, 157, 161, 162, 163, 170
The Three Musketeers 131, 161, 162
The Three Musketeers (color movie) 83
The Three Musketeers (silent movie) xi
Three Texas Steers 163
Thunder River Feud 79
Thundercloud, Chief 156
The Tiger Woman 31, 67, 99, 125, 139, 213, 237, 238
Tim Tyler's Luck 85, 179
The Time Tunnel 199
Tomei, Louis 91
Tonto Basin Outlaws 79
Topeka 115
Towne, Aline 236
Tracy, Spencer 199
Trader Tom of the China Seas 92, 144, 145
Treasure of the Sierra Madre 15, 116
Trendle, George W. 156
Trowbridge, Charles 5, 117
20th Century–Fox Film Corp. 15, 49, 80, 82, 85, 91, 104, 141, 168, 193, 195
26 Men 145

The Twilight Zone 234
Tyler, Tom x, 44, 54, 81, 82, 86, 99, 111, 150

Undersea Kingdom 1, 42, 99, 106, 138, 140, 150, 151, 162
Union Pacific 12
United Nations 183
U.S. Steel Corp. 91

The Valley of Vanishing Men 32, 67, 79, 85, 97, 109, 197, 241
Van Sickel, Dale 54, 120, 177
Vengeance of the West 79, 109
Victory Pictures Corp. 127
The Vigilantes Are Coming 99, 138, 157, 162, 197
Villegas, Lucio 152

Wagner, Richard 172
Wakely, Jimmy 116, 152, 153
Wales, Wally 140
Walker, Johnny 177
Wallace, Edgar x
Wallace, George 236
Waller, Eddy 109
Walt Disney Studio 49, 63, 170, 171
Walt Disney World 49
Walton, Jeff 229
War of the Worlds 185
Ward, Burt 82
Warde, Anthony 30, 78
Warner, H.B. 111
Warner Brothers Pictures Corp. 83, 91, 161, 167, 170, 171
Washburn, Bryant, Jr. 57
Washburn, Bryant, Sr. xi
Wayne, Carol 109
Wayne, John 38, 53, 60, 62, 77, 131, 161, 162, 163, 164
Weaver, Doodles 167
Wells, H.G. 185
West, Adam 82, 195
West Point Military Academy 235
The Western Film Fair 36, 37, 38,

39, 40, 42, 43, 47, 48, 49, 53, 71, 80, 103, 104, 105, 112, 114, 121, 163, 200, 239, 240
The Western Film Preservation Society, Inc. 36, 239
Western Union 12
What? No Beer! 20
Wheeler, Howard 176
The Whispering Shadow 127, 133
White, Pearl 51, 52, 67, 112
White Eagle 96, 97, 125
Whitley, Ray 93, 152
The Whitman County Fair 60
Who Was That Masked Man? (book) 154
Who's Guilty? 128, 143
Wild West Days 25, 97, 162, 172
Wild, Wild West 234
"William Tell Overture" 156, 170
Williams, Maston 124
Wilson, Ben 53
Wilson, Lewis 105, 107
Wilson, Stanley 26
Wilson, Whip 115, 198
Windsor, Marie 111
A Wing and a Prayer 126
Winners of the West 15, 23, 25, 42, 85
Witney, William xi, 67, 70, 75, 80, 143, 238, 239, 240
The Wizard of Oz 146

The Wolf Man 177, 178
Wolfe, Bud 91, 120
Wonder Woman (TV movie) 81, 82
Wood, Ward 117
Woodbury, Joan 43, 112
Woods, Harry 138
Worth, Constance 120
Worth, Harry xi
Wright brothers 223
Written, Produced and Directed-By Oliver Drake (book) 153
Wyatt, Edgar 239
Wyler, William 71, 76

Yates, Herbert J. 79, 148, 153
Young, Carleton xi
Young, Loretta 140
Young, Tammany 20

Zahler, Lee 25, 173
Zombies of the Stratosphere 144, 185, 198
Zorro Rides Again 15, 125, 151, 204
Zorro's Black Whip 67, 89, 139, 215
Zorro's Fighting Legion 15, 25, 85, 131, 143, 197